DELIVERANCE
AT LOS BAÑOS

DELIVERANCE
AT LOS BAÑOS

ANTHONY ARTHUR

ST. MARTIN'S PRESS
New York

Design by Kingsley Parker

Library of Congress Cataloging in Publication Data

Arthur, Anthony.
    Deliverance at Los Baños.

    1. Los Baños (Los Baños, Laguna, Philippines:
Concentration camp) 2. World War, 1939–1945—
Prisoners and prisons, Japanese. I. Title.
D805.P6A77 1985   940.54′72′52095991
85–1868
ISBN 0–312–19185–5 2827 6011 1-03

First Edition
10 9 8 7 6 5 4 3 2 1

This book is for my wife, Carolyn,
and our children, Reagan and Owen

CONTENTS

A sixteen-page photo section follows page 146.

ACKNOWLEDGMENTS

For their continued encouragement and support, I am particularly grateful to Ben Edwards, George Mora, and the late Harold Bayley. Their full and enthusiastic responses to my original questionnaires and their continuing willingness to contribute to and comment on the manuscript made the task easier than it would otherwise have been.

I would also like to thank the following for their comments on various portions of the manuscript: Henry Burgess, Lou Burris, E. M. Flanagan, Jr., Bob Fletcher, Glenn McGowan, Henry Muller, Grace Nash, Carol Terry Talbot, Agnes Yamada, and Fred Zervoulakas. Any inaccuracies that remain are, of course, my own.

George Doherty's contributions to this book go well beyond the maps he did for it. A former member of the Eleventh Airborne, all the way from basic training through the fighting in the Pacific, George was inspired by the rescue at Los Baños at the time and has lived with it ever since. He has brought together hundreds of the participants in the rescue, both ex-prisoners and ex-soldiers, at the several reunions he has organized, and he was the first person I talked to about doing a book on the subject. His personal contacts, his industrious pursuit of obscure reference materials, his close scrutiny of the manuscript at various stages of preparation and, perhaps most of all, his unflagging enthusiasm were of great value to me.

I am grateful to The Honorable Gregorio Areneta, Deputy Minister of Tourism for the Philippines, for his invitation to visit Manila as a guest of his government in January 1982 in order to do necessary research for this book. While there, I was fortunate in being able to use the resources of the historical collection at the

American Embassy and to meet the director of the embassy library, Lewis Gleeck, whose several works on the recent history of the Philippines were extremely helpful.

To my old friend Joe Roseman, then the manager of the Sheraton Hotel in Manila, and his wife, Sally, my thanks for their warm hospitality during my research visit to the Philippines.

My colleague, Bob Oliphant, deserves special mention for his early and continued encouragement of this project. He shared his considerable knowledge about writing and publishing unselfishly. Finally, I appreciated the enthusiastic and expert secretarial help of Carol Nadler and Bobbie Coleman—including their editorial suggestions.

INTRODUCTION

If a single star appeared only once every thousand years, wrote Ralph Waldo Emerson, the world would be transfixed in wonder. The stars are not less wonderful because there are many of them, visible every night. But the principles of context and contrast mean they go unappreciated.

If 2,000 American civilians were rescued unharmed tomorrow by means of a daring raid from an enemy feared for its ferocity, it is not hard to imagine what an event for national celebration it would be. But because the rescue by the Eleventh Airborne Division and Filipino guerrillas of 2,147 civilian internees at Los Baños happened in the midst of other intensely dramatic events, it was all but ignored at the time. For on the same day that the internees were rescued, February 23, 1945, the single most striking moment of World War II was captured on film: the raising of the American flag by six marines on Iwo Jima's Mount Suribachi. Iwo Jima cost America more than 27,000 casualties—8,000 dead—and the pathos and valor represented by its capture were more compelling to the nation's editors than the rescue several thousand miles away in the Philippines.

Nor was the rescue given more than passing notice in the Philippines. There, the largest concentrations of Japanese and American forces ever to face each other were locked in battle. For the Japanese, the Philippines were the last redoubt before they had to retreat to the sacred home islands. For General MacArthur, the liberation of the Philippines would redeem American honor, shamed three years earlier by the fall of Bataan and Corregidor. In February 1945, the Japanese were resisting American efforts to capture Manila to the last man in what was one of the most destructive city battles of the Second World War after Warsaw and Leningrad.

The rescue at Los Baños was a humanitarian diversion from the primary mission of the American forces. It pulled battle-tested troops out of the line and sent them with a few days' notice thirty miles behind enemy lines, within an easy day's march of an 8,000-man Japanese division that had been honing its battle skills since the invasion of Manchuria. The rescuers and the rescued would have an eight-hour window of opportunity, as we would call it today, to get in and to get out. There would be no ground gained, no strategic objective seized. There were no opportunities to practice. Any failure would result in probable disaster. Any success would have to be total, the result of competence, daring, and luck. When and if it was over, the troops would go back to the front lines and resume their proper mission of killing, not rescuing, people.

The fact that the rescue was a complete success was, naturally, of lasting importance to those who were freed that day; some were near death from starvation, and others were convinced that a mass execution was in store for them later that same day. For the Eleventh Airborne Division, the rescue represented one of their most satisfying achievements. And for military historians and tacticians, it is of continuing interest as a unique and imaginative solution to a problem.

But all that was long ago and far away. Other problems concern us now, including those who were there and are still alive. What is there about the rescue at Los Baños that should interest us today?

First of all, there is simply the human story. Dorothy Johnson, the short-story writer, once defined her basic plot: "I put a man I like in a hole and throw stones at him." How good people survive and overcome hardship is of continuing interest; of the several thousand people who were involved with the rescue at Los Baños, I have selected a relative handful whose experiences seem both representative and interesting and tried to put them together in a coherent narrative. The result is a work that relies entirely on fact but reads, I hope, like a novel.

Beyond the human appeal of the story, many readers will,

perhaps, find it instructive in various ways. No event in an individual life or in the history of nations can be understood without reference to the past; for that reason, the rescue itself occupies only the final third of the book. Life in the camp before the rescue —the homely details of cooking and sanitation, the student production of "Singin' in the Rain" and debates on the rights of women, the death of a dog and of an Eagle Scout—provide a necessary prologue to the rescue. Even earlier, life in Manila before the Japanese invasion of the Philippines, and the relations between Japan and the United States that ultimately led to the internment of the civilians at Los Baños—these, too, have their place in the story.

Those who were involved, then, or who know something about Los Baños, may enjoy having the immediate context of a part of their past reconstructed. For those readers to whom World War II is as distant as World War I is to this writer's generation, an effort has been made to provide enough information and background about the war in the Pacific to be helpful. In dealing with information about both the camp and the rescue, the author has relied entirely on the sources acknowledged at the end of the book. I hope readers whose memories differ from those described will understand that a complete rendering of everything that happened to all concerned was not possible.

More than simply a good story or an interesting history is involved here, however. The Los Baños rescue tells us something about ourselves as a people, both then and now. In and of itself, it is about two groups of Americans who behaved well under difficult circumstances: the internees, who survived an extended period of hardship with grace, humor, and ingenuity, and the soldiers, who risked their lives to help them.

But the question remains: Why is this story of such interest *now?* One obvious answer is suggested by the recent events in Iran. Many of the persons interviewed for this book made pointed comparisons between the mortifying failure of the mission to rescue the embassy hostages in Tehran and the successful Los Baños mission. However, it seems clear now that the situations were not really comparable; political constraints on American power not relevant at Los Baños doomed the Iranian mission from the first.

Another reason for interest in the Los Baños rescue may be simple nostalgia for a simpler time, when the issues were clear and unambiguous. Many of the books and films appearing now about World War II in both Europe and the Pacific seem to share this feeling.

But more to the point than either recent events or memories of a supposedly simpler time is a powerful change in the American mood. The story told in this book celebrates American virtues rather than flailing our vices; ten years ago it might not have found an audience. But the legacy of Vietnam—the miasma of cynicism, self-doubt, and distrust of virtually all American ideals and institutions, including the military—has begun to give way to a healthier perspective on what this country has done and is still capable of doing. We are, it might be said, mature enough now to be able to appreciate a story with a happy ending. The author is grateful to the men of the Eleventh Airborne Division and to the internees at Los Baños for having lived that story.

DELIVERANCE
AT LOS BAÑOS

The strategic location of the Philippines guaranteed its role as a battlefield both at the beginning and at the end of World War II. Japan had to retain control of the islands to protect her shipping lanes to the Dutch East Indies and Southeast Asia. Moreover, it was clear that if the Philippines fell, the next assault would be on the sacred home islands. The Allied command was persuaded by General MacArthur that recapture of the Philippines was essential for American honor and for establishing air bases and staging areas for the invasion of Japan. Map done for this book by George Doherty.

1

THE LAST DAWN

Los Baños Internment Camp, The Philippines: February 23, 1945

Harold Bayley, Trinity College, 1934, United States Navy and Marine Corps Flight School, Pensacola, 1936, assumed his position as assistant keeper of the pigs at Los Baños in the spring of 1944. Major Iwanaka had consented to let Carl Myers, a stocky, taciturn farmer from Waterloo, Iowa, build a pen for the fifty pigs donated by the Philippine Red Cross to the internees, and also to fashion for himself and an assistant a rude nipa shack next to the pigpens. Bayley volunteered to help—he had grown weary of prodding the camp garden's cantankerous Brahman bull through the rocky soil, his previous post. He was also more than willing to move out of the oppressively crowded barracks, jammed with more than 2,000 fellow prisoners of the Japanese, into the relatively roomy pig keepers' shack.

Although conditions at Los Baños had been worsening since the later months of 1944—many of the prisoners were convinced that the Japanese intended to starve them all slowly to death—the gift of the pigs was seized upon by Bayley and others as a hopeful sign that better times were at hand. The sows had obligingly dropped teeming litters early in the summer, and it looked as though the specter of starvation could, if not dismissed entirely, at least be held at bay a little while longer. Destined for the cooking pots of the camp kitchens, the squealing piglets were the object of fond attention not only from their keepers but from some of the guards as well. Farm boys themselves far from their villages in Honshu

1

or Hokkaido, too sick, too old, or too inept for combat, they would stop by the pens en route to their watchtower about fifty yards away to toss bits of rice and candy at the pigs, giggling like children at the zoo.

In the minds of many, particularly the hundreds of "religious" —the Catholic priests and nuns and the Protestant missionaries who inhabited the section of the camp known as Vatican City— the pigs in fact represented a kind of religious mystery. Like the loaves and fishes of the biblical parable, they were going to be transformed into enough food for the multitudes. But late in the summer the piglets began to droop listlessly, and the sows no longer snorted and rooted in the mud; they merely gazed steadily through the sheeting tropical rains until the water rose to their bristly chins. On a particularly wet and steamy September morning, Bayley, Carl, and the Japanese veterinarian who had been sent for huddled together in the pig keepers' shack. Corporal Masaki, the commandant's best interpreter and the one most friendly to the Americans, was there too, but his presence was unnecessary. The language of medicine is international, like that of mathematics, and the deadly word *anthrax* was appallingly plain to all.

So all that came of the generous gift of the pigs and their fine litters—all the dreamed-of rashers of bacon and the pork roasts, sausage, and scrapple that the fevered imagination of the prisoners had already cooked and served and devoured—all of this fine fare was reduced to a few buckets of boiled blood mixed in with the evening rice.

Bayley and Carl still camped in their shack, though they no longer had anything to do. The guards no longer stopped on their way to the watchtower—except, as the year drew to a close, to warn the prisoners not to watch the flights of American B-29s flying up from Mindoro to bomb the Japanese positions in Manila and on Corregidor. Even the parody Jap, as some of the prisoners thought of him—the smiling, buck-toothed boy with steel-rimmed spectacles who had spent a month in San Francisco, considered himself an expert on American slang, and constantly whistled an off-tune version of "St. Louis Blues"—even St. Looey shunned the prisoners now.

For it was obvious to all, guards and internees alike, that the

Japanese empire was being threatened with collapse as 1944 drew to a close. By February of 1945 Douglas MacArthur had kept, at last, his famous promise to return to the Philippines. The sounds of battle in Manila were commonplace now. It was only a matter of days—or at the very most, a couple of weeks—before the U.S. Sixth Army broke through General Yamashita's defenses and swept south to rescue the Americans at Los Baños.

If, that is, anybody remained alive at Los Baños to rescue. It was typical of American misunderstanding of the Japanese mind for at least some of the prisoners to assume that the Japanese would treat them better as American forces drew closer. Surely the Japanese could see that they would soon be prisoners themselves. Their lives might well depend on the judgment that those Americans now in their custody would pass on them. But such had not been the case. At least a dozen bodies recently buried in the camp graveyard proved that the Japanese were not reacting according to Western logic. Many more internees would die soon unless help arrived.

These and similar melancholy thoughts occupied Harold Bayley's mind on the morning of February 23, 1945, as he sat outside his shack waiting for the 7:00 A.M. roll call. He and Carl shared a thin gruel flavored with rice that had been laboriously husked. That was the last straw, Bayley thought, giving starving prisoners unhusked rice. If they ate it as it was given to them, the husks would slice like tiny razors through their intestines, and they would die writhing in agony. But to husk the rice with the only tools available—rolling it between two pieces of wood—used up more calories than the food would provide. In the end, he had managed to knock enough kernels of grain loose to supplement his meal. He would survive.

He would survive, as he had for more than three years as a prisoner of the Japanese, in part because he was a single man, without the nagging worry of caring for a wife and children, and in part because he knew how to adapt, to relax. Even now, after his scanty breakfast, he could sit back and watch with pleasure as the morning mist rose from the shallow lake that reached endlessly beyond the neighboring village of Los Baños. He could stretch his legs contentedly under the warm touch of the morning sun as it topped the forested crest of Mount Makiling behind him. And, shifting slightly, he could look to the north and see the native farmers wending their way up the terraced hillsides as they had done for hundreds—perhaps thousands—of years. The scene looked, he thought, much like a Japanese painting.

Bayley puffed contentedly on a cigarette. It was a Lucky Strike —for weeks the pleasantly familiar aroma of Virginia tobacco had been drifting through the camp. The cigarettes were part of a series of shipments smuggled behind enemy lines from American submarines to Filipino guerrillas. Like the thousands of newly minted dimes, recent issues of *Life* magazine, and newspaper stories about the Battle of the Bulge, they were designed to let it be known that liberation was at hand. But what, Bayley wondered idly, did the letters on the cigarette pack—LSMFT—mean?

During the past weeks there had been so many American planes flying overhead that now, when Bayley sensed the droning throb of engines, he didn't even bother to look up. Besides, those who did look and wave and cheer often found themselves spending the next six or eight hours staring into the tropical sun as punishment. But Bayley didn't need his pilot's ear to tell him that these were not B-29s at 10,000 feet flying north, their silver bodies gleaming distantly in the azure sky. No, these were the lumbering converted cargo planes, C-47s, and they were coming *from* the north—and, Bayley could see without raising his head, they were crossing the shallow lake and approaching Los Baños at what looked like treetop height—no more than 500 feet! There were three planes, Bayley thought at first, in a single V-shape formation. No, there were four—six, seven, eight—nine, all told, three Vs; as the first plane passed overhead he saw a tiny figure drop from a hole in the side. It was followed at once by scores of others.

For a split second Bayley thought he could hear the snap of their chutes as they cracked open. Then he realized that the Japanese guard at the nearby post had been shot. His body crumpled to the ground. The staccato of small-arms fire replaced the roar of the C-47s as Bayley and Carl leaped into the ditch they had dug behind their shack and crouched under the iron caldron they had placed there when it was no longer needed to stir the pigs' food.

If they were lucky, Bayley thought, the pigs might save their lives even yet. . . .

As usual, Louise Craven and her husband, Coit, had risen early the morning of February 23. It was the only way to beat the lineup in the latrine, and with twelve toilets and twelve sinks for ninety-odd people, some way of coping with the needs of nature other than patience was essential. This morning it was Coit's turn to stand in the breakfast line. Not much food would be forthcoming, they knew. The cornmeal and grated coconut that they had been saving had been depleted last week, and the most they could expect in their battered tin cups was a few boiled camotes that looked and tasted like red clay. When Coit returned the two would share their breakfast in their eight-by-twelve cubicle, sitting on the daybed that their wooden bunks became when folded into each other every morning.

Louise Craven's chief worry was not the cramped living conditions. Not even, so far as she was concerned, the sparsity of food —though she feared that her husband's recent bouts of beriberi and dengue fever would drain yet more weight from his spare frame. Her greatest uneasiness was for her infant son, one of about eighteen babies born to internee couples in spite of official Japanese frowns. Born on December 18, 1944, Henry Truxton Craven had survived mainly through the generosity of his parents' friends, who contributed the condensed milk they had received in Red Cross "comfort kits." Others had donated blood when Chad Vinson—Dr. Charles Vinson, in more formal doctor-patient circumstances—told Louise that her hemoglobin count was dangerously low. Lying in her bed, listening to the rain lashing against the thin walls of her barracks, Louise Craven had given thanks to God for her Christmas baby, and for the understanding that people were basically good. Her fellow prisoners would not stand by and watch someone suffer if they could help.

But now, as Henry Truxton Craven entered his third month of life at Los Baños, everyone's resources—both material and spiritual—were giving out. The canned milk was long since gone; the baby clutched at his mother's breast and squalled with frustration at finding it dry. Louise rocked him gently and waited for her husband to return from the breakfast line. What could be taking him so long, she wondered—and what in the world was all the commotion outside her window. . . .

Bill and Polly Yankey were sociable people who got along well with the other forty-seven couples in barracks No. 1, so it was only natural that the husky mining engineer and his cheerful wife were elected barracks monitors. Their duties were light; Bill still had time to work as the camp blacksmith, and Polly did a daily stint in the laundry. Their most important duty was morning roll call. This was especially true, Lieutenant Konishi had told Bill with a stern scowl on his broad, pocked face, since so many men had turned up missing in recent weeks. Konishi reminded Yankey that it should be clear to everyone that the punishment for such behavior was immediate execution; the American should remind the others in his barracks of that.

Yankey rubbed a razor blade gingerly against a piece of glass as he stood before his shaving mirror—after a year of use, the blade was so thin and brittle that he daily expected it to shatter in his fingers or to break in half on his tough beard. This was no way to live, Yankey thought, wincing as the blade tugged at his lip. He wondered about the odds against the men who had slipped through the fence into the surrounding jungle. Chances were they would be picked up by Jap patrols or turned over to the Japs by *makapili*—Filipino sympathizers with the invaders—and shot on the spot. Only the lucky ones would be taken in by the various guerrilla units that were said to be all around them, though they were still thirty miles behind Jap lines.

Yankey rinsed his razor blade and sighed. He would have gone with Ben Edwards, the Pan Am mechanic, and the others despite the odds against making it. He was afraid, though, that Konishi would vent his wrath on Polly's elderly father, who had been a professor, honored and respected, not 200 yards from the camp where he was now forced to bow to men who in the best of times would have been his inferiors.

Bill Yankey tucked his razor blade carefully into a slit he had made in the side of his shaving kit—not, as he had first done, in his soap dish, because soap was too likely to be stolen. Then, at one minute before seven o'clock, he stepped into the hall of barracks No. 1 to blow his whistle for roll call. . . .

They were almost all awake, all 2,147 of the people at Los Baños on the memorable morning of February 23, 1945. George Mora, who was nineteen, had studied hard in the Santo Tomás Internment Camp high school and had won a college scholarship at Los Baños. He was almost always not only awake but alert, taking notes and planning to become a journalist. Hank Johnson, another teenager, a Chinese-American whose middle name was Sioux and whose sixteen or so brothers and sisters bore such tribal names as Cheyenne, Arapahoe, and Apache, was awake; he was still thinking about the tasty lizard he had lost yesterday to a speedy Catholic priest. Floyd McCarthy, the brother of a United Press International correspondent who was at that moment poised in the doorway of a C-47 directly overhead, was awake. Isla Corfield, an acerbic, witty Englishwoman who kept her wits and her voluminous diary intact, was awake. William Donald, last seen in public helping Madame Chiang Kai-shek step out of her car in Peking, where he was a top adviser in her husband's government, was awake. Robert Kleinpell, a professor of geology at California Institute of Technology, and Alex Brockway, a petroleum engineer who was his appreciative student at Los Baños, were both awake.

Of course Sniffen and Shapiro, the raffish gamblers who seemed to have stepped straight from the pages of Dickens' Victorian London into Los Baños by way of Manila, were awake. So were the Army wives who had hardly had a decent night's sleep since their husbands disappeared into the death camps at Cabanatuan and Palawan three years earlier. Merchant seamen marooned in Manila Harbor when the war broke out . . . various executives of the Manila utility companies, banks, churches, and the YMCA . . . and a wide assortment of hustlers, thieves, pimps, whores, and vagabonds swept from the city streets by the Japanese authorities, who were nothing if not thorough—all these were awake, and all were ready for the day of their deliverance. For the day, as one of them would later put it, when the angels of the United States Eleventh Airborne Division landed at dawn.

2

THUNDER 'CROST THE BAY

Manila: November–December 1941

There were, during the foreboding autumn of 1941, some 15,000 American civilians in the Philippines. Many had been there for years. George Mora's father, Ernest, was born in New York. His family, originally from Spain, had settled in Cuba and lost its sizable sugar plantation during the Cuban rebellion that preceded the Spanish-American War of 1898. Ernest had then started anew to recoup the family fortune in the Philippines, on the other side of the world. Polly Yankey's father had helped to make his small agricultural college south of the city at Los Baños famous for its animal and crop research. George Grey, a young career foreign service officer, had joined the staff of the American high commissioner in 1936. They were accomplished and intelligent people. Like the representatives of the American Tobacco Company, General Motors, General Electric, Pan American Airways and scores of other companies, not to mention the electric company, the water company, the telephone company, and all the banks, they knew that the United States might soon go to war with Japan —maybe, some said, as early as the summer of 1942.

Because of its location, Manila had long been a major port of departure for the United States. Recently, large numbers of Americans and Europeans, fleeing other parts of Asia that lay open to the Japanese armies if war should come, had crowded into the city. Among the new arrivals in mid-November was a well-traveled ex-marine named Harold Bayley who was en route from Java to San Francisco. Comfortably settled for a week in the

Manila Hotel, Bayley was in no particular hurry for his ship, the *Coolidge,* to leave earlier than its scheduled date, November 20— if the locals were content to live in Manila with their heads in the mouth of the tiger, he should be safe enough for a few days of well-deserved vacation.

At twenty-nine, Harold Bayley had seen a good deal of the world that lay beyond the ivied halls of Trinity College in Hartford, Connecticut. Graduating in 1934 with a degree in literature at the very bottom of the Depression, he had joined the Navy as an aviation cadet and been commissioned as a Marine pilot in 1936. After four years of active duty with the Marines in San Diego and Quantico, he was hired by the Curtiss-Wright Company in Buffalo as a P-40 test pilot and sent to Turkey for eight months. Early in 1940 he was sent to the Netherlands East Indies to help supervise the assembly of seventy-two Brewster "Buffaloes" and nine Curtiss trainers as well as to test-fly them—the ultimate test of whether or not they had been assembled properly. Late in 1941 he was ordered to return home to take charge of the delivery of another batch of planes to Java.

Harold Bayley had grown up reading the adventurous travel narratives of Richard Halliburton and the novels of Somerset Maugham, Joseph Conrad, and Pearl Buck, and he wanted to see as much of the storied Orient as he could. Like most Americans, his understanding of the American connection with this remote island nation was vague. He knew that the United States had acquired it in 1898, along with Cuba and Puerto Rico, as part of the spoils of what Teddy Roosevelt called the "splendid little war" with Spain. He knew—but only because as an aviator he loved to read maps—that the Philippine archipelago included thousands of islands, anchored by the large islands of Luzon in the north and Mindanao in the south, an easy day's flight from Manila to Tokyo in the north and a figurative stone's throw to Borneo in the south via the Sulu Archipelago.

Bayley could also see from the map that the citizens of Manila would be in trouble if war came. It was obvious that the Japanese would have to consider the American presence in the Philippines intolerable: in one sense as a roadblock to their planned expansion throughout Southeast Asia and in another as a dagger pointed at

the heart of Japan. Either of these reasons would have been sufficient cause for an attack. Combined, they made an attack inevitable. But he also knew, through an Army buddy stationed at Clark
Field north of Manila, that President Quezon had been assured by
General Douglas MacArthur, his grandly named "Field Marshal," that the Japanese would not attack before April 1942. And
by that time the defense force that MacArthur had been laboring
mightily to put together for the past six years would be ready to
repel the invaders.

There was no reason, then, for Bayley to return home by way
of Australia, which he had no special interest in revisiting, when
he could safely visit Manila en route. Accordingly, he spent a
relaxing week wandering through the ancient walled city of Intramuros, around the grounds of the Malacañan Palace, and along
Dewey Boulevard. One evening a few days after his arrival he sat
with his feet upon the iron balustrade of his balcony at the Manila
Hotel. The aroma of his cigar, an excellent local blend, mingled
with the scents of jasmine and honeysuckle from the gardens
below. The sunset, obscured by haze the first few days of his visit,
was at last as spectacular as he had been promised—a clustered
mass of golden clouds that gave way as the sun, now a brilliant
orange, vanished behind a line of palm trees edging the bay. From
the nearby Luneta Park drifted the sounds of the constabulary
band bugler sounding retreat. Alone on his balcony, Bayley stood
at comfortable attention until the last notes had faded away.

Then, across the water to the west, the lights of the villages on
the Bataan Peninsula flickered on, a few isolated patches in the
dark shadow of the jungle that formed the eastern shore of Manila
Bay. It was clear enough to see the Mariveles Mountains that rose
4,000 feet above the southern edge of Bataan, some twenty-five
miles away—and, as well, the legendary fortress of Corregidor,
where dozens of gun batteries that could hurl 100-pound shells for
ten miles lay hidden in concrete bunkers poured into folds of solid
granite. An impregnable bastion, the Gibraltar of the East, Corregidor was manned by hundreds of the most skillful artillerists
ever trained by the United States Army.

The shiver of pride that Bayley felt as he stood listening to the
lingering notes of retreat and gazing at Corregidor was a symptom

of unambiguous patriotism. It was a feeling shared by most Americans then in Manila. Few were troubled by invidious comparisons of the United States with Great Britain as an imperial power. Even fewer would have subscribed to the notion that they were depriving an alien people of their right to direct their own lives—a common charge in the Japanese press. We had, admittedly, been motivated by considerations of global politics when, forty years ago, the opportunity appeared to gain a stronghold in Asia. Neither was there any question that American businesses had profited handsomely from their trade in the Far East. And the American military, especially the Army, had long regarded the islands as a training ground without peer—as evidenced by its habit of sending its most promising officers, from John Pershing to Dwight David Eisenhower and Douglas MacArthur, to the Philippines for extended tours of duty.

But the benefits that the United States had conferred upon the Filipinos—some 17,000,000 in 1940—were also considerable. Except for those remote areas of the south where only Stone Age tribes and headhunters lived, public-health officers had cleansed the islands of typhoid and cholera. Teams of civil engineers had built commercial docks, railroads, highways, and sewer systems. Thousands of teachers, lay and religious, had fanned out through the country, bringing education to the remotest hamlets and quintupling the literacy rate within ten years. A middle class of Filipino managers who would eventually run their country had been created as a deliberate matter of United States policy.

The contrasts of American rule with that of its Spanish predecessors was obvious in many ways, but this last was the most important. For the Spanish had discouraged the growth of a responsible middle class as incompatible with the needs of a medieval monarchy, which is what Spain then was. They had feared, rightly, that the agitation for basic reforms, for freedom, would destroy their hold on the Philippines. The American policy of encouraging ultimate independence was a welcome innovation, not merely because it contrasted with the three centuries of subservience to Spain but because it represented a dramatically different course from those of England and France, whose leaders were dragging their feet on independence for India and Indochina. The

Filipinos, by contrast, had been promised full independence in 1946, even though many doubted they would be ready for it. All of this had been accomplished with a minimum of hostility between Americans and Filipinos. There were no signs in Manila such as the one on the garden gate next to the British consulate in Shanghai: "No Dogs or Orientals Allowed." There was, it was true, a degree of social and economic discrimination that neither group would have tolerated in later years (witness the condescension and paternalism implicit in President Taft's fondly intended reference to "our little brown brothers"). And there was clearly a division of classes according to privilege and caste. A stroll through the Luneta Park on any given afternoon would reveal squads of filthy street urchins relaxing from their labors at petty theft and panhandling by playing checkers with bottle caps on charcoal-marked squares. Meanwhile, not twenty feet away, a cluster of well-scrubbed American children, the girls in pinafores, the boys in sailor suits, would play on the closely clipped grass surrounded by a ring of Chinese *amahs*, all chattering merrily away in Cantonese. The mothers of the street children, if they were lucky, would be ironing or cooking in one of the foreigners' houses in Makati or Paco; the mothers of the pale children within the protective circle would be sipping gin and tonics at the "nineteenth hole" of the golf course, in the lounge of the Manila Hotel.

Despite these obvious differences in privilege and prestige there was, by and large, an easy relationship between Americans and Filipinos. Certainly there was nothing of the servility and barely concealed resentment toward whites that were common in other parts of Asia; nor was there much of the Colonel Blimp bigotry toward natives so common among the British. Open-mindedness was aided by the fact that the Filipinos were an attractive people. Slender, graceful admixtures of Malay and Polynesian strains, with high cheekbones, large, almond-shaped dark eyes, lustrous black hair, and a burnished mahogany complexion, many Filipinos were not merely comely but strikingly handsome. In addition, they had a gaiety and charm—a heritage from the Spanish—that made them seem to be both livelier and more Western to American eyes than other Asians; it was greatly to President Quezon's advantage that he was a wonderful ballroom dancer, particularly expert at the tango.

It was true that the Filipino could be vengeful and violent, for both the Malay and the Spanish heritage demanded that affronts to manly pride be redeemed in blood. The unofficial national sport of cockfighting was revolting to Western eyes, as was the custom, still common in the provinces, of raising dogs to be slaughtered for their meat. And the importance that Americans attached to punctuality and dependability was far less pervasive than the Latin sense of mañana. It was hardly surprising that the American soldiers charged with the task of developing a national defense force capable of resisting the dedicated soldiers of Imperial Japan were not always sanguine about their prospects for success. Overall, though, the Filipinos were widely regarded as competent and loyal, free from malice and incapable of the kind of treachery that most Americans had come to associate with other Asians—particularly, in recent years, the Japanese.

For their part, the Filipinos admired and envied Americans. They sent their brightest and most promising young men to become doctors at Johns Hopkins, teachers at Columbia, infantry officers at Fort Benning, and engineers at Carnegie Tech. The movies they watched in the grand theaters along the Escolta were *The Great Ziegfeld, Mr. Deeds Goes to Town,* and *Naughty Marietta.* Their popular music was played by Harry James and Glenn Miller. Their sports idols were Ted Williams, Bobby Jones, and Bill Tilden, the tennis star who had stayed at the Manila Hotel just two years earlier. And their official language was English.

All this Bayley was to learn during his leisurely week in Manila and, through his Air Corps friend, from the Cotterman family, longtime local residents. Like most pilots, Bayley was a reflective man who could be contentedly alone for long periods of time, but the Cottermans were a comfortable group. Mr. Cotterman had established a successful business selling bottled oxygen and medical supplies to local hospitals, and he and his wife had raised two daughters in a rambling white-frame house in the Paco section of the city. Ozzie Lunde, Bayley's pilot buddy, had been dating the younger Cotterman sister, Catherine. The older sister, Elizabeth, was married to an oil company engineer named Jim Morgan. During the week before Bayley's ship was to sail the five Americans proposed to show him the night life of Manila—before all the lights went out for good, Elizabeth had said glumly.

The day before the departure of the *Coolidge,* Bayley sat on his balcony and listened to the constabulary band's evening concert. Though a cool breeze from the South China Sea had sprung up at sunset, his forehead was clammy with sweat. He pressed his damp gin-and-tonic glass against it and listened to the band. It was playing familiar tunes—Sousa marches, Strauss waltzes, and a mournful version of "The Road to Mandalay." He filled in the words, those he could recall: "For the wind is in the palm trees, and the temple bells they say . . . and the dawn comes up like thunder out of China 'crost the bay . . ." Suddenly chilled by the night breeze, Bayley stood up to get a jacket. Was General MacArthur, two floors above him in his penthouse suite, also listening; and was he, like Bayley, looking north toward Japan and thinking about "thunder 'crost the bay"?

That night Bayley was seized by a wracking intestinal disorder, a high fever, and a weakness that barely allowed him to crawl out of bed. Lunde visited his old friend, shook his head gravely, and called in Dr. Pope Noel, a mutual friend. Noel looked Bayley over carefully, said he had dengue fever, and consigned him to bed for three days. He was scheduled to sail tomorrow, Bayley protested. Not possible, Noel said. Catch the next ship out.

Dengue fever, it turned out, was merely an easily curable form of influenza, and Bayley was almost back to normal in five days. He could certainly have recovered as easily on board the *Coolidge,* and he suspected that his friends had conspired with each other to keep him with them a little longer. But that was all right—there was another ship leaving for Seattle in two weeks, on the afternoon of December 8.

It was about 3:00 A.M. on December 8 (the date was a day later than at home because of the international date line) that the shocked citizens of Manila heard about Pearl Harbor. Nine hours later, despite the warning that the raid on the Pacific Fleet should have given MacArthur's staff, the Flying Fortresses and fighter planes that were supposed to protect the Philippines were caught on the ground at Clark Field and immediately wiped out. The Japanese had refused to oblige MacArthur by waiting until April 1942 for their attack—the date by which he said an attack could be repulsed—and 50,000 troops were poised to land on the beaches of Luzon and to march on Manila.

During the anxious days and weeks that followed Pearl Harbor, Bayley spent most of his time with the Cotterman family. Jim Morgan was busy devising plans to sabotage the oil and gasoline storage depots that ringed Manila Harbor. Ozzie Lunde had survived the raid at Clark Field; he and the other pilots, he said bitterly, had been ordered into the air at dawn. For some reason, they had not been allowed to attack the Japanese staging areas on Formosa. Instead, they had flown in circles for three hours above Clark Field until their fuel ran low. Then all seventeen Fortresses and almost fifty P-40s had landed and lined up for refueling. While the pilots were having lunch and the planes were sitting like explosive ducks in a row, the Japanese attack bombers burst upon them. The Japs had been fogged in at dawn, Lunde learned afterward. Their departure, two hours late, had allowed them to hit us at precisely the worst possible time. Our stupidity was criminal, he said.

Now Lunde was on Bataan, flying one of the surviving P-40s in dogfights with Jap Zeroes. Most of the other pilots had been sent to Australia to regroup—and to wait for new planes. The grandly named Asiatic Fleet under Admiral Hart, which consisted of a few heavy cruisers and a dozen destroyers—not a single battleship or aircraft carrier—had also fled for safer waters. Clearly, the pathetic remains of American naval and air power in the South Pacific were being saved for a better day. The implications of their departure were not lost on the 600,000 inhabitants of Manila who did not have the luxury of flight available to them.

With Lunde gone, Morgan busy, and Mr. Cotterman ill with heart trouble, Bayley did what he could for the Cotterman household. There was never any thought of arming themselves against the Japanese troops who would soon march into the city; it would be enough merely to survive the bombing raids blasting the military targets that lined the Pasig River and the bay, particularly the Cavite naval base. It helped somewhat that the Japanese were methodical in their attacks; Bayley learned soon enough that his noon shower at the Manila Hotel coincided with daily bombing runs on the remaining ships in the harbor and adjusted his schedule accordingly.

A more pressing concern was presented by Elizabeth Morgan. High-strung and imaginative, she had magnified both the present and the potential horrors of the war to the point of hysteria. Her three children, the focus of her concern, were beginning to absorb their mother's fear, which only worsened Elizabeth's state of mind. In a quixotic effort to face down her terror, she had asked Bayley to escort her at noon one day early in the Japanese attack to the lounge atop the Bayview Hotel. The hotel, one of Manila's finest, was on Dewey Boulevard, not far from the U.S. high commissioner's office. There, sipping Bloody Marys, the two watched a formation of twenty-seven Japanese bombers circle Cavite, ten miles away. The distance and the thick window glass deadened the sound of the falling bombs, which exploded with an eerie, incandescent beauty, like poison flowers. The bottles behind the teakwood bar rattled from the concussion. Then the bombers circled and dropped a dozen bombs on the remaining ships in the harbor —making no distinction, so far as Bayley could see, between military vessels, intercoastal steamers, and passenger liners. As the planes flew north toward their bases in Formosa, white clusters of fire from the antiaircraft guns on Corregidor spotted the sky far below them, harmless as powder puffs.

Elizabeth's experiment in acquiring grace under pressure was a failure, and she became a growing irritation to Bayley in the days that followed. But personal destinies now seemed trivial in the face of the Japanese juggernaut that rolled relentlessly toward the city. General Homma, the burly Japanese officer who led the invasion, had held diplomatic attaché posts in Washington, London, and Germany. Like all the Japanese military leaders, he had studied the German concept of blitzkrieg—lightning war—both in theory and in practice. Just as the Germans had overwhelmed Poland, Czechoslovakia, and the Low Countries within a matter of weeks in 1939, so the Japanese could penetrate and control Southeast Asia. An American army that still mounted its cavalry on horses instead of tanks would not stand in their way for long.

On December 22 Homma landed his Fourteenth Army in strength at three places on the Lingayen Gulf. With total command of both sea and air the Japanese landings were unhindered, despite reports to the contrary in the Manila press. Two days later, a 7,000-man contingent landed south of the city at Legaspi Bay and slashed northward through token opposition. It was obvious to all that MacArthur's ill-equipped and undertrained forces, though numerically superior to the enemy, would soon be annihilated by Japanese tank and mobile artillery units. MacArthur would be forced to fall back on War Plan Orange.

War Plan Orange had been formulated before Bayley's birth, shortly after the United States took possession of the Philippines. It rested on the assumption that there would never be an American force large enough, so far away from home, to defend the islands against a determined aggressor—which was already, in 1910, seen as Imperial Japan. If a strong force attacked, then the USAFFE units—U.S. Armed Forces in the Far East—would make an orderly retreat into the Bataan Peninsula. Twenty-five miles long and fifteen miles wide, a nearly impenetrable tangle of jungle and mountains, Bataan could be held indefinitely against a larger force—long enough for assistance in the form of troops and ships to arrive from Hawaii.

Douglas MacArthur knew Bataan well. As a young lieutenant assigned to the Philippines before the First World War, one of his first assignments was to survey the entire peninsula as part of the planning for War Plan Orange, or WPO. But he scorned the premise of the plan: wars, he said, were won by attacking, not by retreat. He would have nothing to do with War Plan Orange.

He persuaded the American military command and President Quezon that, given enough time, he could build a defense force that could repel the invader at the beaches, refusing to allow them a foothold. The Japanese would come to see that it would cost them too much in time, men, and matériel to take the islands. Instead, they would bypass the Philippines entirely and move on to their primary targets: the oil-rich Dutch East Indies, the trading centers of Hong Kong and Singapore, the rice fields and rubber plantations of Malaya, and the vast plunder of China. So certain was he that War Plan Orange would never be implemented, that

MacArthur neglected to create the required depots of food and medical supplies on Bataan—food and supplies that would keep a beleaguered army alive until help arrived. And, of course, there would be no help in any case, the Pacific Fleet having been all but destroyed at Pearl Harbor.

During the first days after the disasters at Pearl Harbor and Clark Field, there was no talk in the press of pulling back into Bataan. The Japanese army was too contemptible to make Americans run—"an ill-uniformed, untested mass of boys between fifteen and eighteen years old, equipped with small-caliber arms and driven forward by desperate determination to advance or die," one American officer was quoted as saying. Most of them died because their .25 caliber rifle and machine-gun bullets could hardly stop a man. A squirrel, maybe, or a rat, but not a Yank. So why, the American was asked, were the Japanese still coming? "We licked the pants off them three times," was the response, "and were beaten only by their planes and tanks. When our planes and tanks go into action we'll chase them back to the sea."

But there were no tanks to speak of, and the planes were all destroyed or in Australia. One of them had been piloted by a brave man named Colin Kelly. When his Flying Fortress was hit he ordered his crew to bail out to safety and then single-handedly destroyed the great battleship *Haruma* by diving straight into its stacks. Bayley would not learn until much later that while Kelly had indeed been a hero in saving his crew, his plane had crashed harmlessly into a dirt road. His was the only life lost, for the *Haruma* was safe at anchor 1,000 miles away. The American press, sensing the country's need not merely for stories of heroism but of successes, had manufactured a triumph that would become a legend.

It was already obvious, though, that such whistling in the dark would not drown out the wail of the air-raid sirens and the chatter of antiaircraft guns in Manila as the city was pummeled by Japanese bombers. Ships still tied up in the broad, yellow Pasig River, which cut through the heart of the city, were blasted by high-flying Japanese bombers whose deadly freight crumbled the ancient walls of Intramuros. The beautiful Dominican Church, shrine of the patron saint of the Philippines, was destroyed, along with the treasury building, which had housed the first Philippine senate: symbols of government and religion tumbling before a soulless mechanized onslaught. The government itself, along with MacArthur and his staff, fled the city for the tunnels of Corregidor on December 24. On Christmas Day the newspapers of Manila published a statement from the U.S. high commissioner, Francis Sayre, and President Quezon. General MacArthur, it said, had asked that they remove themselves to the island fortress with him so that the government of the Philippines might continue even if the city fell to the enemy.

On December 26 MacArthur declared that Manila was an open city, hoping thereby to prevent its destruction by the Japanese. USAFFE forces totaling some 80,000 men continued their painful and dangerous withdrawal into the refuge of Bataan. Oddly, the Japanese seemed not to have considered American retreat as a likely strategy and did not try to prevent the retreat until it was too late. General Homma, embarrassed, put the best possible face on this temporary setback by gloating that he had the USAFFE forces where he wanted them—"like a cat in a sack." Homma could hardly be expected to know that it would take him four long months to bag the cat. It was a delay that would fatally disrupt the Japanese timetable for securing the Philippines and the rest of Southeast Asia.

But there were no silver linings, no hints of later trouble for the Japanese, in view after MacArthur's statement on the afternoon of December 26. A group of prominent American citizens who had formed to discuss plans for dealing with the Japanese issued a dire warning: all "Europeans" should prepare to be interned. They should gather together whatever valuables and essentials they could carry in a few light bags and be ready to move at once.

Bayley borrowed the Cotterman car and drove to the Manila Hotel to retrieve his belongings the next morning. For once driving in Manila was easy, for about one third of the city's population had fled to the surrounding countryside. He saw an occasional electric trolley but not a single one of the thousands of horse-drawn jitneys that normally clogged the streets, arousing the histrionic fury of Manila's maniacal taxi drivers. All the schools had been closed on December 8, and there were no children to be seen.

In a morning lull from bombing, the city lay quiet and still, motionless beneath the bright blue December sky.

Shortly after dinner on December 28 Mr. Cotterman and Bayley stood by the rocky stream that flowed through the backyard of his spacious lot. One by one, with ceremonial precision, they broke all the bottles from Cotterman's liquor cabinet. In the distance they could see the flames of burning fuel depots, ships, and military installations that had either been bombed by the enemy or deliberately destroyed by our own retreating forces. The dull, heavy concussions were punctuated by the sharp splintering of glass against rock as dozens of bottles—Irish whiskey, scotch, a few liqueurs—were destroyed. Neither man spoke—there was no need—of the reason for getting rid of the liquor. There had been too many accounts of Japanese troops in China and Manchuria going berserk with alcohol and the fever of victory to make any comment necessary. And there were three women in the house.

That night Bayley cut his naval aviator's identification card into tiny pieces and flushed it down the toilet.

On December 30 the Cottermans read a terse announcement in the Manila *Times:* inauguration ceremonies had been held for President Quezon's second term in office. No mention was made of the contrast between this ceremony, held in the dusty gloom of the Malinta Tunnel on Corregidor, witnessed only by a handful of military and civilian officials, and Quezon's first inauguration four years earlier. Then there had been great rejoicing at Malacañan Palace, for no less a personage than the vice-president of the United States was in attendance, along with the honorable speaker of the United States House of Representatives. The Philippines was being recognized, in 1936, as a sister in democracy by the world's greatest nation. It was an occasion for celebration, and the speechmaking and the dancing and the fireworks had lasted until very late in the night.

But the fireworks that now accompanied Quezon's second inaugural ceremony were provided by the Japanese and by retreating USAFFE demolition teams. On the evening of December 31, the remaining oil storage tanks at Pandacan were torched. At eight o'clock that evening the local radio stations signed off for the duration—they were to be destroyed, too. Listeners were given a few words of advice: they should stay in their homes, no matter what happened, until the invading army arrived with further instructions.

At midnight Harold Bayley and Mrs. Cotterman—the rest of the household had gone to bed—toasted each other with ice water and watched the flames of the burning fuel tanks leap into the sky above the darkened city.

The new year of 1942 was ushered in with an orgy of looting. Government warehouses had been opened to the populace to let them take what they needed. Other warehouses were opened by force. Refrigerators and rugs, diesel generators and canned milk were carted away, along with hordes of cracked wheat, rice, and drugs, which would soon surface in the black market. Nothing was left unappropriated, not even a large box found near the docks that a distressed looter laboriously carried home, only to find that it contained a corpse, presumably shipped from abroad for burial in home soil.

On the morning of January 2 the sun, barely visible through the asphyxiating pall of smoke that now shrouded the city, looked like the moon. The Cottermans' two pet canaries dropped from their perches, fluttered feebly in the noxious air, and died. An eerie stillness pervaded all.

Shortly before noon a boy on a bicycle tossed a Manila *Bulletin* onto the porch—an oddly normal occurrence. The paper had received a statement from what it described as an "official source." Japanese authorities had promised that no troops would be quartered in private homes. "We don't propose to interfere with civilian activities," the Japanese source said reassuringly, "much less do civilians any harm."

Shortly after lunch a truck pulled to a halt in front of the Cotterman house. Seated in the shuttered living room, they heard a heavy shuffle of booted feet on the proch. Mr. Cotterman answered the peremptory knock on the door. A slender young Japanese civilian in a black serge suit identified himself as Mr. Harumi. In flawless English, he ordered everyone out onto the porch. Their house was needed to quarter Japanese troops, Harumi said briskly. For their own safety, all civilians of enemy nations would be interned by Japanese authorities until further notice. They would leave immediately for the University of Santo Tomás, with no more than two bags each.

Harumi read the names of the family from a checklist as they prepared to board the truck. "Who are you?" he demanded of Bayley. "Why are you in Manila?" The ex-marine and commercial test pilot identified himself as a Ford salesman. Harumi looked suspiciously at Bayley's trim, erect bearing. Bayley groped wildly in his mind for something to say about Fords if Harumi pressed him, but at that moment one of the soldiers approached their leader with a question. Relieved, Bayley looked over the Japanese soldiers who were now lounging on the porch, making themselves comfortable on the rattan furniture. How small they were, he thought—less than five feet five inches, most of them, and skinny. Their coarsely woven uniforms were stained with grease and sweat; their rifles pocked with rust, webbing frayed. The report he'd read by American soldiers looked right enough, he thought: man for man they wouldn't last long with most American soldiers. They were a puny and repulsive lot. But taken in the mass—and even the dozen who were there seemed a lot—they reflected an alarmingly implacable hostility for their prisoners. And, surprisingly, an unnerving feeling of contempt for them—contempt for Americans!—as well.

Harumi nodded as the soldier spoke and turned to Mr. Cotterman. Where was the key to the safe in the house, he demanded. Cotterman was indignant. The authorities, he said, had promised only today that no troops would be quartered in civilian houses and that the citizens of Manila would not be interfered with. Already these promises were being broken. Were the Japanese thieves, too? Harumi made a guttural noise and slapped the old man's face twice, middling hard. Cotterman paled, not from the pain, Bayley thought, but from the shocking indignity of the reprimand. Mrs. Cotterman quickly told Harumi where the key was, and the soldier disappeared inside the house as Harumi translated for him.

Elizabeth Morgan had watched the humiliating treatment of her father with each of her three children clutching fearfully at her white muslin skirt. A young soldier, trimmer and friendlier than the others, approached the children with a broad smile and offered them candy. The little girl reached eagerly for it, but Elizabeth pulled her arm back sternly. "We don't want anything from you or your men," she said coldly to Harumi. "Just go away and stop bothering us." Bayley was amazed. The same woman who had cowered in terror a week ago at the possibility of Japanese occupation was fearless when she stood before the real thing, the enemy who had just demonstrated how ruthless he would be. But her children, and the need to be strong for them, had given her courage, and both Harumi and Bayley could see it was no bluff.

Harumi shrugged indifferently and ordered them all onto the truck. Their route did not take them directly to Santo Tomás, for other families and households still had to be picked up. It was almost more of a shock than the actual presence of Harumi on their front porch for Bayley and the Cottermans to see the Imperial Japanese flag, a blood-red sun on a white background, flying from the U.S. high commissioner's flagpole. Throughout the city, the rising sun had replaced the stars and stripes: the Army and Navy Club, the Elks Club, the Manila Hotel, U.S. Army headquarters at Santiago—soon to become the headquarters of the Japanese Gestapo, the Kempetai—all were visibly under Japanese control.

In front of each of these buildings, and before every hotel, apartment house, and office building, stood soldiers with their weapons at port arms, and there were four soldiers posted at every major intersection. The few Filipinos who were on the streets ducked their heads awkwardly as they passed before the watchful gaze of the Japanese: they had already learned that failure to bow to every Japanese soldier, no matter what his rank, would result in brutal reprimands, such as the one Mr. Cotterman had experienced.

The city had been quickly brought to heel, Bayley thought as the truck ground to a stop before the massive arched entrance to Santo Tomás. The Japanese had assumed responsibility for the destiny of thousands of noncombatant civilians, at the same time trying to oust an American Army from the fastness of Bataan. When, he wondered, would the constabulary band hold its next concert?

3

ARRIVALS AND DEPARTURES

Santo Tomás University, Manila: December 1942

Shortly before noon, about two weeks before Christmas, 1942, some 1,400 internees milled about curiously in the Fathers' Garden at the Catholic University of Santo Tomás. A score of cowled Dominican friars peered through the open windows of their adjacent seminary. The raised platform from which the scholarly Anglican clergyman, the Reverend A. O. Griffiths, had throughout the year delivered weekly religious lectures, was now occupied by a dozen American and Japanese figures familiar to most of the internees. There was also a portly, nervous Japanese, dressed in a dark suit, who was not known to them.

In the center of the internees stood a stocky white-haired man in his mid-sixties. An observer might have noted the man's heavy shoulders, corded forearms, and thick wrists, and seen only someone whose life had been spent doing heavy labor—until he looked more closely at the eyes that squinted in the tropical glare behind heavy bifocal lenses. They were the eyes—cool, gray, alert—of a man who had survived the bizarre twists and turns of Asian politics for three decades, a man who knew that the Japanese had put a price of $10,000 on his head but were as yet unaware that they had already netted their big fish by accident.

Bill Donald had understood from the first that elaborate disguise would not protect him. Even today he wore the white broadcloth shirt and rumpled cotton slacks that he had worn on that day in Nanking with Madame Chiang. The *Time* magazine pic-

ture that had been taken of the burly Australian emerging from
a limousine was a very good one, and it had been widely distributed by the Japanese throughout Asia. The face was a High-
lands Scot face: square hewn, with a heavy chin, wide, thin-lipped
mouth, jutting beak of a nose. A forceful face, easy to recognize,
easy to remember.

The Japanese wanted very much to talk to William Donald at
length: they believed, rightly, that he could tell them some interesting things about Chiang Kai-shek's war plans. In fact, Bill
Donald had been on the scene in China almost as long as Chiang
and had entertained some of his fellow prisoners—those he could
trust to be discreet—with stories of his adventurous life. As an
idealistic young foreign correspondent for the Sydney *Daily Tele-
graph,* he had helped man the guns that blasted the Manchu
Dynasty out of power in 1912—resigning his position with the
newspaper before he got fired. Out of a job, he then took an offer
from the *China Mail* in Hong Kong, an offer made because he was
reportedly the only nonalcoholic newsman in Asia. From Hong
Kong he had gone to work for the New York *Herald,* where he
met Sun Yat-sen. The leader of the revolt against the corrupt and
tottering Manchu Dynasty remembered the fiery young newspaperman and asked him to become his public-relations adviser.

For nearly thirty years after that Bill Donald had moved in the
highest circles in China. After Dr. Sun died he joined the staff of
Chang Hsueh-liang, the marshal of Manchuria. Dr. Sun's daughter remembered Donald, though. When she came home from the
United States, where she had gone to Wellesley College, and
married Chiang Kai-shek, she had sent for him. Soon the young
newspaperman had become a chief economic adviser to Chiang
and a close friend of Madame Chiang.

It was, indirectly, due to Madame Chiang that Donald was now
in Santo Tomás. She had asked Donald to write her biography and
had assigned her young secretary, Ansie Lee, to assist him. Donald and Miss Lee had been working on the book at his home in
New Zealand and were en route to China via Manila when they
were interned. They barely had time to hide Madame Chiang's
papers and the partly completed manuscript in an apartment in
Manila before being hustled off to Santo Tomás. Fortunately, their

internment was treated as a matter of routine during the sweep of the city by the Japanese in the first hectic days of the occupation. None of the authorities realized that the "William Donald A. Scot" who signed the register at Santo Tomás was the notorious Australian-born Scotsman who was being sought throughout China by them for interrogation.

Despite—or because of—his long acquaintance with powerful men charged with shaping the fate of nations, Donald did not know any of the Americans on the lecture platform very well. Unlike many of the British internees, he didn't begrudge the Americans their eminence—Santo Tomás was a Yank show, after all. Three out of four internees were Americans. But it was wise for him to keep his distance from the "Executive Committee," as it was called. They had their hands full without having to worry about him.

It was Japanese policy, the internees had learned immediately, to allow those being detained to organize themselves as they saw fit. Challenged to prove that their democratic Anglo-Saxon traditions would function even in these dire circumstances, the internees had early elected a group of men who were then charged with dealing directly with the Japanese commandant and his staff. Some prisoners with a sense of irony noted that the democratically elected leaders of the internees were the same men who had "ruled" Manila before the war—the heart of the city's business establishment. Carroll Grinnell, the head of the Executive Committee, had graduated from Union College as an electrical engineer twenty years ago and had spent his entire career in Asia, most recently as Far East division manager of the International General Electric Company. A. D. Calhoun—"Alex" to the relatively few people who were on a first-name basis with him—was the distinguished, aloof vice-president of the National Bank. Ewald Selph was a prominent Manila attorney; O. G. Steen was vice-president of the American President Lines, and Sam Pinkerton was general manager of an Australian company, Philippine Cold Stores. All were comfortably seated today with their Japanese masters.

Some of the internees did not object to the composition of the committee so much as to their apparent docility, their fear of offending the Japanese. One of these was Ben Edwards, a husky young Pan American Airways mechanic with a blistering fastball. Edwards had been approached by a committee member before a softball game with the guards earlier that fall. The Japanese commandant, the captain of the guards' team, was a man of great pride but indifferent ability as a hitter. "It might be best if you could take it easy on him," a committee member had suggested mildly. "Let him get a single, it can't hurt. You know how they are about saving face."

Edwards had smiled. Yes, he knew how they were. He eased up appreciably in his delivery to the commandant: he allowed him at least two foul tips before he fanned him with a ball that the catcher had to pry loose from his glove.

But the committee had worked wonders during the first hectic months of "the Pacific War," as the Japanese called it. With their influence in Manila and their financial connections, they had helped to work out plans to feed some 4,000 people. (This was a responsibility that the Japanese had denied entirely until July 1942, when they had grudgingly agreed to contribute a daily allowance of about seventy centavos per person toward feeding the camp—enough for a modest breakfast of boiled rice, papaya, and coffee without sugar.) Thanks largely to the efforts of the committee, the "package line" of Filipino friends was allowed to bring food and other supplies to the prisoners; garbage was collected and buried; mosquito netting was supplied and malaria averted; vegetable gardens were planted and tended—in spite of arguments that they would all surely be rescued before the crops came up; regular classes for children and even college-credit courses were taught; Hollywood movies were shown along with the Japanese propaganda films; intramural sports were arranged, hospital passes secured, and shanties authorized to expand the overcrowded living quarters of the campus buildings. To a degree that surprised everyone, Santo Tomás in many ways came to resemble a small town peopled by, among others, an extraordinarily talented number of mining engineers, agronomists, biologists, businessmen, medical missionaries, and others. All of these men—and women —possessed some of the qualities that professionals who live abroad often have: competence, initiative, restlessness, and adaptability.

They did not have the one thing they wanted most: freedom. And that, for many like Ben Edwards and Harold Bayley, was the most galling aspect of the committee's rule. But the Japanese had made it clear that no dissension, no disruption of any kind among the internees, would be tolerated. Rules had to be established and enforced by the committee to guarantee order. Otherwise the Japanese military would step in and impose its own kind of order —the kind, committee members knew, that was killing seven out of ten men in the camps that had been established for prisoners of war elsewhere in the Philippines. Camps run by the same soldiers who had marched 80,000 men from Bataan in April 1942 after their surrender, for forty miles to Camp O'Donnell, and who had left 18,000 of those men dead in the roadside dust—many of them bayoneted, clubbed, buried alive.

The camps set up for civilian internees at Santo Tomás and Baguio, in the north, were not yet under the direct authority of the Japanese army, but the least sign of disruption would bring the army down upon them heavily—just how heavily had been tragically illustrated by the execution of three British sailors who had stolen away from Santo Tomás early in February of the first year. Within a few hours they were caught, tried, convicted, taken by truck to the Chinese cemetery, made to sit with their feet dangling over a common grave, and shot. It was then that many internees began to think of themselves more as prisoners than simply as detained civilians.

Carroll Grinnell and the others on the committee reasoned that their captors were themselves the prisoners of a nation that had, like Germany, become a psychopath; the only way to survive was to avoid antagonizing them. The result was a series of committee rules and edicts designed to keep a bored but assertive population under control. In some ways Santo Tomás came to resemble a Puritan village of seventeenth-century New England. A court of order was established; violators of the public order who were hauled before it for pilfering or malingering could be sentenced to hard labor or solitary confinement in the camp jail. Behavior that in different circumstances would have been only annoying—stealing a neighbor's soap or refusing to help with an assigned work detail such as cleaning toilets or pulling weeds in the camp gardens

—became a punishable offense. Able-bodied adults who refused to help out were told to choose between working and starving. A morality squad outlawed shorts for women as provocative and patrolled the grounds to warn "huggers" away from each other, for the Japanese disliked public displays of affection. A building committee established the height of the naked light bulbs that dimly lit the rabbitlike warrens thrown up in the various college buildings. A member of the committee previewed the entertainment skits put on by the prisoners to make sure the Japanese staff, comfortably ensconced in the front row, would not be offended.

The chief means of communicating among the prisoners was the camp newspaper, staffed by an illustrious group of journalists from *Life,* the International News Service, and the Hearst chain. There was also the public-address system loudspeaker, a device that one young prisoner, Robin Prising, never thought of except in capital letters. Each sunrise arrived with the Andrews Sisters harmonizing, with stunning inappropriateness, "Good morning, good morning, we've danced the whole night through. . . ." Then the needle would be lifted from the worn groove of the record and a guttural, staccato series of orders in Japanese would be issued to the camp guards—a juxtaposition that removed any illusion that this was summer camp in the Poconos. Throughout the day, until "Day Is Done" played at 10:00 P.M., the loudspeaker entertained and harangued the internees, and summoned them to their appointed or unappointed rounds.

The summons this December morning had been the first of its kind—the first time, too, that so many prisoners had gathered in the same place since those terrible first weeks after Pearl Harbor. Through the waiting crowd scampered bands of small children. Their parents, aware that the Japanese were surprisingly indulgent toward children, let them roam. Similarly indulged were the very old, the rheumy-eyed Spanish-American War veterans who lounged contentedly in the sun toward one side of the speakers' platform. There had been great resentment against the Japanese earlier that summer when the old soldiers were forced to move from their comfortable retirement at the Army and Navy Club into the teeming university. But most of them seemed happy to be once more at the center of things. They had gone from being historical artifacts to becoming part of the drama of current events. Bill Donald, who was not much younger than some of the old soldiers, thought he understood how they must feel.

There were five Japanese on the platform, three in uniform and two civilians. Commandant Kuroda, a thin, austere man with baggy pants and wire-rim glasses, sat in the center. To his left were the two civilians. One was his interpreter, Ahiro Watanabe, a smiling, cheerful young man who had graduated from Yale in 1936 with a degree in economics. To the right of Kuroda sat the two most despised men in Santo Tomás, Lieutenant Abiko and Lieutenant Konishi. Abiko might have posed for a recruiting poster. Darkly handsome, broad-shouldered and deep-chested, he had competed as a swimmer in the 1936 Olympics. Now, sleek and powerful, he looked as though he had been poured into his spotless uniform with its knife-edge creases and gleaming brass.

Lieutenant Abiko's particular passion, as many of the internees knew, was the proper bow. At the same time, it was a point of pride to most of the Americans to avoid having to bow to the Japanese, and the ruses they employed were many: when it appeared that a guard's path would be crossed, a prisoner would stop, cock his head as though hearing a call, and retreat before making eye contact with the enemy; mothers would pinch their babies to make them squall at the critical moment; and if all else failed, the prisoner who met a guard and was forced to bow would drop an object on the ground so that he would have to bend over to retrieve it—thus saving his face while satisfying the demands of the enemy. But for all their guile, not a day passed without Lieutenant Abiko haranguing some hapless and forgetful internee. "From the hips, not the waist!" Abiko would shout. "Head to the ground! Back stiff!" Lieutenant Abiko was fondly known as "Shit-face."

A startling physical contrast to the handsome and unrevered lieutenant was offered by Lieutenant Konishi. Reputedly a wounded veteran of the Manchurian campaign, Konishi had been assigned to Santo Tomás as a supply officer in the summer of 1942. His eyes, deeply set under close-cropped, gray-flecked hair and heavy brows, were furtive and sly, his face heavily pocked. His blouse was stained with rings of dried sweat under his arms, which indicated, like the rings of a tree, its age—in this case, since last washing. Konishi smoked incessantly, holding the cigarette far back between his third and fourth fingers and knocking the ash off by letting his fist fall heavily onto his knee. His fingers and teeth were stained a blotchy brown, and a heavy, rattling wheeze riffled through his broad chest.

Two weeks earlier, on Thanksgiving Day, Lieutenant Konishi had refused to allow the Philippine Red Cross to bring in a contribution toward the internees' Thanksgiving dinner. When a member of the Executive Committee complained, Konishi laughed. "Before I'm done with you," he said, "you'll be eating grass."

Kuroda smiled uneasily and spoke slowly, in English. He had been a factory manager in civilian life, accustomed to harmonious cooperation and deferential submission. The resentful curiosity of 1,500 people amounted almost to a physical force pressing against him. He said that since he had been appointed commandant in February he had "kept behind the curtain"—that is, he had not met with them as a group, but he had always had their welfare in mind. "Some people," Kuroda continued, "might be quite sarcastic about what I have done for you, but I hope you will understand the situation. The reason why I appear here today is that I have the unique opportunity to introduce one of my friends who was chargé d'affaires in Panama. He was interned in America"—here Kuroda paused significantly—"and I am sure that all he will say will be very interesting to you. Mr. Izzawa."

The tall man in the dark suit cleared his throat audibly and apologized for his poor command of English. "I have live many years in South America and do not visit your country until late," he said. It soon became apparent that Izzawa had not enjoyed his visit and was there to tell them all how badly their countrymen in America were treating the Japanese, especially the Japanese-Americans on the West Coast. He explained how he had been sent, along with other Axis diplomats, to the Homestead Hotel at White Sulphur Springs, Virginia. Seeing some raised eyebrows among the Americans—the Homestead was one of the half dozen grandest resorts in the country—Izzawa hastened to add that he and the others had been restricted to their rooms and not allowed to visit the lobby or walk in the beautiful gardens—not until they got the Spanish ambassador, "after the many fights," to intervene on their behalf.

When the war began, Izzawa said, all of the Japanese nationals in the Canal Zone were taken to a police station, where they waited for thirty-six hours without food or water. They were then taken to New York, where their money was confiscated, and they waited in a cold and drafty immigration detention room to be questioned. After that, he said, they were forced to live in "open fields in the middle of winter with the windows open" and many times stripped naked and searched.

Izzawa was especially indignant in recounting the experience of the Japanese-Americans. All of the Japanese nationals living in Hawaii were sent to internment camps in the United States, he said, and many of the more than 200,000 Japanese-Americans in the country were being interned. "They have no houses, furniture, and everything. Their money is all freezed." Deprived of their means of support, Izzawa said, they were forced to live as laborers or farmers, building roads under bayonets in Montana, cultivating rocky soil in California and Texas that had never grown anything but sagebrush and mesquite.

Were the Japanese internees in the United States, Izzawa was asked, allowed to write to friends and relatives in Japan?

Yes, once a month, the Japanese diplomat said. The woman who had asked the question nodded grimly: for ten months there had been no letters, no communication of any kind other than that smuggled in at great personal hazard to the Americans by their Filipino friends. Tens of thousands of Americans at home had lived in suspense for nearly a year, wondering what had happened to prisoners of the Japanese in the Philippines, one of the bloodiest theaters of war.

Kuroda, embarrassed, interrupted to say that it was only right for the Japanese in the United States to be allowed to write more often because they were "very far from home and friends." "And we're not?" the woman muttered audibly. "Next question!" Kuroda said briskly.

What chances were there for repatriation? Izzawa and Kuroda smiled. There had been two exchanges already, Izzawa said, and a third was being negotiated between the governments of Japan

and the United States. Unhappily, it had been temporarily post-
poned because of "war battles in the south."

What battles? the prisoners wondered. Deprived—most of them
—of any news about the war aside from the Japanese-controlled
Manila *Tribune,* the curiosity of the internees was piqued by
Izzawa's slip. According to official Japanese propaganda, the empire had established its dominion over all of Southeast Asia and
was now ready to sit down to discuss a negotiated peace with the
American government. There were not supposed to be any "war
battles in the south" according to this scheme.

Izzawa concluded his remarks by assuring the internees that he
was sure they would receive "fair treatment. When I was interned
in the United States we had the same conditions that you have
here. I hope you will all soon go home."

Kuroda thanked the internees for their attention, and the crowd
wandered away. Bill Donald was relieved that the questions left
hanging in the humid noontime glare had not been asked of Mr.
Izzawa: How many Japanese, either American citizens or nationals, had had their toes crushed with rifle butts? How many had
been forced to drink water until their stomachs were distended,
then jumped on by soldiers in combat boots? How many had
routinely been slapped, kicked, and clubbed? How many had suffered and died from beriberi, malaria, dysentery, and other diseases
preventable with proper medical provisions and decent food?

Donald and many of the other internees thought, in short, that
it was the sheerest hypocrisy on the part of their Japanese captors
to compare the situations of the Japanese-Americans to those of
the prisoners of Santo Tomás. Granted that it was sad that the
loyalty of American citizens who happened to be of Japanese
extraction was assumed doubtful. Granted even that thousands
were being subjected to unprecedented inconvenience, even hardship. But looked at coldly, there was a rational argument to be
made for what the American government had done, unpalatable
and unpleasant though it was. Even so, the Japanese might well
have succeeded in persuading the Americans at Santo Tomás that
their government had been unfair—if they themselves had not so
ruthlessly imposed a reign of death and terror throughout their
part of the world, upon people who had done nothing to injure

them. It really was a bit much, Donald thought, for the Japanese to complain that the Americans were bending the Bill of Rights during a time of such national crisis.

The worst part of the situation for the internees at Santo Tomás, though, was not the physical privation but the uncertainty of their future—an uncertainty compounded by ignorance of what was happening in the world beyond the walls of the old university. When would it all end?

For the first few months of 1942 there had been hope: Bataan had held out until late March and Corregidor even longer, both against all expectations. General MacArthur, widely viewed as the only American who was capable of leading the war against the Japanese, had escaped to Australia. "I shall return!" he had vowed, and no Filipino or American doubted his word. The Japanese navy had been dealt a disastrous defeat at Midway in June, barely a month after the fall of Corregidor and only six months after the American humiliation at Pearl Harbor. There was no question in anyone's mind that the United States could quickly annihilate a nation that was smaller in size than the state of California.

But it gradually, painfully dawned on the Americans at Santo Tomás during that first year of the war that their plight was not Washington's primary concern. The word had begun to slip through the net of Japanese censorship during the siege of Bataan: President Quezon's anguished pleas to President Roosevelt were being received with sympathy, with compassion, with admiration —and they were being studiously ignored. The primary enemy for America was not Japan but Nazi Germany. The primary immediate military goal was the capture of North Africa in order to take the pressure off Great Britain. Outraged, Quezon had wired Roosevelt an anguished protest from the Malinta Tunnel on Corregidor: the United States was helping its cousins across the Atlantic while its daughter across the Pacific was being brutally raped. The father—America—was as culpable as the rapist—Japan, Quezon implied. Only with difficulty was President Quezon prevented by MacArthur's eloquence from immediately surrendering to the Japanese.

Not until much later would it become common knowledge that

the Pacific theater would receive only fifteen percent of available money, men, and matériel until after Hitler had been crushed. But one thing was clear to the people of Santo Tomás by the time of Izzawa's visit: they would celebrate Christmas of 1942—and perhaps that of 1943 as well—in Japanese custody despite their initial optimism. With a collective mental sigh, the 4,000 prisoners of Santo Tomás had seized on the one certainty that was available to them: for the duration of the war they would be living at Santo Tomás, and they simply had to learn to make the best of it.

Even that certainty was shattered just a few months after Izzawa's visit with the Japanese decision that the entire camp, all 4,000 and more, would soon be moving to an isolated agricultural college campus thirty miles to the south, called Los Baños.

4

SHUFFLING OFF TO LOS BAÑOS

Los Baños, The Philippines, May 1943

One of the major sources of amusement for the internees at Santo Tomás since the beginning of the war was the Manila *Tribune*. Reading between the lines of the Japanese-controlled newspaper, they had learned about MacArthur's dramatic escape to Australia in March 1942 ("a cowardly flight, but to be expected from the leader of a mongrel army"); about the Japanese defeat at Midway ("heroic sacrifice of the sons of Nippon"); and about the surprise and uneasiness felt by the Japanese over America's lack of interest in negotiating a peace that would allow the empire to keep what it had stolen ("stubborn refusal to accept Japan's rightful dominance in Asia"). Separating the wheat from the chaff had become a minor art by the time the 800 pioneers at Los Baños came to read the glowing account in the *Tribune* of their experiences on May 16, 1943.

The first part of the story was accurate enough, describing the departure from Santo Tomás of the men and the twelve nurses who accompanied them. So was the description of Los Baños and its environs, travel-agent prose notwithstanding. The town was indeed a resort, named after its hot springs, "the baths." Located as it was on the shore of a huge inland lake, the Laguna de Bay, the setting was admittedly "superb"—especially with the backdrop of Mount Makiling, the terraced, emerald-green hillsides, and the blue waters of the lake shimmering in the brilliant sun. The "spacious lawns" of the agricultural college, a mile from the village, were graced by palm and mango trees, and the faculty bungalows with their red-tiled roofs and white stucco walls were surrounded by a profusion of exotic flowers—jasmine, hibiscus, wisteria. The aroma of the flowers, mingling with the scent of fresh-cut grass, was—the newspaper neglected to add—a welcome relief from the pervasive stench of Santo Tomás, a compound of garbage, sewage, and too seldom bathed bodies.

Even some of the details about the mood of the departure were accurate. It was true that the 800 had been sent off by their friends on "motorcars and trucks which were placed at their disposal" by the Japanese authorities. And there had been "phonograph records played to create a cheerful atmosphere," beginning with "Tiger Rag Bugle Call" at 5:00 A.M. and continuing through the morning with "Onward Christian Soldiers," "The Battle Hymn of the Republic," and—a whimsical selection—"Shuffle Off to Buffalo." But the *Tribune* had stretched the truth when it explained how "happy the men were to move to one of the best-known health centers in the Philippines" and how cheerfully they piled onto the dozen trucks that would take them to the Tutuban Station. Only about one in four of the men on the trucks had volunteered to go to Los Baños; the rest would have greatly preferred to remain where they were.

This was only natural, for despite its obvious drawbacks the old university had been made reasonably livable. Thousands of pesos had been spent from Red Cross funds, augmented by the belated Japanese per diem allowance of seventy centavos and individual contributions from prisoners and their relatives. The money had gone to provide medical facilities, efficient kitchens, and supplementary housing. Many of the prisoners had worked out arrangements with Filipino friends that provided them with laundry, food, and medicine—in some cases even with check-cashing privileges. Passes in and out of STIC—as Santo Tomás Internment Camp was known—were still possible during that first year to visit family and friends. As Commandant Kuroda put it, "While we are winning, we can afford to be generous." To be deprived of these hard-won adaptations would be a cruel blow for many.

Kuroda did his best to assuage the fears of the prisoners in his initial statement. He stressed that "this change of location is entirely based upon the humanitarian consideration of your own welfare, and fairness to the treatment to be accorded to internees shall always be maintained." A special committee of three men, including Alex Calhoun, would leave the next morning with Lieutenant Colonel Naruzawa for Los Baños; they would "work out a program adapted to the needs of the internees that will ensure them of at least the same degree of comfort as now enjoyed." This was not meant to be ironic, the prisoners feared.

"In carrying out the above plan," Kuroda said, "the first group of 800 men, to be selected from volunteers, will be dispatched to Los Baños by train on the sixteenth of the month. Let me conclude by reminding the internees that you are warned not to make careless utterances that will distort the true intention of the military administration regarding this plan." The listeners understood perfectly: go without making any noise, they were being told.

But despite the commandant's assurances, there were few men who wanted to be separated from their families at Santo Tomás, if only for a few months. Thus fewer than 300 men volunteered, mostly young bachelors such as Bayley and Edwards. The rest had to be "press-ganged," as Isla Corfield put it in her diary. The names of all the eligible men, including the unattached or the young married, were dumped into a barrel. When they were pulled out and read aloud to the assembled prisoners, it looked to Isla like a scene at a mine disaster, with the women waiting in anguish to see if the names of their loved ones would be included in the toll.

Now, the morning of May 16, 1943, the men were about to board the trucks that would take them to the train a mile away. Major Kuroda appeared in the plaza and took the microphone to address the departing group. He cleared his throat and searched for the words he wanted. "I congratulate you boys on good behavior here," he said. "I hope in new camp you will be good also and acquaint yourself with new rules. I congratulate, too, on short time you are being ready. You will have hard work to get new camp ready for your fellow internees. I myself soon go back to Japan. This is probably last time I speak to you. I wish you good luck and much health."

The newspaper account did not include mention of the distant strains of "The Star-Spangled Banner," played somewhere in the village by a native band of three trumpets, a violin, and a tenor saxophone, that drifted over the camp as the men loaded onto the trucks—nor the Japanese soldier at the gate who returned the V sign flashed him by one of the prisoners and then promptly burst into tears. Neither was there any account of the three-and-a-half hour ride in closed metal boxcars so crowded that everyone had to stand. Even those whose stomachs churned with nausea from the 120-degree heat, the enervating press of bodies, and the lurching, stop-and-go motion of the train could not sit or lie down. Those in the middle of the press of bodies were more fortunate than those on the edges. They could at least lean against other bodies, but the walls of the boxcars were so hot from the sun that touching them for longer than a few seconds was unendurable. There were, of course, no latrine facilities and no water at all. The only relief to be had was from taking turns standing at the narrow crack in the door and urinating through it. Another two or three hours and some of the older prisoners such as Harry Fonger might not have made it to Los Baños alive.

The *Tribune* account of the arrival after this wrenching journey did include some delightfully dubious dialogue, supposedly uttered by the arriving prisoners: " 'Say, this is not bad at all!' Their eyes focused on the vegetable gardens. 'We'll grow our own vegetables!' they agreed unanimously." In fact, the pioneers had arrived in a torrential afternoon downpour. The college administration at Los Baños, not expecting them so soon, had no place for the men to stay, and they sat for two hours in their trucks while accommodations in the college gym and other buildings were improvised.

Alex Calhoun was particularly interested to read the remarks he was reputed to have made on Los Baños as reported in the *Tribune*, since he was the newly appointed chairman of the Executive Committee for the new camp. Life at Santo Tomás, he discovered he had assured the readers of the *Tribune*, had been "not bad at all. In fact," he continued, "we were grateful of [sic] the considerate treatment we received from the Japanese authorities. However, we believe that we can all enjoy a happier and healthier life at the new camp here."

"Calhoun" went on to praise the surroundings at Los Baños,

where "the air is pure and campgrounds are spacious. There are hills, streams, playgrounds, and gardens. The place is ideal from the point of view of health provided we internees lead a disciplined life. I would like to express my gratitude to the Japanese authorities for their thoughtful consideration of our welfare."

All of this was the purest fabrication. What Calhoun had actually said, in a report to Carroll Grinnell, was that 600 men were housed in a gymnasium with four toilets; that a test for B coli bacteria in the water supply had proved positive, and that widespread dysentery must surely result; that 200 men had slept in the rain that first night; that the evening meal had consisted of two hardtack biscuits and six ounces of corned beef per man; and that forty cases of malaria had been treated at the college infirmary within the past month. It would be hard enough for the mostly healthy and hardy younger men who had come to Los Baños to stay well. To move the elderly, the sick, the very young, and the women from Santo Tomás to Los Baños would be a murderous folly.

Not everyone, however, viewed the transfer to Los Baños as a hardship. Some, like Alex Brockway's wife, Sue, a nurse, thought it was their duty to go with the men and help out. Some, like Harold Bayley, had had quite enough of Manila by May 1943. Some, like Dr. W. H. "Harry" Fonger, head of the American Bible Society in Manila, knew that Los Baños was indeed a beautiful spot and that despite the drawbacks noted by Calhoun, it was likely to be a healthier place than Santo Tomás.

Harry Fonger, who would become one of the central figures in the dramatic story of Los Baños, was a patient, soft-spoken man, considerably older than most of his fellow pioneers. Born in London, Ontario, in 1891, he was past fifty years old when the war began, and the perspective of his age and his experience in the Philippines gave him a quiet authority. His authority did not rest upon the "Donated Dignity" he said his ecclesiastical "D.D." (Doctor of Divinity) title really meant but on some deeper reserve of character, a reserve that had been tested long before the Japanese trucks reached Los Baños.

Harry Fonger had already been in one war. In 1916 he graduated from tiny Eureka College in Illinois as an ordained minister.

He was older than most of the other graduates because his father, a farmer near London, had pulled his son out of school at the age of twelve to help him in the fields; not until he was seventeen did the boy return to complete his high school education. Through a friend of the family who knew about Eureka College, the strapping young man was allowed to attend the academy affiliated with the college to finish his college preparation (he much preferred to be away from home instead of sitting through classes with the neighborhood children).

After graduation Fonger took a pastorate at a small church in Cooksville, Illinois, near Bloomington. The church lost its pastor and a large proportion of its congregation when Fonger and eleven farmers went together to join the U.S. Army. Though totally ignorant of any weapons larger than shotguns or deer rifles, they volunteered for the artillery: the big howitzers were pulled by horses, and they all knew a lot about horses, so the choice seemed logical.

The Army sent Fonger off to stand guard in Panama for eight months, then to officers training school at Old Point Comfort, Virginia. He was in the third class to finish the three-month course —thus one of the original "ninety-day wonders"—and was set to go overseas when the Army tapped him to be an instructor in "gas defense." Someone figured that a man who could preach the gospel ought to be able to lecture on the principles of surviving a gas attack, and Fonger spent the next two years leading gasping troops into and out of small houses filled with chlorine.

When the war ended Fonger married his college sweetheart, Leith Cox, an Illinois girl, and the two set out for Kansas, Illinois, and a new pastorate. Kansas was only a temporary stop, though; as a student at Eureka Fonger had applied to the College of Missions of the Christian Church Disciples. He wanted to be a missionary, and in 1923 he and his wife sailed for the Philippines. For the next ten years they worked in the northern province of Abra, among the Ilocono tribes, and doted on their only child, Burton, born in 1925. In 1933 Fonger transferred to the American Bible Society in Manila, where he directed the translation of the Bible into various Philippine dialects and saw the editions through the printing and binding process at the Bible Society's own facilities. His wife, meanwhile, looked after Burton, gave music lessons and Bible instruction, and played the organ in the Union Church.

When the war began, Harry Fonger's placid life was disrupted to an even greater extent than those of most of the Americans then living in Manila. From their first days in the Philippines the Japanese authorities had attempted to enlist the cooperation of the Catholic and Protestant religious leaders there. A Buddhist Lieutenant Colonel named Naruzawa had been named head of the "Religious Section" of the Propaganda Corps and had fashioned a statement of cooperation that he wanted all clergy to sign. The population of the Philippines being overwhelmingly Catholic, Naruzawa had directed his first efforts toward winning the support of the archbishop of Manila, Michael J. O'Doherty.

On January 20, 1942, the Manila *Tribune* reported that a harmonious meeting had been held at the palace of the archbishop between the representatives of eleven Roman Catholic religious orders and Lieutenant Colonel Naruzawa. The Japanese officer had "explained the aims of the Japanese army with regard to the religious activities of the Filipinos." He noted that "the fundamental principle underlying Japan's actions is the spirit of universal brotherhood, which is the same as that of the Catholic Church." The archbishop, the report concluded, had "expressed the desire to cooperate with the army in endeavoring to establish peace throughout the world." The archbishop had, in fact, merely asserted that "the Holy Father has expressly and strictly forbidden us from engaging in any other profession or activity but the religious," and the Japanese would have to be content with that assurance. In the meantime, he said, he would like to call to the colonel's attention the wanton destruction of the religious printing press at the Good Shepherd Sisters orphanage, the theft of the sacred chalices from a parish priest in a southern village, and a number of other incidents.

Naruzawa agreed to look into these matters, but the initial cordiality between the Japanese Buddhist and the Irish archbishop soon diminished. Late in January Naruzawa asked O'Doherty if he would agree to give a radio talk about the "Co-Prosperity Sphere" from the Catholic perspective. He was furious at the archbishop's refusal: O'Doherty had seen fit to make a speech against Nazism the previous November, a demonstrably political topic, had he not? Then he should be able to make one now for him, Naruzawa said. When O'Doherty said nothing, Naruzawa restricted the archbishop to his quarters and turned his attention to the Protestant leaders.

Far less numerous and powerful than their Catholic brethren, the Protestant clergy were not coddled initially, as the Catholics had been. It was not necessary to be diplomatic, Naruzawa probably felt. And in any case, that approach had gotten him nowhere with the Catholics. He would have slightly better results with the Protestants.

Like the other clergy, Harry Fonger had been interned with his family in Santo Tomás early in January 1942, but they had all been released to their homes after a few days. On January 26 he received a phone call from a Japanese Christian, the Reverend Dr. T. Aiura. Aiura told Fonger that he was "invited" to a meeting the next day at the Manila Hotel with Lieutenant Colonel Naruzawa. The invitation was repeated more gruffly the next morning by a military aide, Lieutenant Mihara: attendance was required, not optional. At two o'clock that afternoon, Fonger arrived at the Manila Hotel, along with twelve other American religious workers, one Englishman, and twenty-six Filipinos. A Japanese guard checked off their names on a clipboard as they entered the palm-fringed lobby. They were then all ushered outside into the garden for a picture-taking session, after which they were taken into the Walnut Room. The tables there had been arranged in the form of a D. The Japanese were seated at the vertical shaft of the D, and their "guests" were seated by alphabetical order around the curve, every seat marked by a large number. An aide called the roll and Dr. Aiura introduced Lieutenant Colonel Naruzawa, who delivered a carefully prepared speech through his interpreter.

Naruzawa thanked the clergymen for leaving their holy duties to join him. It was important, he said, that they realize that the present war was the holy war required of the army of Japan in order to build the stability of Greater Asia. Its aim was emphatically not to fight against those Filipinos who would cooperate with the Japanese army but rather to bring about the downfall of the

American and British forces that "would ever uphold the status quo by keeping the anti-Japanese policy and denying, under the cloak of world peace, the living rights of the ever growing races in East Asia, and also to exterminate communism, which aims at the conquest of the world by destroying and confusing all cultures, religions and orders . . ." and so on.

Try as he might, Harry Fonger found it impossible to keep his mind focused on Naruzawa's interminable harangue. This was siesta time, not meant for windy speechmaking, and under the disapproving glare of Dr. Aiura he felt himself nodding in the midafternoon heat. Occasional phrases cut through the humid air, though, and caught his attention: ". . . Japan is willing to sacrifice anything in order to fulfill her mission of creating the Greater East Asia Co-Prosperity Sphere . . . Japan marches on, on the road of justice and humanism . . . you must trust in the power and mercy of Japan . . . you must sign the five-point pledge that is before you . . ." Pledge? Fonger came to with a start as Naruzawa's interpreter read the pledge. The first point presented no problem: "Although we are granted the freedom of faith, we will gladly offer our buildings and their equipment whenever they are needed and are requested through proper channel for military strategy." "Gladly" was hardly accurate, but the provision did no more than admit that what they had kept was at the suffrance of the invader. Also acceptable were the second and third points, which said that the clergy agreed to hold services only at Santo Tomás and not to hold other—i.e., political—meetings. Again, no problem. The fourth and fifth points, however, raised some questions.

Point four committed those who signed it to "lead and instruct our members of the church, trusting in the Japanese army, understanding that the great ideal of the Great East Asia Co-Prosperity Sphere is according to the will of God." Point Five said "we would positively cooperate with the Japanese army and would not fail its generous considerations toward us." Lieutenant Mihara, head of the Protestant subsection of Naruzawa's group, said the pledge would now be passed around so that the men could read it and ask questions.

"What does 'positive cooperation' with the Japanese army in paragraph five mean?" Fonger asked politely.

"The meaning is perfectly clear," Mihara said. "Next question."

"Doesn't the sense of the fourth and fifth points," asked Simon Reyes, a Filipino clergyman, "seem to go against what we were earlier advised to avoid—that is, involving ourselves in politics?"

"These points do not involve politics at all," Mihara responded shortly.

The Reverend H. S. Spackman questioned the phrase "according to the will of God" in the fourth point. The Reverend Doctor E. E. Tuck agreed: "Even my own bishop cannot interpret the will of God for me," he laughed nervously.

"Perhaps we could substitute something more agreeable," suggested Dr. Aiura. "Something having to do with world peace."

The Reverend Spackman and Dr. Aiura were directed to draft a compromise statement, and for several minutes there was only silence in the dark, humid room. When the two men returned with a harmless statement about all present being agreed to the need for peace in the world, Lieutenant Colonel Naruzawa smiled contentedly. "Now you can have no further objections," he said. "You will each be given the opportunity to come forward and sign the pledge."

Seat number one was occupied by a Japanese whom none of the other clergymen knew. He was, they learned later, not a clergyman at all but a lumber contractor from Ilocos Norte. He signed with alacrity and was followed by the Filipino clergymen in seats two and three. The next three seats were occupied by American ministers who refused to move.

"Okay, anybody sign," Aiura said, after an uneasy silence. "No need to go in order." A few more went up to sign, but most milled around aimlessly. Harry Fonger stood off to one side with two or three colleagues, including Dr. Holter, president of the Union Theological Seminary. Holter commented that after all those years of teaching their students about Becket and More and the conflict between church and state, they were now getting a chance to see it in action for themselves.

By six o'clock all but one of the Filipinos had signed the pledge, along with six of the thirteen Americans and the one Englishman, and the clergymen were all allowed to go home. But the holdouts were brought back the next day, and the next, and the next. . . . By the following week, only four still refused to sign the pledge: Holter, Fonger, Reverend Brush, and Reverend Bomm— two of the first three men to stay in their seats originally. Aiura was outraged at their "petty nationalism" when they said the pledge demanded that they renounce both their religion and their country.

"You can have no objection to point four now," Aiura said. "The phrase you objected to, 'the will of God,' has been struck."

"That is not the problem," Fonger said. "The problem is in the phrase 'trusting in the Japanese army' to lead the world to peace. I for one would find it difficult to sign even if 'American army' were substituted. Armies do not lead the way to peace. Wise and humane governments do, by directing the armies in proper ways."

"Forget the words and sign the pledge," Aiura said. "You have until six o'clock. If you delay you may not be permitted to sign the pledge in any event."

Fonger and the others left. None of them returned by six o'-clock. The following morning Aiura called them into his office. They were to see Lieutenant Colonel Naruzawa shortly, Aiura said. "Please, gentlemen, reconsider," he pleaded. "You are taking too much on your individual consciences. The whole future of Protestantism in this part of the world may be at stake. If you refuse to sign, we may have to turn you over to the military. There is strong sentiment already in the army to erase all traces of Protestantism from the Philippines. Your Bible Society, Dr. Fonger, would not be able to function. Your seminary, Dr. Holter, would be closed." Aiura hesitated, then continued, as if embarrassed. "And I must confess that we would not be able to guarantee your personal safety, or that of your families. . . ."

"Dr. Aiura," Holter said, "you are asking us to do the impossible. Consider: what would you do in our place?"

Aiura smiled wanly. "We will have to wait until after the war to discuss that further," he said.

The conversation with Lieutenant Colonel Naruzawa was brief and less than cordial. He glanced at a substitute pledge that the stubborn four had drafted and tossed it back at them. "Your version leaves out the essential word," he said. "Cooperation."

Naruzawa sat back and tugged thoughtfully at his short mustache. "We have been very patient with you gentlemen. We are not the Kempetai, and we do not employ their . . . methods of persuasion. We will not ask you to sign this document again. You will understand, of course, that certain amenities provided to those who *did* sign will no longer be available to you."

The four men waited silently for Naruzawa to continue. The sun shone through the windows of the French doors and dazzled them, while the Japanese officer sat immobile, in shadow, behind his polished teak desk. A minute went by, two minutes, then three, and the only sounds were those of the city, slowly returning to a semblance of normality and, in the distance, the heavy concussive thuds of Japanese bombs falling on Bataan and Corregidor. Finally Naruzawa spoke, just one brief sentence: "This discussion is finished."

The following morning a black Pontiac sedan pulled up in front of the Fongers' residence at the American Bible Society. Two Japanese officers knocked on the door of the small apartment that had been converted from the second floor of a warehouse behind the main office. Harry Fonger kissed his wife, Leith, good-bye and embraced his son, Burton, by now a tall, handsome boy of sixteen who was trying, without much success, to grow a beard. The officers led Fonger to the car, which was soon joined by three other black sedans in a procession to Santo Tomás. It was part of their punishment for refusing to cooperate to return the four men to the internment camp; the other part, far more onerous, was to separate them from their families.

So it was that when the chance to leave Santo Tomás for Los Baños arose, Fonger took it. He had seen his wife and son only fleetingly for more than a year; he might as well be forty miles away as three for all the good proximity had done him. Then, too, there was the possibility of being reunited with Leith and Burton after a few months at Los Baños, when facilities there had been established. It had concerned him greatly from the start that they had been thrown on their own resources, alone in a city that had become dangerous for anyone except the Japanese, while he enjoyed the relative security of Santo Tomás. There had been too many reliable accounts of "Europeans" still outside the walls of the university being harassed by Japanese soldiers, even of Japanese truck drivers trying to run down white pedestrians for sport.

There was one more reason for Fonger to do whatever he could to get himself and his family out of Manila. At fifty-two he had accumulated a knowledge of the Philippines and a sense of the ebb and flow of Asian politics. His age and experience allowed him to view the long months, even years, of internment as a temporary aberration, not as a permanent condition. But Fonger knew two things would surely happen before long: MacArthur would keep his promise to return to the Philippines, and the city of Manila would once again become a battlefield. And when that day of deliverance arrived, Los Baños, for all its drawbacks, would be a healthier place for himself and his family than Manila.

5

A TYPICAL AMERICAN TOWN

Los Baños Internment Camp, The Philippines: May 1943–June 1944
I

Many of the 800 pioneers whom Harry Fonger had chosen to join would come to regard the slow, sultry summer of 1943 as a period of calm between two storms—the beginning and the end of the war. Few of them knew then that Alex Calhoun, the Manila banker, had spent the summer fighting his own war for their survival. It was a fight that pitted him against both the Japanese and some of his own colleagues on the Executive Committee at Santo Tomás.

The problem faced by Calhoun had its roots in Carroll Grinnell's originally rather timid reaction to the Japanese plans for Los Baños; and particularly his response to the dramatic change in plans that the Japanese decided on early in the summer. The original announcement in April had indicated that Los Baños was intended to accommodate the overflow from Santo Tomás, but shortly after that the word came down that Los Baños should become the central camp for all of the northern Philippines. The 4,000 prisoners now at Santo Tomás would go there, plus the scattered hundreds of civilians being held at various other locations. The internee population at Los Baños would be 4,000; seventy barracks, each to contain ninety-eight people, would be built on a site of twenty-five acres.

It was glaringly obvious to all that the Japanese plan was not only absurd but dangerous. Clyde DeWitt and George Grey of the U.S. high commissioner's office objected that the Japanese were violating "a well-established principle of international law—that military necessity should govern the actions of an occupying army in dealing with the inhabitants of an occupied territory." The Japanese had failed to explain how military need required such a move, the diplomats argued—but to no avail. Privately, the Americans suspected that there were two reasons for the move to Los Baños, neither of them humanitarian and neither admissable by the Japanese. The first was that the obvious sympathy of the Filipino people for their deposed "masters" was embarrassing. The package lines, the food and supplies, and the moral support offered by the Filipinos had remained at their original high peak despite Japanese harassment. The only way to discourage such displays of sympathy was to remove its provocation—to send the Americans far away. The second suggested reason, particularly appropriate for the exile of the 800 men between the ages of eighteen and forty, was Japanese fear that they might escape and join the guerrilla bands that continued to bedevil the Japanese. It would be better to have all the potential troublemakers in one place.

Dr. Charles Leach, under orders from Kuroda to take over as the medical director at the new camp, tried to explain to the Japanese the dangers posed by disease and lack of water at Los Baños. The surface water was thoroughly contaminated by the farm animals in the area, Leach said. The reservoir on top of Mount Makiling to the rear of the camp supplied only 20,000 gallons daily at present, with a tiny reserve of only 10,000 gallons. There was barely enough water for the 2,500 native residents of the area: already the water was rationed, the main valves being turned off at night. The additional burden of 800 men on the system, plus the Japanese guards, would by itself bring the daily demand to 85,000 gallons. And it would be utterly impossible ever to provide the minimum of 300,000 gallons daily that would be needed for a camp of 7,000 people.

Moreover, there was no sewer system planned. Septic tanks for 1,000 or even 1,500 prisoners at Los Baños might be tolerable, but the waste from 7,000 people would certainly contaminate all area wells. A major outbreak of typhoid would be inevitable. The suggestion that water could be boiled was ridiculous, Leach said, except on a very short, interim basis: Kuroda need only think how long it would take to strip the surrounding land of everything burnable to boil enough water daily for 7,000 people. Finally there was malaria. This was a disease that knew no favorites, as the Japanese were well aware (it was responsible for more Japanese deaths on Bataan than were American bullets). Leach had done a malaria survey in and around Los Baños some years earlier. "I can assure you," he said, "that there was an abundance of the anopheles mosquito at the time. I understand that the streams on the college campus were treated with Paris green until the outbreak of the war. This would indicate anopheles breeding, as Paris green is not used in exterminating other species of mosquitoes. I am informed that forty cases of malaria have been treated in the college dispensary recently," he concluded. Given the conditions at Los Baños, Leach hoped that Commandant Kuroda would understand his reluctance to assume the post of medical director there—though "if a military order is given me, I will have no choice and will do the best I can." The order was duly given, and Dr. Leach assembled a medical staff of several doctors and a dozen nurses.

Calhoun, Grey, DeWitt, and Leach had never been unfavorably disposed to the plan to move 800 men to Los Baños. Much of their problem now in resisting the unreasonable expansion of the camp was that they had received only halfhearted support from Carroll Grinnell. Even though he agreed with the others in conversation, Grinnell simply observed to Kuroda that he "would like to confirm formally our verbal protest against any transfer of internees from this camp to any location that is not properly equipped to protect the lives and welfare of civilian internees to a degree at least equivalent to that afforded by Santo Tomás Internment Camp. . . . We believe that this is a very serious matter that merits full and careful consideration by all concerned. . . ."

It was hardly a forceful protest. Indeed, by mid-June Grinnell's fears had been sufficiently allayed to allow him to give a rosy report to the internees at Santo Tomás. Everything was going very well at Los Baños, he said. It was true that there was a water shortage and that all drinking water had to be boiled. But "exhaustive studies were being taken to guarantee an adequate supply of water." It was also true that all cooking had to be done on wood fires, which was somewhat inconvenient; however, several men had been heard to say that the wood-smoke improved the taste of their food.

There was, Grinnell said, plenty of free time for "study, reading, and athletics," and morale was high. He also reported that construction was beginning on the new barracks. Each barracks would hold ninety-eight persons, with space amounting to sixty square feet per person, including the center aisle, or forty-eight square feet excluding the center aisle. There would be flush toilets, one for each fifteen prisoners (versus one for seventy at Santo Tomás), one shower for each seventeen, and laundry facilities. The buildings would be 30 by 198 feet, of wood-frame construction, with nipa roofs and sawali sides. They would have concrete floors. A six-foot veranda covered by *"media-aguas"* to carry off the rain would extend around the barracks.

Despite Grinnell's sanguine appraisal, on July 18 the Los Baños Executive Committee submitted a formal protest to Kuroda. Not only were the Japanese planning to cram thousands of people into an area half the size of Santo Tomás, itself admittedly over-crowded, but they had now severely altered the building plans that had prompted Grinnell's optimistic report: there would be no electricity; no flush toilets; and no upgraded water-supply system, the internees were told. They would have to make do with what they had.

These changes meant that hundreds of people—later, thousands—living in barracks built with grass walls and thatch roofs would have to use oil lamps, an incalculable fire hazard; that box seats over earth trenches would have to serve as toilets and would have to be emptied manually every few hours; and that water for drinking, cooking, bathing, and gardening would have to be carried in buckets from distant wells. The new camp would quite obviously be unsafe, the committee charged, for "the health and lives of a congested population consisting of men, women, and children ranging from infants to the extremely aged and in varying conditions of health." The committee took a collective deep breath and plunged forward. From this "inexplicable alteration" of the original plans, its members could only infer that "there has evidently been a reversal of official policy governing the treatment of non-combatant civilians." This was a reversal that, the committee said, "tended toward deliberate persecution." There was no reply from the Japanese.

Alex Calhoun pondered his problem. Tall and thickly built, with deep-set blue eyes and a ruddy complexion, he had become vice-president of the Philippines National Bank by virtue of his ability and his natural authority. He had kept his composure and his dignity even when, on January 3, 1942, a Japanese lieutenant had held a pistol to his temple and forced him to open the bank safe. Afterward, when he was paraded in an open car through the streets of Manila with other leaders of "the corrupt American plutocracy," he had kept a portion of himself removed, inviolate. It was not in Alex Calhoun's character to plead for, or even to request, anything of anybody: he had been accustomed to give orders, not to receive them. It may have been this as much as the eloquence of his personal appeal that finally saved the day for the internees at Los Baños.

Early in August 1942, Calhoun wrote a letter to Lieutenant Colonel Kodaki, chief of the section of external affairs of the military administration responsible for civilian internees. His letter was written to Kodaki rather than Kuroda, who had been unresponsive, out of "sheer desperation," Calhoun said. If some changes in policy were not made immediately, then "several thousand" people, including women and children, "will be faced shortly with intolerable conditions, which may easily lead to a serious epidemic, with a number of fatalities."

Calhoun went on to summarize the problems of health, housing, and water at Los Baños, and to remind the Japanese officer that these were problems that could easily be solved by the "many educated and practical engineers of wide experience" among the internees. He then referred more personally to his own situation as that of a typical internee. On January 3, 1942, Japanese troops had entered his home and ordered him and his guests (Calhoun's family had returned to the States before the war) to Villamor Hall "with only a supply of clothing and food for three days. On January 6 we were transferred to Santo Tomás with nothing other than the original supplies quickly gathered together. In Santo

Tomás we were crowded into bare rooms but at least had adequate shelter, running water, gas, and electrical connections. We were interned there with no beds or bedding, no mosquito nets, no food, no kitchen equipment, and no hospital. Through our own resources and efforts Santo Tomás was gradually made livable."

After summarizing their efforts in this regard, Calhoun said, "In the meantime, our homes were occupied, and we lost our possessions which, in most instances, represented the accumulation of a lifetime. We, enemy aliens, it is true, but noncombatants, have suffered all of this without complaint. But we have now reached what threatens to be a fatal blow to our health and perhaps our lives. Alone and powerless" in this new camp, Calhoun said, "I do not know where to turn next. To bring women and children, the aged and the sick, to the new camp in its present condition would be a fatal blow to all of us. I believe," he concluded, "that there has been a serious mistake somewhere along the line. I feel confident that when the true facts are known, adequate facilities will be provided for our health and safety. It is in this faith that I appeal to you."

Calhoun's personal and emotional appeal succeeded where earlier appeals to international law and medical common sense had failed. Variations on the previous plans for adequate water, electricity, and waste disposal were reinstated—and, even more significant, plans to expand Los Baños beyond 1,500 or 2,000 prisoners were scrapped. The internees at Los Baños had won their first battle to stay alive even though few of them were ever aware that it had even taken place.

II

Part of the reason for the success of Alex Calhoun's efforts lay in the fact that they were approved, not opposed, by Major Tanaka, the first commandant at Los Baños. Tall for a Japanese at nearly six feet, he was not at first sight a reassuring figure. His lean, wan face was deeply etched, not from age but from the incessant pain where his left arm had been before it was shattered by a Chinese grenade in Manchuria. The last surviving male in a samurai family whose origins stretched back to the fifteenth century, Major Tanaka had been a warrior, dedicated body and soul to the emperor. Now his final duty had been decreed, far from the fields of battle where he belonged.

But if Tanaka was resentful at being posted to such a distant backwater as Los Baños for the last few months of his career, he did not take it out on the internees in his charge. Both with Calhoun and with Harry Fonger, who would succeed Calhoun as chairman of the Executive Committee in December 1943, he was as fair and as humane as circumstances allowed him to be. He permitted the internees to trade with the natives for food, allowed the Philippine Red Cross to deliver its "comfort kits" for the prisoners, and encouraged the Executive Committee to handle the governance of the camp to as great a degree as possible.

A brave man himself, Tanaka respected the strength and single-mindedness of Calhoun and the moral courage of Fonger. His approbation showed itself in small but significant ways. One day Fonger was to go by truck to Manila, where he would purchase food in the open markets for the camp. The guard curtly ordered the white-haired minister into the rear of the truck, where he would have to sit on the splintery, hard bench for the duration of the two-hour trip over shell-pocked roads to Manila. Tanaka happened by as the truck was leaving, stopped it, and ordered the guard, who had taken the comfortable seat beside the driver of the cab, to trade places with the American.

Another more important intercession by Tanaka occurred when he received orders to require a head-count roll call twice daily instead of only once. The procedure had already been instituted at Santo Tomás. Tanaka asked Fonger on his next supply run to Manila to find out what had been the response of the internees at Santo Tomás to the new rule. When Fonger reported that the extra roll call was seen without exception as pointless harassment of the internees, Tanaka refused to require it at Los Baños.

By the early autumn of 1943, when the next batch of 850 internees arrived from Santo Tomás, the residents of Los Baños had their lives fairly well in order. Filipino laborers had been hired by the Japanese to build twenty-six barracks on the athletic field near Baker Hall, the gymnasium, on the upper part of the old college campus. (Tanaka had concurred, after some hesitation, with the internees' arguments that they should not be used as laborers in building the new camp; to do so would be a violation of the Geneva accords.) The 200 men who had initially been housed in old student dormitories—buildings so riddled with termites and wood-eating ants that nails could be pressed into the walls with a forefinger—were now mostly in the new barracks, as were about three-quarters of the 600 who had been jammed into Baker Hall.

The barracks had turned out approximately as Grinnell had described them. They were built in pairs, each pair being joined by a combination wash house and latrine. In some ways, though, the new quarters were worse, not better, than the facilities at Santo Tomás, where the walls and ceilings were constructed of durable stone and concrete and the water supply was ample. Here, the nipa roofs of the new barracks leaked and the sawali walls rotted with the first prolonged rains. Another problem, the result of living in the middle of a jungle, was insects, especially mosquitoes and bedbugs. Mosquito netting strung over the eight to ten bunks in the larger cubicles, or the two to four bunks in the smaller, worked well enough to keep flying insects out. However, the bedbugs used the netting as highways from one bed to the next, and infested mattresses and bedding were inevitable. There was only one cure for bedbugs, and that was to kick over one of the many ant hills that dotted the compound and leave the infested bedding on top of it. The ants would feast on the bugs, after which they could be evicted themselves by a hearty shaking. And if a few ants remained for company during the night—well, an ant's bite was much smaller than a bedbug's.

The bathing and toilet facilities were Spartan but sufficient. The sheds that connected each pair of barracks contained six showers, six water taps and sinks, and six toilets for women, and the same number for men. Although there was never to be enough water at Los Baños, just as there was never enough food, even at the best of times, enough wells had been dug to augument the reservoir so that the internees could make do. The flush toilets never did materialize, despite Kodaki's promise, but a brilliant invention by an unsung engineer had solved the problem of waste disposal.

The toilet facilities consisted of a long, flat board with six holes that were covered with lids. Below the plank was a metal-lined cement trough, pitched at a five-degree incline toward a concrete-lined septic tank to the rear of the barracks. At the high end of the trough was a large water closet, a tank into which water trickled constantly. The tank was balanced in such a way that when the water reached a certain level it would tip forward and empty into the trough, flushing it effectively and cleanly. It was an incalculable improvement over the Japanese plan to have it emptied by hand every few hours, but the arrangement was not quite perfect: toilet paper and feces could cause miniature dams to build up directly under the holes. The pressure of the sudden release of water would then send it gushing upward when it hit a "dam," creating a very unpleasant sensation for anyone who was using the facilities at that moment. Thus, whenever the bucket tipped there was an immediate reaction—as many as six bottoms would rise as one, in a salute of sorts to American ingenuity.

Privacy in such intimate circumstances was, of course, only a memory, a prewar luxury. "If you want privacy, shut your eyes" was the watchword for this and a number of other activities at Los Baños.

The feeding of some 2,000 people, or even of 1,000, who had little money and no means of earning any, was a problem that would later turn into a disaster, but in those early months at Los Baños it was still in hand. The machinery for borrowing money through the Red Cross and other charitable and corporate sources had been put into operation early at Santo Tomás by Alex Calhoun and others experienced in such matters. The same sources of funds had helped the Executive Committee to obtain enough food for Los Baños, both from the Manila markets and the local natives. Rice, mangoes, papayas, camotes, coconuts, and bananas were all abundant; milk and dairy products somewhat less so; and meat, even at the beginning, was available only infrequently. Any red meat that appeared was probably carabao; pork was more easily obtained than beef by far. Whatever its source, meat seldom appeared by itself, only as part of a stew or hash in order to make it stretch as far as possible.

Calhoun had turned the thorny problem of food preparation and distribution over to Frank Bennett, an affable, jug-eared businessman from Manila whose integrity was visible: he lost as much weight as anyone else, though he had complete access to all the food in the camp. But Bennett had been hungry before and had survived. Born in northern Idaho, he quit college in Washington to join the Navy during World War I; after his discharge in 1922 he was washing dishes for his meals in Seattle when he ran across his former commanding officer. Asked what he was doing with himself, Bennett said wryly, "Trying to make one dollar do the work of five." His former CO put him on to a job as baggage clerk with the *President Grant,* sailing that week for Shanghai, and within three years he had worked his way up to assistant purser.

Bennett's seagoing career ended in 1925 when the Dollar Line bought the *Grant* and ordered him ashore in Manila to take charge of their office there. Eleven months later Bennett, piqued at being shoved from ship duty to clerking on land, took a fifty percent pay cut to join a mineral-exporting firm, Atlantic Gulf and Pacific. In twenty years, he promised his wife, he would be on the board of directors. Bennett beat that timetable handily; by 1939 he was not only on AGP's board of directors, he was, at forty-two, one of Manila's leading citizens—a member of the board of directors of the Chamber of Commerce and of the Wack Wack Golf and Country Club, and privy to the highest circles of the government and business establishment.

One night a few months before Pearl Harbor, Bennett and his wife were out walking the dog through their elegant walled suburb of Makati. They met and chatted briefly with "Miles" Standish, an old friend who had been with National City Bank in Japan and had recently returned to Manila. The next day Standish called Bennett at his office. He was shocked to see that Bennett's wife was still in Manila, he said. "Get her back home right away, along with your boys," Standish advised. Bennett thought about the advice for one day and, over his wife's vehement objections, sent his family back to California on the next available ship.

But he himself stayed, moving into the Manila Hotel. His neighbor at the hotel was Admiral Hart, chief of the Pacific Fleet, and over quiet dinners that the reclusive Hart preferred, Bennett came to feel that he had made the right move. Hart was convinced that the Japanese planned to attack the Philippines by early 1942, if not before. But he was equally convinced that a sea lane from Pearl Harbor would allow the Sixth Fleet to arrive within sixty days and that the Philippines would not fall.

Bennett had occasion to recall Hart's words one day early in 1942 when he was called in for the fifth time to see Captain Kato at Santo Tomás. One of the major products manufactured by Bennett's firm was creosote, which it shipped in great quantities throughout the world, though it also shipped iron ore, bauxite, and other minerals. Captain Kato did not speak much English, but he had an excellent Japanese interpreter, "an arrogant young whelp," in Bennett's words, who had grown up in Manila. The Japanese had found in Bennett's office a diagram shaped in the form of a tree that showed the company's various branches, products, and production quotas. Somehow the concept of such a diagram escaped Kato, and the questions he put to Bennett through the interpreter had to be repeated several times. It didn't make any sense: "Where does the creosote tree grow?" Kato asked.

Bennett swallowed hard to avoid laughing. There was no such thing as a creosote tree, he said. Kato interrupted angrily, and the interpreter told Bennett that if he did not tell where the creosote tree grew he would be severely punished. Disgusted, Bennett said they could do what they liked, but that the interpreter would look pretty stupid if he didn't tell the captain that creosote was a derivative of coal. He'd be happy to point him in the direction of the coal mines in Baguio.

Captain Kato took this information quietly. Then, as if to change the subject, he tossed a stack of glossy eight-by-ten photographs across the desk to Bennett. "Here pictures of Pearl Harbor," he said. "You like to see?"

Bennett's heart sank as he looked at his old ship, the *Oklahoma,* clouds of smoke billowing from its decks, and the *Arizona,* lying on its side. He riffled through the photographs and handed them back to Kato without comment. At supper that night he told Alex Calhoun and several other internees that there was no doubt in his mind they would be prisoners for at least three years, and maybe as many as five. Admiral Hart's optimistic estimate of sixty days to open a sea lane from Hawaii to the Philippines had been blasted, along with a large part of American naval power, at Pearl Harbor. All the rumors about Pearl Harbor they had heard and had been denying were unfortunately true.

Bennett paid for his candor by being told the next day that he was practically collaborating with the enemy. A group of angry internees said it was defeatist and unpatriotic to tell the people they would be prisoners for three years. Bennett shrugged and walked away. He had already learned that the behavior of people under extreme stress was not predictable from what it had been before the war, and that paranoia was rampant. Some preferred to remain blind to the truth, and everyone in a position of influence, either before or after the internment, was suspected of having access to special treatment or extra food.

It was with no great enthusiasm, then, that Bennett agreed to Calhoun's request that he handle the food distribution at Los Baños when he arrived with the original group of 800 pioneers. But Bennett was liked and trusted by everyone, even those who had reproached him at Santo Tomás, and he felt he had no right to refuse the job. Under his direction a workable system evolved. There were only two meals a day, breakfast at 8:00 A.M. and dinner at 6:00 P.M. When the barracks were completed, one was set aside as the kitchen. Half of the building was open on three sides, sheltered only by the roof; the other half served as a storage room. All the cooking was done in half a dozen huge caldrons that were set within concrete forms with fire pits beneath them. Along one side of the cooking area was a long grill for cooking fried mush and "hamburgers" generously extended with cornmeal. Two thirty-foot galvanized smokestacks rose above the kitchen, providing the draft necessary to make the green wood gathered daily from the jungle burn beneath its caldrons. After the food was prepared, two men would carry twenty-five-pound buckets full of food to the waiting food line, wearing protective mittens fashioned by the women of the camp so they could grasp the handles of the pots, and there the food servers would ladle out the meal—each recipient carefully watching the person in front of him to make sure that no one got any more than anyone else.

Fortunately, Bennett got some good people to work for him—men like Bill Lowery, who had been chief baker on the *President Grant* and could make horse taste good, and Johnny Oppenheimer, who had been the Manila agent for Pan American Airways, to handle the food distribution. But he had to replace Lowery after a while because the cook didn't seem to be losing enough weight, even though Bennett was sure he wasn't using his position to his own advantage—no more than was justified, at any rate, by the enormous service he was providing in making their slender rations palatable. And Johnny Oppenheimer begged to be relieved of his duties; the tension of dealing with 2,000 hungry and suspicious people every day was getting to him. Bennett appointed a substitute for Oppenheimer who nearly caused a riot the first day on the job and had to plead with Oppenheimer to take over the job again. He didn't have to touch a ladle, Bennett promised; he just had to be there.

Bennett's activities, like everything else at Santo Tomás and now at Los Baños, were supervised by the Executive Committee. The first committee, consisting of Calhoun, Dr. Leach, John Manning, Jim Muckle, Bill McCandlish, Sam Pinkerton, and Bob Cecil, had, in the interest of efficiency, simply been appointed by the committee at Santo Tomás. Late in 1943 the internees at Los Baños requested the opportunity—demanded the right, as some put it—to choose their own committee. It was then that Harry Fonger, George Grey, George Watty, Dr. Dana Nance, and Hank Heichert were elected and that Fonger became head of the Executive Committee. Regardless of who filled the positions, the same duties had to be performed both by the committee and by the internees, and the same reactions from the governed toward the governors could be anticipated. The committee assignments were what one would expect in any small town: finance and supply, health, public works, personal welfare, and safety and order. There was one more committee assignment not commonly found in small American cities: food.

Under the Executive Committee, and largely separate from it, were the barracks monitors, each elected independently by the residents of the barracks. The monitors were responsible for enforcing curfew, taking roll call, assigning cleanup and latrine details, and distributing food, which meant ensuring that people got into the food line in an orderly fashion. Infractions of camp rules beyond the power of the barracks monitors to deal with were considered by the court of order, appointed from the committee membership by the chairman.

In the best tradition of American democracy, the Executive Committees at both Santo Tomás and Los Baños received a generous share of abuse from their constituents. It was rumored that committee members got extra food and other perquisites for themselves and their families; that the list of internees from Santo Tomás who had been repatriated in November 1943 had been shamelessly stacked with the rich, the famous, and the well connected; that the committee members tried too hard to please "the damn Japs," that the court of order was a star chamber.

Throughout the duration of the war, it was the unhappy lot of the executive committees at both camps to be given responsibility without power. They were lightning rods for the irritations, anxieties, and fears that the internees all felt, and for which they dared not reproach the Japanese, who were the source of the problems. At the same time as they tried to mollify their fellow prisoners, the committee members had to deal with the Japanese, not all of whom were as fair-minded as Major Tanaka—and even when officials were amenable to internee arguments, they were rotated so frequently, along with the guards, that any continuity of relationships was difficult to establish.

III

Lester Yard, who served as Alex Calhoun's secretary during those early months at Los Baños, saw close up how dangerous the life of a committee member could be. A cheerful, bouncy little man with bright blue eyes and pale blond hair, Les Yard had always gotten along well with people. Born in Philadelphia in 1901, he majored in journalism at the University of Pennsylvania for three years, then left to handle public relations in Shanghai for the Studebaker company there. By 1932 he had returned to the United States via Los Angeles, where he was hired by the *Hollywood*

Reporter. It was the heyday of Hedda Hopper and Sheilah Graham, when the star and studio system was at its peak, and for the next two decades Les was in the middle of it. He worked for some stars—John Wayne and Joan Crawford, among others—and hobnobbed with more, in particular the raffish group that gathered around John Barrymore and Gene Fowler, and which Fowler would later describe in his book, *Minutes of the Last Meeting.* The decade-long party with Errol Flynn, Thomas Mitchell, W. C. Fields, Red Skelton, and the notorious Sadakichi Hartmann at the house on Barrington Place ended for Les Yard in 1941, when he accepted an invitation from Tony Rocha to go to Manila as a commissioner for the Steamship Association of the Philippines.

Tony Rocha was a Filipino whom Les had met years before through his association with Dewey Smith, head of Studebaker in the Philippines. He was now the head of the Waterman Steamship Line in Manila, where Les would be working. Rocha had suggested that Les might like to get to the Philippines a month or so before the man he was to replace left. It seemed to be a good idea, so Les departed in late August 1941 only to learn when he arrived in Manila that the man he was to replace had decided to stay on until January. Eight thousand miles from home and unemployed, Les talked himself into a job with the NBC affiliate in Manila, doing their 5:30 P.M. newscast and a siesta hour movie review and celebrity report, using material sent to him from Hollywood by Hedda Hopper.

It was a great job, probably better than the one he was waiting for with the Steamship Association, Les thought. On occasion he would even snag the great man himself, General MacArthur, alighting from his air-conditioned Chrysler limousine en route to his suite in the Manila Hotel. Even when there were no movie cameras around, Les noticed, the general kept his head thrown back so that the wattles of age around his neck would not show —though at age sixty-five he was certainly entitled to some sagging skin. Since Les was only about five foot seven inches and the general was closer to six feet, this habit made it difficult for the reporter to look into MacArthur's face as he talked. And Les never did get to ask him the one question that was on his mind: Why was the general so confident that the Japs would not attack when Filipino fishing boat captains were regularly sighting Jap warships within a day's sail of Corregidor?

Everyone could see that something bad was going to happen. Even so, Les had laughed when Stan Brothers, an old friend who was in charge of Pan American Airways, called him at 4:30 on the morning of December 8 to tell him they were at war. The Japanese had bombed Pearl Harbor! "What're you drinking, Stan?" he said. Les had pulled Stan out of bed twice during the past month to join him for a late drink at the Bayview, and he was sure that his friend was drunk and out for revenge. "Must be good stuff. Send some over."

But it was no joke. Les Yard's next work assignment was not as glamorous as the previous ones had been. During that summer of 1943 when Calhoun was fighting for a policy that would keep them all alive, Les was responsible for sending supply requisitions up to Manila. To do this he had to deliver the requisitions in writing to the commandant's office, where Major Tanaka would receive him courteously. Yard had barely noticed Tanaka's aide at the time, a sullen, flat-faced Korean named Han, but he knew enough to stay out of his way. The Koreans were despised by the Japanese as an inferior people. Naturally, with the perversity of human nature, they outdid the Japanese in brutality to the Americans, trying to prove their worth to the emperor.

One day late in August, Les came to Tanaka's office with a requisition form. Neither the commandant nor his aide was there, so he left the form on the desk and walked out. Before he had reached the steps of the barracks he heard an angry shout. He turned in time to see the thick, calloused palm of Lieutenant Han just as it crossed his right cheek. Two guards stood with bayonets on either side of the officer as he struck Yard repeatedly across the face with his horny palm. The American staggered against the wall but did not go down, though blood poured from his nose and mouth. Han turned abruptly and walked away, the guards following. Mr. Masaki, the interpreter, emerged from his office and offered Yard a handkerchief.

What had he done? Yard asked. He couldn't hear Masaki's reply because the beating had left him temporarily deaf in one ear, and Masaki repeated himself. The American had been impolite;

he had not bowed when he entered the commandant's office. Such lack of respect was offensive to Lieutenant Han. Yard stared at Masaki, incredulous, his vision clouded by tears of pain and anger. He had learned his bowing lessons well from "Shitface" Abiko at Santo Tomás, and he had never failed to bow properly, from the hips, when he visited Tanaka's office. But this was ridiculous. There was nobody in the office to bow to, for Christ's sake! Was he supposed to bow to an empty desk?

Yes, Masaki said apologetically, that would have been the proper thing to do. He added that it might be best for Yard to stay clear of Lieutenant Han from now on; he should ask Mr. Calhoun to replace him. Later, when some members of the Executive Committee at Santo Tomás paid with their lives for the privilege of representing the internees, Les saw how fortunate he had been to escape with only a beating. For now, though, in the middle years of the war, the daily routine of the Executive Committee at Los Baños was for the most part not much more dramatic than that of a village council anywhere in the United States. The minutes for this period are revealing not so much of tension and strife as of simply making do.

Item: the Executive Committee ordered Mr. Brown to return the geraniums he took without permission. He agreed to do so.

Item: the commandant has noted that he is very pleased with the musical programs and dances that the Entertainment Committee has provided and hopes it will continue to do so.

Item: the recent decision of the Executive Committee to ban the wearing of shorts by female internees is hereby rescinded. But women monitors should endeavor to influence the ladies to use reasonable restraint and good taste in the wearing of shorts.

Item: the commandant wishes the committee to understand that a concern for the internees' modesty was the reason for covering the fence next to the camp garden with sawali grass last week. It was reported to the commandant that the natives had been peering through the fence at internees who were working without shirts in the garden.

Occasionally, however, more intriguing information was revealed by the minutes, such as those dealing with the arrival of about eighteen Italians early in February 1944. There had been rumors in the camp, later confirmed by the Japanese-controlled *Manila Tribune,* that Italy had surrendered in September 1943 after fierce fighting in Sicily and southern Italy. The Tripartite Pact of 1940, which had linked Japan, Italy, and Germany together as the Axis powers, was thus dissolved. The internees were immensely heartened by the defeat of Italy as a harbinger of the eventual destruction of Japan.

When the Japanese, who now considered Italy an enemy, sent the Italian civilians living in the Philippines to join the other enemy nationals at Los Baños, the Americans greeted them eagerly: the Italians would have news and cigarettes. The commandant, however, issued orders that there should be no contact between the newcomers and the other prisoners, and the committee agreed to enforce the restrictions.

Item: the court of order sentences Mr. Hancock to the following for violating the order against talking to the Italians: fifteen days in jail, fifteen days' confinement to quarters, and thirty days at hard labor, chopping wood, for two hours a day.

However, the committee went on record as regarding itself unfairly imposed upon by the Japanese orders concerning the Italians.

Item: the commandant has advised the Executive Committee that we must work with the Italian internees on work details without friction; we must also provide them with medical services if they are required. We are advised, however, that we have no authority over the Italians regarding discipline.

For the most part, the infractions punished by the court of order were minor, though a number of otherwise law-abiding citizens sometimes found themselves in hot water. Geoff Morrison, the Englishman responsible for the Sunday concerts the commandant so enjoyed, had to listen to one of his concerts while doing time —ten days for stealing lumber in order to build himself a cooking shack outside his barracks. Morrison argued that he was performing a public service because the barracks were such firetraps, but the court members were not convinced, and that Sunday's concert was presided over by its host in absentia. He was solaced to a degree by the message of his selections as the music drifted ironically through the camp: "Prelude to the Thief of Baghdad" was followed by "Orpheus in the Underworld," "The Prisoner's Song," and "I Want to Go Back to My Little Grass Shack."

The court of order was not offended by Morrison's irony. Its members knew that their power was largely symbolic, and Harry Fonger was inclined to be tolerant. Adversity tends to magnify the characteristics people already have, he commented to Leith one day. The generous become even more open, the selfish even more acquisitive. And when not merely comfort but survival seems to be at stake, behavior that would be scorned in ordinary circumstances is not merely condoned but defended as righteous.

Whatever the explanation, there was plenty of evidence of normal human failures as well as successes at Los Baños. Petty pilfering was endemic: anything that could be traded either to the Japanese (illegally, of course) or to the Filipinos for food was a candidate for theft, including soap, clothing, and tools. Money and food especially had to be guarded constantly. People clustered in small self-protective groups, eyeing other groups—missionaries, merchant seamen, camp cooks, the British—with suspicion and distrust.

Despite the pilfering and petty thievery, there was little violence. But the threat of it after a distressing incident made Irene Wightman's life miserable for months. John Wightman, her husband, was part of an old Manila family—his father, a Scottish engineer by training, had worked at building railroads in Mexico during World War I until the revolutionary turmoil there drove him out of the country. He settled with his English wife in Manila in 1919 and eventually had a thriving printing business, one of his chief customers being Harry Fonger's Bible Society. George Wightman had done well enough, in fact, to send his oldest son, John, to Exeter for seven years. After graduation, John worked as a radio announcer in Tucson and Chicago, and met his wife-to-be in Indiana. He returned to Manila at his mother's request in 1939 to help his ailing father with the family business and went into radio work there when his father recovered. By the time the war began John and Irene Wightman had two children, a son, John, born in 1938, and a daughter, Algie, born in March 1940.

Though some argued that internees with their families present had an advantage over isolated individuals such as the merchant seamen and passers-through like Harold Bayley, the Wightmans thought the stress of having to tend small children, and to watch them go to bed hungry every night, was close to unbearable. Irene especially lived on the thin edge of nervous exhaustion for weeks at a time. Late one evening in the summer of 1944 she was on her way back to her cubicle after taking a shower when she realized that she had left her watch on the top of the wall outside the shower. As she returned she saw the young daughter of a woman she knew from the next barracks leave the shower. Inside, Irene saw that her watch was gone. There had been no one else in the shower room when she had left it, and it had taken her less than a minute to discover her mistake and to return, so there was no doubt in her mind that the girl had taken the watch. She walked over to the cubicle that the girl and her mother, a slatternly mestizo from the slums of Manila, shared (there was no father in evidence). She only wanted her watch back, Irene said. She did not plan to press charges against the girl. But the woman denied knowing anything about the watch, so John went to get the night guard. The watch was found after a brief search, and the woman was sentenced to ten days in the camp jail. But she had looked darkly at Irene as she was led away and promised to kill her. There was such venom in her voice and gaze that Irene was sure the woman was crazy. She lived in constant fear of attack for the duration of their stay at Los Baños.

Charles Glunz, a Presbyterian missionary who would observe his seventieth birthday at Los Baños, was a gentle man, patient with the frailties of human nature. After two years of living on the run in the southern Philippines with his wife, Henrietta, he was grateful for the assignment to Los Baños. Several of his closest friends had been among the dozen Baptist missionaries who were beheaded by the Japanese on Cebu in 1942. Charles did not realize until much later how near he had been to death, though his treatment was not the kind that would inspire ease of mind. He spent a week at Bacelod in a hospital room that had been turned into a cell. The door had been nailed shut and a hole about two feet square cut into the bottom. When he was taken out for exercise in the hospital yard it was something of a feat for the elderly missionary to crawl through the hole like a dog, knowing that the impatient guard would close the little door on his ankles if he did not hurry. The windows were boarded up so that Charles and his companions, two other missionaries and five Filipino boys, could not look out. The men slept on a wooden platform that was raised a few inches above the concrete floor and beneath which a variety of vermin—mice, rats, centipedes, and roaches—thrived.

The men were not permitted to speak to each other. They were not allowed to use the mosquito netting Charles had brought with him, and at eight o'clock each evening they were required to lie down on the bare platform over the vermin and "sleep." During the day they were required to sit on their haunches, leaning against the wall. They were forbidden to lie down, to sit, or to stand—unless they stood by the window to use the better light there while searching for bedbugs and lice. Charles began to deteriorate physically: his shoulders and arms developed a maddening rash, and his hips and back were excruciatingly sore from lying on the hard surface of the platform. One day, trying to ease his itching shoulders by rolling on the floor, he was discovered by the guard. "Come out!" he was ordered, and he crawled through the hole. That day and every day for a week afterward, the guard struck the elderly minister across his burning shoulders with a heavy rule as he crawled through the hole.

Shortly after Christmas, 1943, Charles and Henrietta were escorted by automobile (a shiny black Chrysler convertible) to the home of a wealthy sugar planter a few miles from Bacelod. The house was a plantation manor that reminded Henrietta of Tara in *Gone with the Wind*, a movie they had seen shortly before the war. The house had been appropriated by the Japanese military, along with the Chrysler. They were escorted in to see the "high command," a shriveled old colonel seated at the end of a long teak table on the third floor. With the colonel were a captain in the Kempetai and a stern, pretty young Japanese woman dressed in an ill-fitting uniform. She introduced herself as Corporal Anaya, the colonel's interpreter; she had been a student at the University of the Philippines before the war, she said. The colonel understood that his guests today were all former faculty members at Silliman University, and he wished to have a "round table" discussion with them today. The Americans were encouraged to be "perfectly frank" about expressing their opinions. Charles and Henrietta exchanged glances: open your mouths very wide, they were being told, so that your feet will fit in comfortably!

The colonel waxed enthusiastic over his glass of whiskey and proposed a toast to which he and the other men drank, something having to do with the quest for peace. The women sipped their coffee quietly. Charles downed his whiskey neat, and a Filipino servant rushed to refill his glass; he let it stand untouched.

The "round-table discussion" that ensued was essentially a harangue by the pretty young Japanese corporal, who interrupted her remarks only to translate them to the colonel, who sat half dozing over his whiskey. The Americans started the war, she said, by telling Japan that she had to get out of China and by cutting off trade from the United States to Japan. No doubt the Americans felt that because they were physically much larger than most Japanese, they had nothing to fear from them. Charles suggested that a small man could pull the trigger of a modern gun as easily as a large one. Corporal Anaya shook her head angrily; that was not the point. The point was that Americans felt racially superior to the Japanese. What about your immigration policies? They pointedly said all Orientals were inferior to all Europeans. Charles said he was forced to agree that his nation was not guiltless. He declined to point out that the Japanese themselves—"the Sons of Heaven"—were guilty of the same kind of prejudice against other races. America should be better than the others, he knew, including Japan. That it was not was shameful.

In any case, the corporal went on, America's contempt for the Japanese was more than reciprocated. The American idea of war, for instance, to stop fighting because the odds were overwhelming, was pure cowardice. The Japanese were fighting a war of annihilation! They would either win or die.

Sitting there in the faded splendor of the plantation owner's mansion with the sodden Japanese "high command" flanked by the cold-eyed military policeman and the fiery young woman, Charles was seized by a feeling that she was right: the Japanese were embarked on the path to annihilation. Beyond reason, beyond hope, beyond even pain, they were well past the point of no return on their flight to destruction.

Charles and Henrietta had arrived in Los Baños during the good time, Christmas of 1943, shortly after the Red Cross had delivered the comfort kits. By carefully apportioning the twelve-ounce cans of corned beef contained in the comfort kits, they could make a can of meat stretch over a week's time, supplemented by vegetables grown in their own tiny plot behind their cubicle.

The elderly missionary couple were not required to work, but they did, Charles in the camp blacksmith's shop and Henrietta sewing socks for the single men who had no one to look after them. They liked to attend the lectures in economics given by Mr. Donald—a gentleman of their own generation, Charles told a friend, an Australian who used to be in Chiang Kai-shek's entourage; and they especially enjoyed sitting on the athletic field on the folding chairs Charles had made, watching the sun set, listening to scratchy recordings of *H.M.S. Pinafore* and *La Bohème* played on the camp phonograph over the loudspeaker.

When all was said and done, Charles considered their situation a great improvement over what they had experienced in Mindanao, or over what they might have experienced on Cebu. But there were two initial disappointments. The first was the lack of tools. A skilled woodworker, Charles longed to make some more comfortable furniture for himself and Henrietta than was available, especially chairs. They were just too old to sit on their narrow beds or on the ground. But the camp tools were reserved for official tasks, of which there were many, so Charles fashioned and scrounged his own: the leaf spring of a Ford sedan found in the blacksmith's shop became a serviceable plane; the end of a drill a cold chisel; a heavy bolt a hammer.

Even when he had solved this first problem, Charles came up against the second: a lack of sharing. It was not simply because he was a missionary, Charles knew, even though he was aware that missionaries were widely disliked by many people for having been allowed to live out of the camp at Santo Tomás until midway through the war—their reward for signing the document Harry Fonger had refused to sign. He had vowed when they entered Los Baños that no one would be able to mutter "damned missionaries" in their direction. What they did, Charles said, would "speak so loud that people would not hear what we said." Later he would note with pardonable pride that some of his neighbors had over-come their aversion and "learned to like us very much."

But Charles knew that his being a missionary had nothing to do with the selfishness of the man who owned most of the wood appropriate for building chairs. He had his tools, Charles ex-plained to the former teacher from Manila, one of the 800 original pioneers. All he needed was a few of the one-by-two cedar strips that were stacked against one wall of the teacher's cubicle. The pioneer said he would like to help, but he was putting a new kitchen floor down in a few weeks and would probably need all the wood he had. He did have some extra nails, though, the teacher added helpfully. "Come back and see me if you find some wood."

The nails were sixty centavos each, Charles told his wife indig-nantly; a keg at that price would cost $8,000. The profiteering did not bother him as much as the unwillingness to share at any price. The idea that someone who had nothing to sit on might have a greater moral right to the lumber than someone who wanted a wooden kitchen floor "never even entered his head."

IV

Charles eventually found the wood to make his chairs; it is fortu-nate that he never had any occasion to visit Sniffen, who was a far less admirable citizen than the stingy teacher. Sniffen's origins were obscure. He retained a slight trace of a Cockney accent, but nobody knew where he was from originally. He had simply ap-peared one day in Manila during the mid-1920s. He was very good with numbers. For a time he worked for a small American import-ing firm whose manager was abruptly ordered home (it was later learned that somebody close to the manager had passed along to the home office some unflattering reports about quirky sexual habits on the executive level). Sniffen had assumed the manager's role and, for the next decade, nibbled persistently around the edges of the business community in Manila. His special talent was gathering information that could be sold to the highest bidder, trade secrets as well as personal tidbits. By the time the war began, Sniffen had acquired a villa in Makati with half a dozen servants, a wife who was twice his size, and the unanimous loathing of the respectable business establishment he had so skillfully exploited.

The Sniffens lived very well at Los Baños. Their cubicle not only had oak parquet flooring but Oriental throw rugs and an ottoman for Harry to lounge in after a hard day's work. And Sniffen kept very busy. When the old men began to arrive from Santo Tomás with their comfort kit supplies of useless—to them—cans of *klim,* or processed milk, Sniffen bought the milk for a few packs of carefully hoarded American cigarettes. He then sold the milk to mothers whose children needed it desperately. The watches, the pens, the jewelry contributed by the mothers—few had much cash left—passed through Sniffen's hands into those of the Japanese guards who padded in and out of his cubicle during the night.

Each morning, as the rest of the barracks lined up in the food line for fried mush and watery tea, Sniffen and Genevieve enjoyed their sausages and eggs, their toasted rye bread with marmalade, and their Maxwell House coffee. Most infuriating to Sniffen's neighbors was his utter indifference to their low opinion of him, not to mention common decency. On Sundays the Sniffens always had waffles. Small children would gather outside his door, drawn by the aroma of butter and syrup and hot waffles, only to be taunted: "Smells yummy, don't it, kiddies? Sorry there ain't enough for you." Sniffen charged an old man who had an ulcerated sore on his ankle ten dollars for a dab of sulfa powder when the hospital could not provide it. And when the hospital appealed to the internees for sugar for a sick woman, Sniffen said he would be happy to donate two spoonsful for every one given by the others in his barracks—knowing full well that he owned the only sugar to be had.

Sniffen was a stickler for legal form. He had plenty of cash on hand, in Philippine pesos, of invasion money—or, as it was more commonly called, "Mickey Mouse money"—and he was happy to lend it to deserving and trustworthy citizens who would sign a proper note, and then to take it back in return for food, so that no money ever actually changed hands. The note itself was testimony to Snitten's long experience in business affairs. "For value received," it said, "ten days after demand we jointly and severally propose to pay the sum of ————, United States currency, without interest, if paid at maturity, but with interest at the rate of six percent per annum if not paid at maturity. In the event of necessity to begin action in any court for the collection of the above-mentioned sum, we jointly and severally further promise to pay all court costs, including a reasonable attorney's fee, and all expenses incident to such action."

Sniffen's generous provision eliminating interest was easily affordable since it took $100 in invasion money to buy six cans of corned beef from him. Tens of thousands of dollars in promissory notes were issued by Sniffen from his cubicle at Los Baños. Many would be honorably paid when Sniffen presented himself after the war to collect them; he would be one of the few businessmen to turn a profit from the war.

Even the other netherworld inhabitants now at Los Baños—the gamblers, prostitutes, small-time thugs—shunned Sniffen. "That son of a bitch, begging your pardon, gives us all a bad name," a raw-boned, scraggly-bearded card shark named Gypsy had complained to Father William McCarthy, a Maryknoll priest. But there was nothing anybody could do, he said, except maybe kill him. It didn't matter that the court of order could never pin anything on Sniffen and send him to jail. Jail worked fine with somebody like himself, Gypsy said, because the only thing that kept normal people going in circumstances like these were friends. Gypsy, a jolly, gregarious type who had wound his way through the Far East as a bartender, taxi driver, stevedore, and merchant seaman, found his true calling at Los Baños in running the camp's crap game and poker table. More than one player had literally lost his shirt in Gypsy's games, along with his watch, his ring, and his razor blades, but the games were honest and Gypsy was always good for a touch. He liked people, and he wanted people to like him, so his periodic fourteen-day stays in the camp jug were tough on him. But Sniffen didn't have a friend in the world, except his fat wife, Gypsy said, so putting him in jail in Los Baños wouldn't have been any punishment at all. Anyway, it was only the amateurs like himself who ever got caught; that's the way the world turns.

Not quite as difficult to deal with as Sniffen, but still a problem, were the prostitutes. Olga, Gertie, Minnie, and three or four others were no shirkers. They took their turns at gathering wood and scrubbing the latrines, and as long as they were reasonably discreet nobody seriously minded what else they did. However, Diana, "the All-American Girl," was something else again. Isla Corfield, the British diplomat's wife with an eye like Hogarth's and zest like Dickens' for the outré, could hardly avoid observing Diana because they lived across the hall from each other. Tall and lank, fond of wearing a carelessly belted kimono and nothing else, Diana would laugh her horsey laugh and shout to the world, "I'm old but not cold!" Then she would break into one of her dreadful Mae West routines: "Wyncha come up and see me sometime, honey?" It did not surprise Isla to learn that Diana's career as a whore in Manila had been interrupted once before, by a stay in a mental hospital at Muntinlupa (a place she would visit again before too long). Los Baños, for all its deficiencies, was much less restrictive for a working girl, even if her room didn't have a door.

Isla used to send her fifteen-year-old daughter, Gill, on long walks whenever one of Diana's gentleman callers appeared. Finally, after considerable agitation, she got Diana to have a door installed, but it was still impossible to avoid hearing her at her work.

There was at least one consolation for Isla in having Diana as a neighbor. It was the continued assurance that the insufferable lady missionary, Mary Harper, had, in the unchaste Diana, clearly met her match.

Isla Corfield had long been convinced that Somerset Maugham, her countryman, had caught the essence of the missionary spirit in his story "Rain." Sexually repressed, self-righteous, humorless, naive—these were the qualities of missionaries as Maugham saw them—and Isla was rather gratified to find in Mary, whom she dubbed "Hallelujah" in her diary, a case of life imitating art. The daily attempts of Hallelujah to convert the unrepentant Diana to Christ were, Isla thought, better than a music-hall show.

"Oh, Christ," she heard Diana groan one afternoon. "I've had a bellyful of your preaching, Mary. Gimme a bellyful of rum any time."

"Now, now, Diana," was the soothing reply. "You don't mean that, and if you had Jesus in your heart you'd not want rum."

"Like hell! I'd sell my soul for rum!"

"Oh no, Diana. Rum cannot help you, the Bible says nothing of rum. . . ."

Diana's addiction to rum, Mary confided to Isla, was not the greatest threat to her spiritual well-being. Far more insidious were her repeated conversions to Roman Catholicism. "That girl's full of demons," Mary said one day. "I try to tell her to stop going with men and the next thing I know she's off to the RC church and hearing a sermon about 'Let him who is without sin cast the first stone.' Now she thinks she's a saint! But I'll convict her. I've convicted worse."

She was sustained in her faith, Mary told Isla, by the memorable conversion she had worked once on a woman lost in an alcoholic stupor. She had looked deeply into the woman's rolling eyes and blasted her with "Praise God, Hallelujah!" It had pleased God to allow the sinner to snap out of her swinish haze and become "convicted for once and all."

"My church is the Church of God," Mary declared to Isla and marched off to the washroom, where the All-American girl was showering for the evening clientele. Isla listened, bemused, to Hallelujah singing "Jesus never fails," and to Diana's irreverent reply, "Swing it, Mary! I feel the spirit about to enter into me!"

It behooved Diana to encourage Mary because "conviction" required more than singing and exhortation: Mary was persuaded to part with an unending supply of material goods for the sake of winning Diana's soul.

Diana was soon to face a more dangerous challenge to her independence than Hallelujah in the form of a soft-eyed, lumpish Indian matron named Rodda. George Grey, who was now serving as the head of the housing committee, had decided to place Rodda, a new arrival to the camp, with Diana—the only woman to have a cubicle entirely to herself. Her several bags and boxes of possessions were neatly placed within the room while Diana was out. Rodda settled herself quietly in a corner, waiting to meet her new friend. Diana appeared shortly, took one look at the stout, dignified Hindu woman, and threw her into the hallway, her boxes and bags tumbling after her.

"I ain't sharing nothing with no Bombay duck!" she screamed. "Quack off!"

George Grey, a wiry, sandy-haired and easygoing westerner, had worked for a year after graduating from high school in Las Cruces, New Mexico, in the federal prison there as a clerk, until an official told him he was wasting his potential and sent him to George Washington Law School. He had seen some tough customers, he said later, but Diana could have held her own with the worst of them. Followed by the hysterical, sobbing Indian woman, he approached the furious Diana. She stood in her open doorway, hands set defiantly on her hips, her mouth set in a grim, implacable line. Her kimono was half open, revealing her naked breasts.

"She stays here, Diana," George said quietly, "whether you like it or not." He picked up two of Rodda's bags and stepped past Diana into the cubicle. With a fierce yowl, Diana leaped on George's back and tore at his face with her fingernails. By the time he had dropped Rodda's bags and pried Diana from his back Grey looked as though he had stumbled through a plate-glass window.

Major Iwanaka, who had replaced Major Tanaka as commandant, was quietly watering the flowers outside his office, still wearing his kimono, when the bleeding Grey, followed by the two outraged women, appeared before him with their problem. Mr. Masaki was called to translate; he looked at Grey and at the women and kept his face carefully blank as he translated Iwanaka's advice. The commandant was disappointed in the Executive Committee, Grey was told. Surely Mr. Grey could see that to allow any single woman to live alone in the crowded camp was out of the question. There was simply not enough room for such luxury. The two women—Iwanaka smiled gently and turned to his flowers—would have to live together and make the best of it. Diana protested: "Dammit, Grey, you tell that slant-eyed bast—"

"The alternative," Masaki interrupted, "is that Major Iwanaka says he will have to ask Lieutenant Konishi to handle the matter."

Diana's mouth shut like a trap. Grey nodded, and the three went back to the barracks. Anything, they all realized, was preferable to having Konishi deal with their problems. So the Indian matron and the American whore declared an armistice, a period of relative calm broken by occasional attacks. "You'd stink on ice, you black-hearted sow," Diana would shout. "If you were cut open and me cut open," Rodda would reply stoutly, "you be more black inside!" "Bombay duck, Bombay duck!" Diana would sing, and the hapless Rodda, her defenses destroyed, would run from the cubicle, weeping noisily. Diana, alone and triumphant, would sing and shout, "I'm an All-American girl, and there are ten thousand million more at home just like me!"

When Grey finally found other lodging for Rodda and her antagonist had departed, Diana grew quite sentimental about her. "That old woman drove me crazy," she told Isla. "I used to count ten, twenty, before I talked back to her and I could have killed her. But," she said piously, "I respected her gray hairs, just like my mother's."

6

SINGIN' IN THE RAIN

Los Baños Internment Camp: June–August 1944

I

The great and immediate danger to be confronted at Los Baños, once survival itself had been assured, was idleness. Little could be done about, or for, the Sniffens and the Dianas, who, in any case, represented only a small minority of the camp population. But there were hundreds of people at Los Baños who had always been accustomed to productive labor. They could not simply sit around doing nothing indefinitely, or doing only menial tasks.

Darley Downs, a Methodist missionary who had spent twenty years in Japan, spoke fluent Japanese and had worked with Alex Calhoun as an interpreter. He and Calhoun discussed the problem of finding something useful for the internees to do with Clifford Bedell, a Manila utilities executive. The product of their discussions was a series of college-level classes, begun, with Major Tanaka's approval, during the summer of 1943.

The class of '47, as they called themselves, did not lack for qualified instructors. Downs himself taught Japanese. Geology and paleontology were the domain of Bob Kleinpell, who had earned his doctorate at Stanford in 1934 and lectured at California Institute of Technology for two years before the war; when the Japanese invaded the Philippines he was looking for oil as a field geologist for the National Development Corporation. Literature and philosophy were taught by Dr. Griffiths, the Anglican priest who had earlier given talks in the Fathers' Garden at Santo

Tomás. Leland Chase, a young business executive, taught freshman English.

Other members of the faculty included Señor da Silva, a graduate of the University of Madrid, who taught Spanish, and Tommy Worthen, born in Iowa but a resident of Manila for thirty years, who went from his prewar post as a radio announcer to teaching Tagalog, the most prominent native dialect in the Philippines. Bill Donald, the former Chiang Kai-shek aide, taught economics, and a Dutch priest named van Slooten taught medieval and ancient world history.

There was, of course, no money to pay this talented faculty, and there were few texts or other materials other than what had been picked up in Santo Tomás (the Los Baños campus itself had next to nothing in the way of supplies). And there were no classrooms at first, only teachers and students, as in the days of Socrates and Plato. During the first months classes were held wherever there was enough shelter for thirty or forty chairs. For a time the best place was under, not in, one of the old dormitories. As was common in the Philippines, these buildings were perched on stilts several feet above the ground for protection against rain and intrusive creatures such as snakes. The students dug down another two or three feet below the dormitory and soon had a snug, cool cellar for the classes. Admittedly there were some drawbacks: the Japanese headquarters were directly overhead, for one. The room also lacked walls to keep out the tropical deluges that, accompanied by crackling lightning and the rumble of thunder, regularly punctuated classroom lectures. And despite their best efforts to build a protective berm around the base of the dorm cellar, enough water would accumulate during a storm to turn the classroom into a sump.

But nobody griped much about the primitive conditions. Darley Downs knew that the physical difficulties were irrelevant, and perhaps even beneficial. Gathering the thirty-odd students together one morning late in June, before classes began, he reminded them of the remark made by a commencement speaker at a New England college many years before. The speaker had praised the qualities of Mark Hopkins, then a renowned professor of philosophy and religion. " 'Give me a log hut, with only a single bench,

Mark Hopkins on one end and I on the other,' " the speaker had said, " 'and you may have all the buildings, apparatus and libraries without him.' "

Los Baños was fortunate in having a variety of gifted teachers on its faculty; one of the most unusual was Bob Kleinpell. Kleinpell not only knew his material and liked to convey it to others but also had a remarkable ability to reach students as different from each other as Alex Brockway and George Mora. Alex Brockway, an engineer with Tidewater Oil, had been in charge of construction and maintenance of all Tidewater oil storage and service facilities in the Philippines. Born in 1899, a veteran of World War I, a graduate of the Montana School of Mines in 1922, Brockway came to Kleinpell's class as a professional colleague, well matched with his instructor in age (six years older) and experience, and himself qualified to instruct a class in basic geology. He would later refer to his days as Kleinpell's student with gratitude and admiration. With about fifteen other students, Brockway was taken through a twenty-week course in historical geology, followed by another in Cenozoic geology. He would compile more than 100 pages of notes and detailed drawings of geologic strata. A typical Kleinpell lecture was the one on the cephalopod mollusks. A detailed classification according to phylum, order, suborder, and descriptive terms was illustrated with detailed sketches of cuttlefish, squid, and the pearly nautilus, then followed by a selected bibliography: Kroeber's *Anthropology,* Burkitt's *The Old Stone Age,* Wissler's *American Indians,* McCurdy's *Early Man,* and half a dozen others, all obviously read and stored in the balding, high-domed head of the acerbic, shambling geologist. Kleinpell had not a single note for reference for this day's lecture; and he repeated the performance, without repeating the material, for forty weeks. It was a phenomenal and extended tour de force of knowledge and memory.

Such a man can be intimidating, especially to a bashful, unathletic boy of eighteen who only two years earlier had nearly failed the tenth grade. But George Mora was encouraged by Kleinpell to persevere through mastering the difficult subject material taught by the geologist. George hoped that he might be able to be restored to his father's good graces. For the next year and a half, in fact, the class of '47 would be the center of George Mora's existence.

Ernest Mora, George's father, was a hard-driving, energetic man who had been born in New York City. His family had come from Spain and had owned a thriving sugar-cane plantation in Cuba. Despite his privileged status as a landholder, the elder Mora, Ernest's father, had supported the cause of the revolutionaries against Spain during the 1890s—at the same time as similar agitation against Spanish rule was going on in the Philippines, halfway around the world. Stripped of his holdings by the government, he fled to New York. There George's father, Ernest, was raised, tutored by the intense, intellectual Cuban exiles who gathered at his father's house in Manhattan. In 1917 Ernest left Columbia College, where he had studied electrical engineering, and took a position with General Electric in Manila. Before long Ernest's Spanish heritage and knowledge of the language allowed him to regard the Philippines as his true home. Here, he thought, he could recoup the family fortune that had been lost so many years earlier in Cuba. Not, however, as an employee of another company. By 1930 Ernest Mora had left GE and prospered with his own business as an electrical contractor. He and his wife, Iberia, a slender, beautiful Spanish girl who never did adapt to the tropical heat of the Philippines, and a son, George, lived in a spacious house with several servants. The arrival of the Japanese in 1941 meant the destruction of all that Ernest Mora had worked for; he would experience the same fate as his grandfather had a half century earlier in Cuba.

The Mora house had been a refuge for a number of Americans who were visiting Manila and were trapped there after December 8, and all the visitors had been taken to Santo Tomás early in January. Although the Japanese did not knock on Ernest Mora's door, he knew that he had to submit to internment for himself and his family—it was simply too dangerous to remain outside—but he waited about two weeks before doing so. When the rest of the Moras finally did report to Santo Tomás, it was in the family car, a LaSalle, not in a Japanese truck, and the car was loaded with everything they could find and carry in the way of foodstuffs, clothing, medicines, and, of course, books. Emilio, an employee, assured the Japanese that the car belonged to him, not to the Mora family, and was allowed to drive it away unhindered. Ernest Mora greeted his wife and son standing in the plaza at Santo Tomás. They stood in the midst of a pile of boxes and suitcases—all that remained of two decades of hard work.

Thanks to his father's intelligent foresight, and to the continued loyalty of Emilio and other Filipino friends, George's days at Santo Tomás were free from the mere scramble for subsistence that preoccupied less fortunate internees. Moody and sensitive, George had failed to live up to his father's high expectations of him. Later the boy would learn that the sons of hard-driving, successful fathers often have difficulties during adolescence. For now, it was enough for George to know that somehow, being in prison released powers of concentration and diligence he had never suspected having. He finished high school at Santo Tomás with no trouble. And having achieved a degree of intellectual independence from his father, he was not terribly disappointed to be included in the pioneer group of young single men assigned to Los Baños.

Once there, he threw himself eagerly into the curriculum established by Darley Downs. Three years before, nothing in school had seemed to speak to him; now, everything he heard and read seemed to be meant for him alone. Mr. Griffiths' lectures on Pope, Dickens, and Carlyle were polished, witty, cultivated assertions of civilization persisting in the face of savagery, like the Englishman of the *New Yorker* cartoons sitting down to tea in a jungle clearing wearing a dinner jacket. Through these writers, George felt, he could take Carlyle's advice to live by the "great law of nature"— that law being that "each should become all that he was capable of being; expand, if possible, to his full growth, resisting all impediments, casting off all foreign, especially all noxious adhesions; and show himself at length in his own shape and stature, be these what they may."

George knew, of course, that Griffiths did not intend Carlyle's words simply as a message to himself alone. They would all, Griffiths was saying, have to resist the attempts of the Japanese to dominate them, to demoralize them. Despite the absence of news from home, of magazines, letters, or radio broadcasts, the prisoners had to assert their own cultural identity, to maintain the forms if not the substance of their lives before the war. This they did—for they really were prisoners, though they were always referred to as internees—through their procedures for self-government (including what to the Japanese must have seemed their incessant electioneering), their elaborate intramural basketball and softball leagues, their concerts, skits, and bridge tournaments, and through the classes taken by not only prospective college students but by many older people as well.

Looked at objectively, most of the internees would have had to agree that the Japanese did not make a concentrated effort to deprive them of their own culture, aside from not letting them find out what was going on in the war. Nor did they try to impose their own. There were no indoctrination lectures other than the occasional visit by someone like Ambassador Izzawa. Every so often there would be a survey of attitudes, with amusingly loaded questions such as, "Which is more responsible for the outbreak of the present war among Japan, America, and Britain—America or Britain?" and "Which treatment is more humane: the treatment naturalized American citizens of Japanese descent have received from the American authorities or the treatment we give to Americans and British nationals?" By and large, though, the Japanese were exasperatingly indifferent to American opinion of them and their actions—though they labored long, and futilely, for the most part, to convert the Filipinos outside the camp and throughout the country to the doctrine of the Co-Prosperity Sphere.

George Mora was piqued by this indifference to his opinion; the Japanese baffled him in ways that he thought the Germans did not confuse their European neighbors, with whom, despite the current belligerence, they shared many cultural values. He had grown up in Manila, George realized, with Japanese constantly in view—as gardeners, busboys, and masseurs at the big hotels, as deckhands on the intercoastal steamers and fishing trawlers, as salesmen peddling cheap watches and bicycles: squat, bandy-legged little men, earnest and polite in their rumpled black suits and sweat-stained fedoras. But he had never actually known any Japanese personally. They had simply been *there,* part of the landscape, ubiquitous and, indeed, inscrutable.

At home, George understood, the Japanese lived in paper houses on tiny islands that were constantly ravaged by earthquakes, tidal waves, and typhoons, and they naturally built nothing to last. Their lives were short and mean. Growing to average heights and weights that led the Chinese to malign them as dwarves, the result of constant malnutrition, these tiny people had nevertheless overrun the capacity of their miserable islands to support them. It was no wonder they wanted to raid their neighbors' pantries in China, Burma, Korea, and the Philippines. But their chances of doing so in the face of American and European opposition seemed nil.

When by 1936 this vaguely comical and contemptible race had somehow managed to subdue large parts of China, many times larger than Japan, George had asked a teacher at his high school to explain. The answer was simple enough: both the Japanese and the Chinese were yellow, not white; they were, to quote Kipling, "lesser breeds without the law," one victimizing the other. It was no affair of ours. By the time he reached Los Baños, George had not suffered personally at the hands of the Japanese in any dire physical sense and bore them no particular animosity. Not yet. But he was frustrated by his ignorance of the people who had managed to humiliate the United States so shamefully. How could it have happened? He yearned with an almost physical longing for an answer in the form of a course in modern political geography, history, politics—something that would give him some clue as to why the world was in its sorry state.

It was exactly at that point that the Japanese drew the line: they allowed only courses in ancient and medieval history. Current events and contemporary politics were forbidden. George would have to settle for a series of lectures on medieval Japan given by the Dutch priest, van Slooten. On the first day of class he resigned himself to a tedious narrative of the establishment of Christianity by Francis Xavier in Japan some 300 years earlier. It did not take him long to realize that the elderly, avuncular Dutch priest was describing a history that Shakespeare might have written. There was no "Japan" before modern times in the sense of a unified political entity any more than there really was a "Co-Prosperity Sphere" today or an "Italy" before 1848. The oldest Japanese records dated from the eighth and ninth centuries, but they were hardly more than a collection of myths and legends such as *The Odyssey* and *The Aeneid,* with less basis in fact than either of those epics. The history of Japan was, until the nineteenth century, a record of feudal warlords, of prolonged and bloody strife between clans and families, of shoguns who were only the puppets of contending chieftains, of emperors who might as well have been stuffed dummies, and of royal lines cut time and time again; of intrigues, murders, and conspiracies, all borne by a long-suffering population of peasants and workers.

What about the claim, George asked, that the empire of Japan was in 1942 celebrating the 2,602nd anniversary of its founding as the Empire of the Rising Sun—a nation that had existed since before the age of Pericles in ancient Athens? The answer to that question, the priest said, lay in understanding the peculiar obsession with time, both past and future time, that totalitarian mentalities have. Look at Germany: Hitler says the Third Reich will last 1,000 years and justifies today's carnage as the price of tomorrow's utopia. The Japanese militarists were trying to justify their actions by placing themselves in an ancient tradition; they could thus more easily ridicule their chief antagonist, the United States, as a mere child in the family of nations: less than 200 years old, a barbarian nation without history, without culture; even, as a conglomeration of peoples from elsewhere, without a clear bloodline, a contemptible assortment of mongrels.

Brutal, fanatical, grasping, dishonest. A new image of the Japanese was now revealed to George to replace the obsequious little men he thought he knew in Manila before the war. Still he was dissatisfied. He could not reconcile everything he had heard about the Japanese, including some horror stories of atrocities he was certain were true, with some of his own observations of Japanese soldiers: the boy who had flashed them the V sign and then burst into tears when they left Santo Tomás; the third-base coach on the guards' softball team who, during a game between the guards and the Americans, saw Mack Todd run into a pole in the outfield while chasing a fly ball and went over and cradled the unconscious American boy's bleeding blond head in his lap; the guard who, when a dog that belonged to an interned family died, left them a haiku poem as a gift—"When a small dog leaves, the space behind is bigger than his wagging tail."

He turned for answers to Darley Downs, who, in addition to teaching classes in Japanese, was a regular at the informal evening discussions held during that first summer outside Bob Kleinpell's quarters. Through his long stay in Japan, Downs had come to admire the Japanese as an adaptive, ingenious people, highly disciplined, stoic in the face of disaster, deeply sensitive to nature, and, very often, gifted poets and painters. He talked about these aspects of the Japanese through the summer evenings, while the fireflies danced among the sawali grass, until George felt that he finally had some sense of the Japanese character.

What he did not learn from Darley Downs was the missionary's certainty of two things, both of which were bad. The first was that the war would be a greater tragedy for the Japanese than for any of their victims, for he knew that nothing short of total destruction would turn the Japanese back from their perceived destiny as rulers of Asia. On Bataan, American soldiers had already learned that Japanese soldiers wounded in action would keep live grenades and blow themselves and their American medics up together rather than be captured. There was no doubt that the Japanese would die almost to a man before they let the home islands fall to an invader. There was no doubt, either, that MacArthur would keep his promise to return to the Philippines, and that to the Japanese, the Philippines would be the last redoubt; the next stop for the Americans would be Japan. The resistance of the Japanese army when MacArthur returned would be without parallel in Western military tradition, which allowed a losing force at some point to surrender before total annihilation.

It was not merely the fact that to the armed fighting men the war would become too terrible for words which concerned Downs; it was his deep conviction that the Japanese, if they saw themselves inevitably headed for destruction, would as a matter of policy take with them to death as many of the enemy as possible, civilian or not. This meant that the closer MacArthur came to the Philippines, the greater were their chances of dying at Los

Baños. The chances of the class of '47 ever meeting in 1950 in Ann Arbor for their scheduled reunion were remote indeed.

Six young women dressed in dark skirts and white blouses adorned with orchids sat primly in the middle of the basketball court in Baker Hall as Leland Chase waited for the crowd to quiet down and chatted with Darley Downs. There were nearly 100 people in the bleachers on this warm May afternoon, fanning themselves with palm leaves and straw hats—a good turnout, Chase was glad to see. He walked to the center of the court and welcomed the guests for the fourth public debate sponsored by the class of '47. The topic for the day was, Chase said, the following: "Resolved, that as a whole the members of the class of '47 have benefited more from the experience of internment than they probably would have if there had been no war in the Pacific." Arguing for the affirmative would be Barbara Coleman, captain, Juanina Fernandez, and Sally Nichols. Arguing for the negative would be Margo Tomkin, captain, Helen John, and Patricia Brambles.

George Mora and Burt Fonger listened intently as the speakers went through the stipulated pattern of presentation and rebuttal. Burt was the coach for the affirmative team, and George for the negative, and each knew the other's arguments inside out. During that first year of college there had been other debates on topics of various kinds: Should a camp restaurant be established? Negative. Would there be world benefit from a political union of all English-speaking peoples? Negative, by a very slight margin. Was a woman's proper place in the home? Affirmative—though as George, who was then secretary of the college club, had recorded in his notes, the conditions for the debate were less than decorous; the arguments against the proposition had reduced a gang of giggling boys in the back row to squealing hysterics, and the scale of emotion during the debate "ranged from the high note of indignant womanhood to the tremolo of bewildered manhood."

But the debate today was not so abstract. George and Burt had argued it out between themselves during their early-morning vigils, tending the kitchen fires, sometimes switching sides. They had each reminded their teams to take advantage of the many guest lecturers they had heard during the past year. Bob Kleinpell on the theory of organic evolution; Michael O'Brien on the power of personality in selling; Dr. Dana Nance on the Japanese advance through China, which he had witnessed; John Manning, Lawrence Hebbard, Betty Salet, and Leonard Michaels, all college graduates, whose topics included everything from how to study to how to pledge a fraternity; and, in particular, visits by Alex Calhoun and Mr. Masaki, and in a strange way, the one by Major Iwanaka.

Burton especially had regarded all of these talks as valuable in terms of providing specifics for the affirmative team he was coaching. He was gratified to hear Barbara Coleman making the same points as Calhoun had—that they were both privileged and condemned to live in the crucible of history and that the world after the war would be a vastly different place from what it had been before. It was clear from the devastation that the war had already wrought, Barbara was saying, that it would have to be the last of such wars. If the human race was to survive, it would have to come closer together. It was no longer enough to quote Kipling's "east is east, and west is west, and never the twain shall meet." They would *have* to meet, and those who were now college students at Los Baños would have unique credentials for providing mutual introductions after the war was over. Far from a hardship, these years should be seen as a privilege.

Much the same point had been made by Mr. Masaki, the commandant's best interpreter, when he visited the college club. Masaki was a generous man: out of his own pocket he had given the students notebooks, pens and points, erasers, typing paper and carbon sheets, and even a special pen for drawing Chinese characters. He had gone to college in Los Angeles, at UCLA, and his English was flawless. His talk had been brief—"a good speaker," he said, "is one who gets up, speaks up, and shuts up." But in his brief talk he made one point that Burt had seized on as essential and that he team was now using to good effect. "You should realize," Masaki had said, "that you are all exchange students, just as I was in California, but on a much larger scale than any I could have imagined: British and American students in Japanese-occupied Philippines. I must leave it to professional educators to discover all the possible benefits of such an association—it makes my head swim!''

Burt looked smugly at George as his team summed up their arguments. There was little that the negative side could do in response to such assertions—not because they were unassailable but because to do so would require overt criticism of the Japanese, who were imposing the unusual circumstances upon them. However, Margo Tomkin had seized upon a comment made by Commandant Iwanaka when he had spoken to their group only a week earlier. Iwanaka was a middle-aged reserve officer recently called from retirement to take the place of Major Urabi, who had briefly succeeded Tanaka. Iwanaka was a mild, muddled man who preferred to let his assistants run the camp while he painted watercolors of Mount Makiling, potted his geraniums, and wrote religious haiku; he was also, like Tanaka, a Buddhist priest. He had smiled uncertainly at the college students before him. He was afraid, he told them through Masaki, that he didn't really know what to tell them about university life in Japan, his topic for the evening; perhaps they would like to look at some magazines about elementary school children that he had brought along. Then, almost as an afterthought, he had indicated his surprise that they should be referring to themselves as the "class of '47." In Japan, students do not make any such references until after they actually graduate, and he was rather surprised at the optimism of the Americans.

"And well he might be," Margo was saying bitingly. "To talk of an exchange program when the classes are held behind barbed wire is an absurdity, and all the wonderful one-worldism of Mr. Calhoun and Mr. Masaki won't do us any good if we're all dead."

Darley Downs and Chase looked nervously toward the door to see if any Japanese were listening in on the debate; this was getting dangerously close to the essence of the matter. But the debate moved to safe ground as Patti Brambles developed the next objection. She observed that the social life at college that some of their guests at the college club had described to them—the Saturday afternoon football games, the fraternity parties, the proms, all the intangible but important things like the acrid, pungent scent of burning leaves on an October afternoon that many would remember long after they had forgotten whatever they learned about

Keynesian economics or the treaty of Versailles—all these were denied them at Los Baños. "We have lost our memories before we ever had them," she concluded.

The judges ruled that Burt's affirmative team had won the debate by a narrow margin and awarded them the prize: a stick of gum for each debater and his or her coach. An extra stick was awarded to Mr. Chase for his valuable supervision. As they walked out of the gym, Burt Fonger grinned that wide, full grin that always got George's goat and handed him half of his stick of gum. "Better luck next time, Georgie," he said. "See you in the morning."

The class of '47 ended its first year with a flurry of activities in June 1944: a dance, a banquet, and most notably, the "Frosh Frolics," a song and dance revue. George Mora had let Bill Kane talk him into being the master of ceremonies for the revue, and he was in a state of semiparalysis, or anticipated stage fright, for weeks before the show.

Thankfully, there were the other activities to distract him from his fears. The dance was held on the old clay tennis court behind the gym. There were bright red and yellow Japanese lanterns strung across the court, and the evening air was heavy with the smell of tropical flowers, Lifebuoy soap long and carefully hoarded, and kerosene burning in smudge pots in an effort to ward off the ever present mosquitoes. The girls, most of them in improvised ballroom gowns fashioned by their mothers from odd scraps and pieces of fabric, clustered together near the refreshment table, where a fruit punch and salted crackers were available, while about twenty boys stood with studied casualness in their slacks and blazers, begged or borrowed from who knew where, waiting for Bill Kane to start "spinning the platters," as he liked to say.

These same boys and girls, about thirty-five in all, had been together for a year now. They had participated in debates, in quiz shows, in weekly meetings, and in class, living within a few feet of one another all the while. They all knew one another as brothers knew sisters. This evening, though, there was a tension between the two groups, a feeling that some kind of transition from adolescence to maturity—a transition that had been delayed by the circumstances of the war—was at hand. Bill Kane, always sensitive to the mood of his audience, fingered through his stack of records, brought with him from the Manila radio station where he had worked, and announced that the evening's entertainment was about to begin—with the bunny hop! The tension was broken in a flurry of bouncing gowns and blazers and dust, and by the time Artie Shaw's rendition of "Stardust" signaled the end of the dance at 9:45, everyone agreed it had been a huge success. They would have to do it all again at Christmas.

The banquet held on June 17 was also enjoyed by all, as Jimmy Fernandez reported in his account of the evening. The menu consisted of fried rice, corned beef, potato salad, peanut butter, dark bread, chocolate cake, and "coffee" made from burned ground peanuts. There were even complimentary cigarettes after dinner. The class president, Ray Beeman, offered a toast to the Allied fighting forces, which was followed by toasts to President Roosevelt, the king of England, and "Premier" Churchill.

Frank Mortlock, class adviser, presented each member of the class with a memento: a small coconut-shell key with a "47" neatly engraved and printed on the head. "Each key," Mortlock said, "represents the key to fellowship and knowledge. I hope you will each keep your key long after we have all left Los Baños and remember its significance."

Then came the surprise of the evening. The students would be happy to know, Mortlock continued, that a scholarship fund had been established by himself, Mr. Calhoun, and a number of other people. The idea was to ask internees to sign pledges for $100 each, to be collected after the war. If all went according to plan, there would be three $2,500 scholarships, one for a British student and two for Americans, reflecting the proportion of each group in the college class. The students were overwhelmed. George Mora rolled the sum over in his mind: $2,500! His father had considered himself a wealthy man with $10,000 a year before the war, and George had always assumed he could go to college whenever he liked. But now his father was financially ruined, and George would have to make his own way. The scholarship, if he could win it, should be enough to send him to the University of Missouri for at least two years (tuition at land-grant colleges was minimal). He could major in journalism . . . his future would be assured. He snapped out of his reverie as Mortlock concluded his description of the scholarship fund. The hardships the students had already met and overcome were great, the adviser was saying, and those ahead promised to be even greater. "But schooling will continue until the last bell rings. This is paramount."

Under the circumstances, the reference to the "last bell" could not help sounding ominous, and an uneasy quiet followed the applause for Mortlock's announcement. But the evening concluded, Jimmy Fernandez recorded in his minutes, with the "humorous and witty presentation" of small gifts such as chewing gum and pencils to the various members of the class. Burt Fonger was the presenter of the gifts, and with each one he made an "amusing remark intended to embarrass the receiver of the gift and consequently entertain the audience. Mr. Fonger's excellent sense of comic timing caused much laughter, and his comments were all taken in good spirit by the recipients."

Watching Bill Kane at the dance and Burt at the banquet, George Mora wondered why he had let Bill talk him into being the master of ceremonies for the "Frosh Frolics." He was certain to be in a stage of rigor mortis when he walked out in front of that audience, George knew; his heart beat faster and his palms grew moist just at the thought of facing a group of people who were there to be entertained. Kane had scoffed at his fears. Short, blond, and freckled, Kane was pushing thirty but looked eighteen; a natural extrovert and ham, he simply had no sense of the fear a shy, introverted boy could feel. It was merely a matter of will, he told George. "Heck, you stand up in debates in front of lots of people and talk about all kinds of fancy stuff, don't you?" he said. "What's so hard about saying, 'We will now hear from so and so who will play such and such on the zither, or whatever?' "

George gave up trying to make Kane understand the difference between being in a debate and entertaining a crowd. One was rational and the other was emotional. You could always put yourself in command of a set of facts and ideas for a debate, but there was no way to tell your heart to slow down. The "Frosh Frolics" of 1944 were held as scheduled on June 27, despite George Mora's fervent hope that the war would end before that date, or that he would at the very least come down with a serious and incapacitating illness. The site was an open area between the gymnasium and the barracks. An improvised stage about twenty feet wide by ten feet deep had been cobbled together and a skeleton framework constructed, using half a dozen lengths of quarter-inch irrigation pipe borrowed from the camp gardens. Gaily painted bunting adorned the stage; Ronnie Laing, a floral decorator in Manila before the war, had made the most of the abundant tropical flowers that local natives had gathered for him, and the homely stage glowed with color. A large sign reading FROSH FROLICS CLASS OF '47 had been painted in red on a white sheet and draped across the back of the stage. George stood beside the backdrop and looked out on the crowd of several hundred internees, all but the oldest seated on the ground (most of the available chairs were occupied by the Japanese commandant, Major Iwanaka, and his staff, who sat in the front, on the left facing the stage). Immediately in front of the stage was a small orchestra, half a dozen instruments, including the camp piano, laboriously trundled over from the nearby practice room. Bill Kane caught George's eye and conducted the band in a brief medley of songs from the new Broadway hit *Oklahoma!* (one of the Italians had brought a recording of the musical with him when he was interned). The music stopped and Bill looked up at George expectantly. George rubbed his sweaty palms on his hips and stepped forward.

"Ladies and gentlemen," he began, his voice quavering, then stopped as he saw Bill vigorously shaking his head and nodding toward the Japanese commandant. Remembering now what he had been told to do, without fail, George began again: "Honored guests," he said, bowing in the direction of the Japanese, "ladies and gentlemen, the members of the class of '47 are pleased to bring you this evening the long-awaited, eagerly anticipated 'Frosh Frolics' of 1944. To begin our program, I would like to introduce Miss Carmen Fernandez, who will play a selection of classical melodies for you on the piano."

George stepped to the side of the stage with a huge sigh of relief. By the time Carmen finished with "Lady of Spain," "Cielito Lindo," and "Sabre Dance," his butterflies had vanished. He breezed through the remaining parts of the program with something approximating enjoyment. "Tobias the Terrible," with Freddy Zervoulakas as a bumbling Cossack, was followed by a

Bill Kane adaptation of a Damon Runyon story "Six Gun Tweeny," starring Burt Fonger as the comic hero. Burt had searched the camp for someone to instruct him in the nuances of Brooklyn grammar and had finally found guidance in the person of Diana, the All-American Girl. Judging from the enthusiastic response to the skit, Diana had done her work well.

Carmen Fernandez returned to the piano for selections from the New World Symphony. Several more skits followed, including an amusingly bad series of exchanges between "ditchdiggers," "hospital orderlies" and the like pretending to fall in love with each other. George squirmed through the awful puns the scholarly Reverend Griffiths had concocted—"I dig you a lot, baby!," "I hope all this pans out," etc.—and laughed at the puzzled expressions on the faces of the Japanese.

Finally it was time for the pièce de résistance, a series of musical numbers concluding with a rendition of "Singin' in the Rain." Burt Fonger strolled onto the stage, twirling a large black umbrella and dressed in a foreign correspondent trenchcoat with a slouch hat, to the accompaniment of Carmen Fernandez. As the introductory bars concluded, Burt cocked an eye upward, as if looking for the rain—and down it came! The irrigation pipes that the audience had assumed were just added framing for the stage had been connected by an unseen hose to the barracks faucet. The effect was not as grand as it would have been in Hollywood, but it was striking. Standing there as the water dripped around him, Burt's clear tenor voice and fresh, open face conveyed, like the lyrics of the song, an unquenchable American optimism. The thunderous applause of the audience for the ingenuity, energy, and hope represented by "Singin' in the Rain" more than justified the recording in the minutes of the evening as a "huge success."

For George Mora, Burt Fonger, and their classmates these were the best of times; the worst were soon to follow.

II

Grace Nash had played the violin for almost as long as she could remember—first as a child growing up on a farm near Cleveland, then, in the depths of the Depression, as a "stroller" in a Chicago saloon, alternating between saxophone and violin to help pay her college tuition costs. In 1936 she married Ralph Nash, an engineer who had worked in Manila for the past ten years, and sailed across the Pacific to begin a new life. For the next five years her life was a full and rewarding round of concerts and recitals, of lessons and reviews written for the *Daily Bulletin,* and of constant and growing delight in her two small boys, Stan and Gale. A third son, Roy, would be born in May 1943.

After they were interned in Santo Tomás early in 1942, Ralph was stricken with an excruciatingly painful series of illnesses, including boils. The task of caring for the family devolved upon Grace, and for more than three years she fought against the threats of illness and disease, sustained by two things: her strong religious faith and her joy in music. She had continued to perform and to give lessons at Santo Tomás. When she was sent to Los Baños in April 1944, one of the first things she did was to set about planning a concert with Rosemary Parquette, an old friend from before the war and an accomplished pianist.

Originally Grace had planned the concert as a celebration of their deliverance from Santo Tomás. Conditions there had become nearly intolerable; food had become increasingly scarce, and illness as a result of malnutrition was increasing dramatically. She had applied for transfer to Los Baños because she knew that the jungles surrounding the camp were filled with food that was free for the taking—trees bursting with bananas, coconuts, papayas—and it would be impossible for the Japanese to starve them, as they seemed intent on doing at Santo Tomás.

For a time the life of the internees had indeed been made easier, in part by the efforts of two young women named Helen Evangelista and Carmen Rivera. Major Tanaka had allowed a commissary to be set up at the rear of the camp, and each day two to four loads of vegetables and fruits would be sold to the internees. The food was brought in on two-wheeled horse-drawn carretas and unloaded under the thatched-roof shelter that was erected there. Approved representatives from the camp kitchen and canteen were allowed to buy whatever provisions they could from the natives. They were closely supervised by Japanese guards. But the guards were easily charmed by the young women, especially by Bamboo-san, as they called the slender, beautiful Carmen. Frequently the girls brought along several of the children who attended the nursery school they operated on the campus, and the guards would play with the children while the camp representatives unloaded the beans, camotes, tomatoes, bananas, papayas, and coffee beans from the carretas.

What the Japanese did not know was that Bamboo-san and Helen were part of an intelligence network established by Filipino guerrillas. They belonged to Terry's Hunters, a group that would later play a significant role in the fate of the American internees, and with each shipment of food they brought in mail, magazines, and communications from resistance forces. But in July 1944 the commissary was closed. Major Tanaka had been replaced by Major Iwanaka, and Lieutenant Konishi arrived from Santo Tomás to take over as supply officer at Los Baños—the same Konishi who had been responsible for the hunger she had hoped to escape at the new camp. Konishi's arrival coincided with a decision reached earlier that year in Tokyo to place the civilian detention camps under military authority. The civilians who had previously been responsible for looking after the internees at Santo Tomás and Los Baños were sent back to Japan. Now the same military men who were responsible for the Bataan death march, for the camps at Cabanatuan and Palawan where seven out of ten Allied soldiers would die before the war was over, were in charge of the noncombatant civilians.

Konishi's first official action at Los Baños was to cut all rations by twenty percent; his second was to forbid any trading with the natives for the fruit that dangled from branches just beyond the reach of the prisoners. By mid-July 1944 his stringent policies had forced the internees to deplete most of the stores they had kept for emergencies. They now ate carabao bones from which the meat had been stripped by the guards for their supper, boiled fish heads, *lugao*—a mixture of rice and water that looked and tasted like library paste, and camote tops so bitter that they had to be swallowed whole without being tasted. The diet, amounting to about 1,000 calories per day, was barely enough to sustain normal energy. The dogs and cats that had previously roamed the camp began to disappear, and small boys looked for lizards beneath the stilted cottages for lunch.

Grace, practicing one day in her cubicle, looked appraisingly at a fat iguana that crawled out of her sawali wall. It peered at her intently, scarlet tongue flickering beneath glittering, beady eyes. She played on, remembering the day when Heifetz some years earlier had charmed a python out of the rafters of the old Manila Opera House. The iguana sat motionless; she could have reached out and rapped it with the tip of her bow, she thought. But she was not quite that hungry. Not yet . . . the iguana, like Heifetz's python, departed safely.

A few days later Grace was practicing with Rosemary Parquette in the empty barracks where the piano was kept, next to the guards' quarters. She was startled to hear a noise at the open doorway and alarmed to see a Japanese soldier staring at them intently. The soldier tugged the heavy door shut and walked towrd them, his boots scraping against the gravel floor. Rosemary's fingers trembled over the piano keys. Grace dropped her bow. She bent down to retrieve it from the baby, Roy, who was clutching one end firmly. When she stood up, she found herself eye to eye with the soldier. She could smell sake on his breath. Sweat beaded his upper lip. His eyes, small and dark, glittered in the dim light. Oh, God, thought Grace, did he want what she feared he wanted? She leaped with alarm as he shouted something at her, her blood pounding so fiercely in her ears that she could not understand what he was saying. He repeated his command. "Play Mozart! Play Mozart!"—and she nearly collapsed with relief.

"Minuet from *Don Juan*," she said quickly to Rosemary, her voice quivering. "Key of C." As the last notes of Mozart faded away, the guard smiled widely: no gold teeth, Grace noted irrelevantly. "Beethoven!" he said. The women played the Minuet in G. The soldier rocked back and forth on his heels, his eyes closed. The plaintive last notes of the Beethoven selection had barely concluded when the sharp click of the catch on the violin case as Grace hastily packed her instrument away jerked the guard out of his reverie. He rushed forward as Grace picked up her baby and Rosemary put their music into the piano bench. Startled at the torrent of words that poured from their strange guest, the women drew back, still fearful. They recognized only one phrase: "*Domo arigato.*" Thank you.

Three days later the guard appeared at the doorway of Grace's cubicle, where she was alone with the baby. He grinned and thrust a sweaty, crumpled note into her hand: "Bring piano friend," it said in legible black letters. "Play more today. Bring baby."

An hour later Grace and Rosemary walked past the sentry post near the practice barracks. There were two guards on duty, small helmeted figures, identical in size and bearing. One of them turned as they passed. It was the music lover. The Handel sonata that she and Rosemary had to practice for the coming concert was a difficult one, and in their concentration the women forgot about the guard standing silently by the door until Grace saw the baby crawling toward the now familiar form of the soldier. "Roy!" she called. But the guard waved reassuringly and picked the baby up. "Boy-san!" he said. "Likee likee!"

For three more afternoons the women played and the guard listened. Each day he added a new phrase, apparently freshly learned, to explain his presence. "Five years soldier," he said. "Cello, Formosa, before war." "Very tired war. Want peace, play cello."

But on the third day he said, "No music tomorrow. Guard duty, different place. *Domo arigato.*"

Due in part to the guard's insistence on their practice, the concert that Sunday evening was a great success. Ronnie Laing had outdone himself with his floral display and had given each of the performers an orchid corsage. Footlights and overhead lights were situated discreetly enough so that the battered piano looked like a concert Steinway. No pythons or iguanas appeared, though a lucky mosquito landed on Grace's bow arm during an adagio that she feared would never end; there was nothing she could do but glare at the engorged insect as she drew the bow before her eyes. It finally lumbered off of its own accord only to be replaced a moment later, during a Fritz Kreisler allegro, by an enormous moth that fluttered down the front of her formal gown. Frantically, she stepped up the tempo of the already fast piece, ignoring Rosemary's puzzled look. The applause was enthusiastic and horribly prolonged, it seemed to Grace. Finally escaping to the makeshift "wing" of the stage provided by two blankets, she dug the furry beast out of her dress and hurled it over the blanket. Returning to the stage, she startled Rosemary with an unpracticed encore: "The Flight of the Bumblebee."

Not long after the concert, Grace was listening to her five-year-old son, Stan, practice on his tiny violin. She heard a tentative cough at her half-open door and turned to see the guard, grinning and bowing. He wanted, Grace finally understood, her son to come down to the main gate now, with his little violin. Later, Stan returned with a bag of fruit that the guards at the gate had given him after he played for them—a coconut, a bunch of bananas, three mangoes! Grace seized the food thankfully. But she knew that Konishi had only that morning issued a new directive: any contact whatsoever between guards and internees was strictly forbidden. She was sure they had seen the last of the cellist.

But not quite. Two days later Stan dashed into the cubicle with a package. The guard had stopped the boy, who had bowed properly, from the waist. He had then thrust the package into Stan's hands, saying, "No tell, give to Mama-san. No tell nobody." The package contained about half a cup of brown sugar and a similar quantity of ground coffee. The sugar became a syrup treat for the boys on the evening bowl of mush and lasted nearly a week. The coffee, shared with the Parquettes, was used and reused and used again until the grounds were finally leached of their last suggestion of flavor and color.

Difficult though life was at Los Baños, then, there were some compensations for Grace Nash, largely derived through her music. The pleasure of performance, the kindness of the guard, the ability of great art to travel from eighteenth-century Salzburg and Vienna to modern Manila, Tokyo, and Los Baños. And, not least, the continuing contact with former students—students such as Burt Fonger.

Grace had known Burt since he had called her before the war in his role as president of the Junior Symphony of Manila. They needed help, he said on the phone. Could she come over to the Union Church on Sunday afternoon? Grace had smiled later at the understatement: the Junior Symphony consisted of five fifteen-year-old boys, one each on piano, trumpet, violin, harmonica, and —Burt's instrument—drums. But with her guidance and Burt's vitality and enthusiasm, the five had grown to forty-five by the first anniversary, in September 1941, of their meeting at the Union

Church. They had met then to work out the orchestration for the new hit song that was sweeping Manila, "God Bless America." "We really ought to try to have it down pat in time for the Christmas concert," Burt had said.

But of course there had been no Christmas concert. Grace had not seen Burt since early December, just before Pearl Harbor, but she wondered, during her own early days at Santo Tomás, how he was enduring the separation from his father. They were much alike, she thought, big-boned, quiet, stubborn, sensitive, and innately kind. The father's religious convictions happened to coincide with his generous character, and the son was very much in his father's image. Each was the center of the other's existence.

Grace's own generosity in helping Burt and his friends had been amply repaid. Shortly after she was interned at Santo Tomás, Grace was terrified to learn that young Gale had contacted bacillary dysentery. Aspirin and castor oil, the only remedies available, were no help: she had to get sulfa. Armed with a medical pass, Grace had visited half a dozen pharmacies on Isaac Peral street, searching in vain for the medicine, when she heard a bicycle bell ring beside her. It was Burt. What was she doing here, he asked? It wasn't safe for American civilians to be out on the street, even with a pass. When she told him, Burt said he knew a couple of places where he could get sulfa. "You go on back to STIC and I'll be there in an hour."

And he was, with enough sulfa to break Gale's 103-degree fever. Grace was certain that without that medicine her boy would have died.

Now it was time for another concert. The weather was astonishing for mid-August in the Philippines. A high-pressure system had lifted the soggy blanket of humidity that usually left all of them drenched in their own sweat. The air was, if not crisp, at least cool. The sky was a deep, cerulean blue, with only a few puffy clouds no bigger than a dinner plate on the distant horizon. Though several hundred people were gathered outside the tiny chapel where Grace stood, invisible to them, the only sound was the cooing of the mourning doves in the flame tree by the graveyard.

Grace breathed deeply and shivered in the unwonted coolness. She looked again at the note from Leith Fonger. "I think Burt would want you to play, Grace," it said simply. She dropped the note and took up the bow. Memories of an earlier concert flooded through her mind—of Rizal Stadium, before 5,000 people in October 1940, celebrating the fifth anniversary of the Commonwealth of the Philippines; of the glittering brass and shining silver instruments of the constabulary band; of her natural fear of performing solo before such a large and important audience; and of Burt and his gang sitting in the front row when she came nervously to the center of the stage; and most of all, of Burt and his crooked grin and his thumbs-up sign. Yes, Grace thought, she would play now for Burt . . . one last time.

Outside the chapel, as the strains of "Ave Maria" flowed from Grace Nash's violin, Hank Johnson stood between the stunned group of cub scouts that he and Burt Fonger had led and Burt's best friends from the class of '47, George Mora and Carmen and Jimmy Fernandez. At sixteen, Hank Johnson had never seen the country on whose behalf he was imprisoned at Los Baños. But he had seen the Japanese in Shanghai and in Peking, and sudden death was no stranger to him.

Even so, the abruptness of Burt's death was startling. Roommates for the past six months, the two had shared many a long evening together. Burt had been fascinated by the exotic background of the tall, athletic Chinese-American boy, who, though several years his junior, seemed to have decided already that life was an impenetrable mystery that had to be faced with a quiet smile. Hank's father was an American who arrived in China after World War I and lived there with no visible means of support until his death in 1936, fathering a child every year upon his Chinese wife. Anxious that his seventeen children should encounter no difficulties in proving their American citizenship if they wanted to do so, he had given each of them, though born in the middle of China, American-Indian middle names, guaranteed to make any immigration officer take notice. Thus Hank's brothers and sisters bore such names as Delaware, Huron, Apache, and Blackfoot; he himself had been christened Henry Sioux Johnson. With two brothers and a sister, Hank had been sent by his mother, who refused to leave China, to Shanghai to begin the long trip to

California and eventually to relatives in Oklahoma. They got no farther than Manila.

Burt Fonger, the farmer-missionary's son, had been awed by his roommate's background—by the boy's experiences, his knowledge of the Japanese and Chinese language and culture. The four-year difference in their ages seemed trivial. Hank, for his part, envied the American his secure sense of belonging somewhere, and to someone. And he liked Burt's sense of play, something he had long since had to repress; he roared with laughter the night Burt told him about the bamboo bombs he and George Mora had made. It was nothing much, Burt had said modestly after half the camp had been jerked out of bed in a panic. You just got the fire good and hot and then popped in a few wet bamboo stalks. The steam builds up in the short sections of wet green bamboo very quickly, and the resulting explosions are highly gratifying—especially to the fire tenders, who are rousted out of bed at 3:00 A.M. for their duties.

Burt would always tumble into bed after his fire-tending detail, every three nights, bleeding from carelessly scratched mosquito bites. Anybody not under netting after dark could count on feeding a lot of anopheles mosquitoes. There was no particular reason he should have been hit by an especially malignant form of malaria that attacks the central cortex of the brain. But he was, and now there was nothing left to do but listen to Mrs. Nash play the "Ave Maria." A Japanese word he had once learned popped into Hank's mind. It had no Western equivalent, but fate, or destiny, or "it is written" came close. The word was *shikataganai*.

Occupied with his own thoughts, Hank hardly heard the traditional Protestant prayers offered by a missionary friend of the Fongers, who stood alone, ashen-faced, by the grave. But when Major Iwanaka spoke, something in Hank responded. He listened intently to Iwanaka's slow, precise reading, and to the translation by Masaki. It was a description of the death of the Buddha. "Among the disciples of Buddha," Masaki translated, "there was a particular favorite named Ananda. As the Buddha lay dying, Ananda stood by him with tears streaming down his face. And the Buddha said, 'How is it that you can still feel grief after all that

I have taught you? Is it so hard to be rid of all suffering? A man's life is like a flame; there is no substance to it, only a process in which the candle becomes the heat and the light and the smoke of the flame. The candle dies but flame persists and from it new candles are lighted. There is nothing to be feared from death, for it is part of each man's karma; and you would do well, my disciple, to remember this haiku:

> " 'My hut in the spring;
> True, there is nothing in it . . .
> There is everything!' "

Iwanaka reached over the grave and dropped into it three bougainvillea blossoms, white and pink. Harry Fonger caught Hank's eye across the open grave. Hank nodded and stepped forward with the papaya leaf that Fonger had earlier asked him to place on his son's coffin. Hank placed the leaf on the coffin as it was lowered into the grave and watched it disappear beneath the first shovelful of dirt.

"*Shikataganai,*" he murmured.

Burton Fonger, Eagle Scout, musician, tennis player, debater, and sometime star of the "Frosh Frolics" of 1944, was dead.

7

THE DOCTOR AND THE DOG

Los Baños Internment Camp, October–November 1944

I

The internees at Los Baños and Santo Tomás were lucky indeed to have a full complement of doctors and nurses interned with them; the loss of life was far less than it would otherwise have been. But some of the gruff, often irascible missionary doctors in particular were notorious for their impatience with less than mortal ailments. John Wightman had worked closely with one of them as an aide at the Santo Tomás hospital, having become interested in medical problems while organizing an ambulance service just before the internment. One night he was on duty at the hospital desk when a man appeared before him, his face convulsed with agony. He had to see Doc Robinson right away, he said. It was a matter of life and death. Reluctantly, Wightman woke the crusty old doctor from his nap, helped him find his glasses, and followed him out to the desk where the agonized patient waited. "Well, what the hell is it?" Robinson demanded. "Doc, Doc," the man cried, "you gotta help me. I haven't had a bowel movement for fourteen days. What can I do?" "Hold on for two more days," the doctor grunted as he turned on his heel and walked away. "Then you'll have the world's record."

Many physical conditions such as constipation that ordinarily would have been easily cured were anything but amusing at the time to those who suffered from them. Carol Terry, the pretty young daughter of a California sea captain who had intended to be a missionary in India, was afflicted with a painful and persistent case of impetigo. One day she was being treated in the hospital, standing naked behind a flimsy partition, all that separated a rough shower stall from the doctor's consulting area. A nurse plucked the scabs that covered her body with a forceps, doused her with buckets of water, and coated her sores with gentian violet. A doctor on the other side of the screen inadvertently knocked it over, revealing the young missionary, naked, wounded, and mortified.

Dr. Dana Nance's temperament and vocation inclined him toward impatience with quibbling about embarrassment. A burly missionary's son who had been raised in China and had first practiced medicine in Shanghai, he was highly competent, even ingenious, as a doctor, but a compassionate bedside manner was a luxury he could not always afford at Los Baños. Though there were other doctors and a number of nurses to share the burden of caring for the sick—including Navy nurses such as Alex Brockway's wife, Sue, and Mary Harrington, the shortage of supplies made proper care almost impossible. Basins fashioned from sheet metal, pillows stuffed with kapok seeds, morphine left over from World War I: the situation was ridiculous.

When Wightman told Nance the story about his colleague at Santo Tomás, he was nervously lying on the doctor's operating table waiting for his appendix to be removed without benefit of anesthesia—the ether had to be saved for life-threatening cases. Nance had responded with a short bark of a laugh and ordered the nurse to tie Wightman's arms to the table; then he stuffed a piece of red inner tube between Wightman's jaws for him to bite on. Wightman watched Dr. Nance in the overhead mirror slicing his stomach open until he passed out.

Two weeks later, in October 1944, Dr. Nance delivered Irene Wightman's baby without a hitch. The couple named the baby William Dana Wightman, after the doctor, and asked him what they could give him in the way of fee since they had no money. A jar of peanut butter when they could get it would be fine, he said. For Dana Nance anything, including working for peanuts or peanut butter, was preferable to idleness and inaction. At Baguio, far to the north, he had been part of the ruling clique of doctors who had dominated the camp government there. And when he was transferred to Los Baños in the summer of 1943 to be the medical director at the new camp, he had promptly set about to shape his role as he saw fit. For a time, before the arrival of Konishi, there was not enough business to fill his days, so Nance performed a variety of tasks to keep his charges well. The ailment for which he was most in demand, curiously, seemed to be hemorrhoids.

An impatient, imperious, hard-driving man, Dana Nance brooked no interference with his hospital and minced no words with his reports to the Executive Committee or to the commandant. He watched with dismay as the health of the camp population gradually gave way before the effects of increasing malnutrition. Besides the malaria that had killed Burt Fonger, there was amoebic and bacillary dysentery as well as beriberi, dengue fever and influenza, pernicious anemia and scurvy—all preventable or treatable with proper food and medication, both of which were, Nance knew, available in the storehouses of the Japanese in Manila.

Nance's report at the end of September 1944 was typical of his tone and his concerns. First, he noted that the sanitation department had continued, as per his instructions, to carry out necessary measures for preventing dysentery and other preinfectious diseases. However, it was time for the camp population to be inoculated again for protection from typhoid and cholera, and although he had been requesting vaccine continuously since July none had been forthcoming. He noted in this regard that there had been no Red Cross medical supplies of any kind for the past three months and that the Los Baños stocks were nearly depleted.

Moreover, Nance said, the food situation was becoming desperate. "The average daily edible meat ration has declined to five grams. The ration of dried beans issued to the camp has fallen to a paltry three grams per person—a negligible figure. The plain fact of the food situation at Los Baños Internment Camp is that everybody is HUNGRY! It will be increasingly difficult to get the necessary work of the camp done on the rations now provided. Hungry internees do not make contented wards—the 'peaceful village' desired by previous commandants will no longer exist unless we get more food." Finally, Nance noted that the Japanese continued to require that a population increasingly debilitated by illness and malnutrition work as though they were field hands getting three square meals a day. A working man needed 3,000 calories to do the kind of physical labor required to keep the kitchens functioning, to gather wood on the hillsides, to keep clean a small city of 2,000 people. They could not function on less than 800 calories per day.

Frank Bennett had agreed to take up Nance's report with Lieutenant Konishi, though he was not optimistic because the Japanese themselves were complaining about the food situation. The cheerful St. Looey had grown more morose as the Japanese rations were cut to nearly the same level as those of the Americans, though, unlike the internees, they still had access to the heavily laden fruit trees growing just outside the camp. "First four cups, then three, then two, now one," he said indignantly to Bennett one day, explaining how his rice ration had been cut. But the guard's spirits revived the next day when he brought in a blacksnake he had killed in the camp garden—much to gardener Pat Hell's distress, because blacksnakes were viewed as the gardener's friend, living as they did off rats, mice, and gophers. St. Looey skinned the snake in Bennett's kitchen, stretched it on the shovel he had clubbed the snake with, and pushed the shovel into the banked fires. When the snake was well roasted the guard devoured it on the spot. "Very strong, eat snake," he announced proudly, and stalked off like an Indian warrior.

Frank Bennett had been kept waiting outside Konishi's office for a half hour when he went with Nance's report. When he was finally ushered in the Japanese officer sat with his bare feet on his desk, munching on a rice bun. Several more buns sat on a plate at the corner of his desk. Konishi looked up from his copy of Nance's report at the tall American. He said Bennett seemed to have too much pride for an American who was being protected by the Japanese army and who was asking for food. Bennett said he was asking only for what the Japanese army had promised, no more and no less. Konishi knocked one of the rice buns from the plate with his toe onto the floor; he rolled it gently underneath his foot until it was gray and mottled with dirt.

"You want rice bun for everybody in camp?" he said. "You eat that one first."

Bennett had eaten the bun, he told Nance, under Konishi's mocking eye. But the special ration of buns was never seen. Instead, almost daily, Konishi gave the internees an added turn of the screw. One day he turned back the pitiful meat ration at the gate because it had arrived late. Another day he gave permission to consume rations that had already been devoured the week before. He took the food grown in the camp garden by the prisoners and gave it to the guards, and he confiscated a new shipment of seeds when it arrived in October. Early in November 1944, he would cut the salt ration: the salt was needed in Japan for making munitions, the internees were told. They would have to eat their stewed morning glory and tomato leaves and pigweed without salt, and endure the agonizing cramps and aches that attend insufficient salt anywhere, but especially in a tropical climate.

Bennett did think one day that Konishi had had a change of heart when the supply officer summoned him and told him to get a group of men together to carry several 100-pound sacks of rice from the Japanese bodega to the camp kitchen. They had been complaining about lack of food, so he would let them have all they could carry. Konishi had watched as the weakened Americans struggled under the heavy sacks for an hour. When they were finished he said he had changed his mind. The rice would have to be returned. Yet another time, Konishi placed a truckload of fresh fruit on the asphalt road in the hot sun. It was noon; the internees could come back at four o'clock and eat it if they wished, Konishi said. By that time, however, after four hours in 110-degree heat, the fruit had already rotted into a fly-blown, putrid pile of garbage.

The internees really began to suspect Konishi's sanity, though, when he jailed the commandant's chicken for ten days. Frank Bennett was the first to see the chicken sitting outside the commandant's quarters in its tiny little cage built especially for the occasion. The chicken's crime had been explained in both Japanese and English on a sign attached to the cage. It had eaten its own eggs. Bennett shook his head in disbelief—the chicken was not maliciously destroying the property of the emperor, Bennett told Konishi; it was just in dire need of calcium, like all of the internees at Los Baños, and it had instinctively tried to eat the nearest source, which was in its own egg shells.

Given the expected shortages of food and the malevolent disposition of the lunatic supply officer, Dana Nance was not surprised when his patients began to die in the autumn of 1944. Irving Posner was one of the first to go. The wonder was that the old man, nearly seventy, had survived as long as he had; after six months at Fort Santiago, Posner's frail body and flickering spirit were too beaten down for him to recover. But Nance had taken the old man on as a challenge. Something in Posner's eyes, a gentle, soft quality, touched the crusty doctor, and he sat with him for hours, listening to his accounts of life in the hands of the Japanese Gestapo, the Kempetai.

Some of the best men in Manila had been held for questioning at Fort Santiago, and Posner said he felt honored to be included among them, though he never did learn what the Japanese suspected him of doing. Bob McCullough-Dick, the fiery publisher of the *Philippines Free Press,* was there, paying for his years of editorial warning against the rise of Japanese fascism. Frederick Stephen, a business leader and head of the Red Cross, was being questioned in connection with his attempt to raise funds for the prisoners at Santo Tomás. There were others, too, in the twelve-foot-square cell he occupied for six months in the old Spanish fort. They came and went, taking up their positions according to their preference. Most crowded as close as they could to the foot-square barred window at the rear of the cell. Two or three always hovered close to the single water faucet; it was contained within a galvanized iron box recessed into the floor, so that the faucet was several inches below floor level. This meant that the only way you could get a drink was by crawling on your belly like a dog, Posner said, and lapping the water as it trickled from the tap. The only toilet was a hole in the floor in one corner that gave off a nauseous stench.

The prisoners were forbidden to talk with each other or to lie down during the day. They were taken out occasionally for short walks in the prison yard and for questioning in the mahogany-paneled room where Rizal, the great nationalist leader, had been held by the Spanish before they executed him. Irving Posner had been questioned by a Japanese major one bright spring morning; two guards had held him still while a third pressed an electric cooking coil against his feet. The major did not believe that Posner was not a member of the Freemasons; he was concerned that the Freemasons, as a secret society, had the potential to undermine Japanese authority, and he was determined to root it out entirely.

Like the other elderly prisoners, like housewives and nuns and priests, Posner suffered through the notorious water torture. Strong young men sometimes died when quantities of water were poured down their throats, after which they were thrown to the floor and kicked and jumped on by guards in combat boots, laughing as water spurted from their victims' every orifice. Posner had suffered so much internal damage to his kidneys, bladder, and intestines that nothing Nance could do would help him. But he survived long enough to see a parade of quiet, desperate men enter his cell, stay for a while, and vanish—some released but most taken to the execution ground in the Chinese cemetery.

He had been spared the worst, though, he told Nance; he had escaped the dungeons. Carved into the base of the old fort were a series of cells with low arched doorways and high metal grills. The rocky ceilings were even with the high-tide level of Manila Bay, which Fort Santiago overlooked. The water was prevented from entering the cells by a door which, on various occasions under the Spanish in the old days and now again under the Japanese, was raised while the cells were filled with prisoners. It was possible for a few prisoners to survive a slow death by drowning if they were willing to stand on the bodies of their fellow sufferers. These few lucky ones could thrust their faces into the topmost recesses of the rocky ceilings, scraping the black granite with their numbed fingers until the tide gradually receded; they would be alive for twelve more hours.

How had he finally been released? Nance asked the old man. Posner's sad, hooded eyes were briefly amused. He had been imprisoned because the Japanese thought he, a devout Jew, was a Freemason—a member of a group that had its roots in medieval Christianity. He was released when a new inquisitor asked him one day why the Jews had always been persecuted in Europe. Posner replied that the Jews had often been reviled as a separate and inferior race by Europeans. The Japanese had sympathized. If that was true, then the Jews were kindred spirits to the Japanese, who had suffered so much at the hands of the white imperialists. Posner had blinked in astonishment but said nothing. The next day he was released and sent to Santo Tomás.

By mid-November 1944, when the typhoon struck, Dana Nance had watched not only Posner die but also a Catholic nun, Mother Superior Sister Mary Glaphyra, and two Americans in their early sixties, Clarence Brown and Arthur Jordan. For the dozen bedridden patients under Dr. Nance's care, and for the hospital staff as well, the dead were almost to be envied when, on November 16, the worst typhoon in ten years hit central Luzon. Winds of up to 200 miles per hour ripped through the camp, stripping the new roofs from some of the barracks; thirty inches of rain fell within two days on ground waterlogged from the torrential July and August downpours totaling thirty and forty inches. Patients lay in their beds listening to the wind roar through their darkened rooms, watching bedpans float away; the kitchen staff saw inundated sacks of rice explode; the sanitation division tried to cope with septic tanks as they backed up and spread sewage through the camp.

Nine days after the storm Nance was picking his way through the still littered ground of Los Baños toward his hospital, fuming over the meeting he had just come from with the Executive Committee. An old man named Green had been caught stealing grain from the Japanese warehouse during the confusion of the storm. The patrolling American who had caught him said the old man appeared to be half crazy, standing there in the driving rain, stuffing grain into his pockets; he didn't even seem to care whether anyone saw him. Nance sat without saying anything as Heichert questioned the old man gently. Yes, Green said, he had taken the grain, and he would do it again. No, he wasn't out of his mind when he did it—was it crazy to want to eat? Yes, he understood that for the safety of the camp he had to punished: twenty days in the camp jail. He left to begin serving his term.

The members of the court of order prepared to leave, but Nance stopped them. It wasn't enough just to satisfy the Japs that we were doing our best to cooperate with them, they had to understand that the conditions they were imposing were intolerable. He read a statement that he had drafted to the other members and wanted forwarded to Iwanaka: The court, Nance read, "emphatically denounces those responsible for the dire straits in which the internee body finds itself. When men are subjected to three solid years of ever increasing hardship and hunger, it is little wonder that some should avail themselves of opportunities to appease an ever present gnawing hunger. When men are reduced to such a state that basic dietary elements such as salt and sugar and beans are denied them, who should appear surprised that they are not particularly careful about observing imaginary barriers and boundaries or making meticulous inquiries regarding the ownership of food—something for which every cell in their body is crying.

"This court denounces the failure of the authorities to erect proper fences around their bodega areas and to mark them plainly so that internees who are unable to withstand the constant anxiety, hunger and despondency of three long years of 'protective custody' will not, in their slow swing from a rational to a less and less rational state, be unnecessarily exposed to the temptation and the dangers deriving from exposed or easily accessible or poorly protected foodstuffs. This court denounces stealing by an internee, regardless of the apparent ownership of the property involved. However, it is infinitely more bitter in its denunciation of the condition that motivates such theft."

Nance overrode objections to the undiplomatic forcefulness of his language. If a man has his foot on your neck, he said, you tell him to move it off, you don't worry about offending his sensibilities. They were all going to be dead soon if the Japs didn't change their ways. The hell with being diplomatic, he said, and stormed out of the meeting toward his hospital.

II

Nobody could ever have imagined that slim, pretty Polly Yankey would be Dana Nance's next antagonist. There was probably not a more equable person in Los Baños, and since her husband, Bill, was of a similar disposition, it was only natural that they should have been elected monitors for barracks No. 1. Of course, as Polly would have been the first to admit, her situation at Los Baños was far different from, and much better than, that of the average internee. When the train had stopped in the village station three miles from the camp early in December 1943, she hadn't minded the rough order issued to the 200 Americans to get out and walk, and not to say anything to anyone until they had seen the commandant. After all, she wasn't just rejoining her husband, who had been here since May; she was literally coming home. She had lived in Los Baños for ten years with her parents—her father was a professor of forestry at the Agricultural College—and she knew many of the faces of the Filipinos who watched the procession of women and children struggle through the village. The smiles and winks and whispered *"mabuhays"* lifted her spirits and lightened her tired feet, and the welcome sight of her two brothers, her mother and her father, and Bill convinced Polly that she was lucky to be here at last.

She had been particularly relieved to see her parents for the first time in two years. Harold Curran and his wife, Mildred, had defied the Japanese at first, refusing to give themselves up, though they were nearly seventy years old. Instead, they joined a group of a dozen Americans who had fled to the forested slopes of Mount Makiling after Pearl Harbor.

Professor Curran was not just an old hand in the tropical forest, he was perhaps the oldest and most experienced man in his field in that part of the world. His first college degree was a BS in agriculture from North Carolina State in 1889, and he received his doctorate from Cornell University in 1902 as part of the first forestry class in the United States. He had been sent to the Philippines in 1905. At approximately the same time as young Lieutenant Douglas MacArthur was mapping the peninsula of Bataan for the Army, Curran was preparing the first forestry map of Luzon. After a decade of field work in Argentina and Brazil, he had returned to the Philippines in 1929 to join the staff of the School of Forestry at Los Baños.

Left to his own devices, the elderly forester could no doubt have provided for himself and his wife indefinitely. But he had deliberately joined a group of other Americans who had fled to the hills with much less expectation of survival—none at all, he grumbled later, dumb tenderfeet didn't know enough to come in out of the rain. Working from dawn to dusk at a pace that would have prostrated a man half his age, the professor established a camp high in the mountains. For more than three months after the fall of Manila they evaded the Japanese patrols and lived off the land, thanks to Curran's expertise and food contributed by the natives. But his labors eventually caught up with him: his hands, though thickly ridged with callous, could not take the punishment of swinging a machete for hours at a time. A blister formed, burst, and became infected, and finally accomplished what the Japanese had been unable to do—forced the stubborn professor to give himself, his wife, and his small band of wanderers up to the enemy authorities.

As this was more than a year before Los Baños was established as an internment camp, the Americans were all sent to Santo Tomás—all except Professor Curran, who was so wracked with fever from his infection that it seemed unlikely he would survive. The Japanese allowed the professor to remain at the small hospital on the college campus, where he was given a room with Mrs. Curran. When—and if—treatment restored him to health, he would be transferred to Santo Tomás with his wife. His tough constitution and the solicitous care of his wife, the medical staff, and, not least, the Currans' Filipino servant, Marimino, allowed Curran to regain his health. Each day Marimino would visit the hospital, bringing with him the family dog, a pudgy black Labrador mix named Poochie. Marimino and Poochie had continued to occupy the family house, about one-third of a mile up the hill from the college. Eventually all of the Japanese who knew that the Currans were supposed to be sent to Manila were themselves transferred, and the elderly couple settled in comfortably.

Even when the Japanese established Los Baños as an internment camp, the Currans were allowed to remain in their hospital room. Not until the new barracks were completed did they have to leave the hospital for a cubicle in barracks No. 1, with their daughter and son-in-law—and Poochie, who now became something of the camp mascot. But after Konishi arrived and the rations began to shrink, the sight of the Currans' fat dog began to strike some inmates as an affront. Polly Yankey knew that Poochie remained fat because her parents were giving her food from their own slender rations. She worried about what to do with Poochie all through the hungry autumn of 1944. Finally she made up her mind: Poochie had to go, as quickly and painlessly as possible. She asked Pete Miles what she should do.

Nobody knew as much about animals as Pete Miles. Though an engineer by training, he had been sent to the Philippines before the war by the St. Louis Zoo to collect animals. He had remained there after his assignment was over to work as a bouncer at a Manila nightclub, though with his clean-cut F. Scott Fitzgerald profile and easy manners he relied more on charm than on muscle to send boisterous customers on their way. Charm didn't work on the cobra snakes he encountered at Los Baños, but guile did, and he soon had the camp clear of all snakes except a few pythons; these he left in the thatched roofs to eat the rats.

Miles suggested poison for Poochie: he still had some arsenic that he had used to kill the snakes, and he could fix it so that Poochie wouldn't suffer. He agreed with Polly that they had to kill the fat old dog: otherwise the Japs could laugh at their claims of starvation. But Poochie was too smart for them. She turned up her nose at the tempting plate of boiled rice that Polly tearfully served her for her last meal. Polly didn't know what to do.

Shortly after noon on the day before Thanksgiving, 1944, Polly heard an agonized yelp, then a soul-piercing animal howl of anguish, followed by an abrupt silence. The noise had come from outside the hospital. She arrived in time to see Dr. Nance administer a final blow to the back of Poochie's skull with a piece of iron pipe. Rushing up to the doctor with tears in her eyes, Polly thanked him for helping her out of her dilemma. She hadn't known that he was aware they had been trying to put Poochie away, she said; she wished it could have been done more gently. But at least it was done now, she said sadly. She would get her brother Hugo from the garden to bury the dog.

Dana Nance peered at Polly Yankey curiously through his wire-rim glasses. He hadn't the foggiest notion of what she was carrying on about, he said. He had killed the dog because it represented sixty pounds of meat and it was going into the camp cooking pot that afternoon. He turned away from the young woman and bent over the dead dog with his scalpel. Polly screamed at the doctor but he ignored her, inserting the tip of the blade near Poochie's sternum and slicing open her stomach. Polly yelled to a bystander to find her husband and raced off to get her brothers, Hugo and Howard. Within minutes the three men converged upon the busy doctor, who by now was up to his elbows in Poochie's blood. The sun glittered on his mud-flecked spectacles as he stood up to confront them.

Before the war all three of Polly's men had weighed close to 200 pounds, and Howard was a giant at 6'6". But by this time none of them weighed much more than 120 pounds. The doctor, big-boned and heavy-muscled, had successfully petitioned the Japanese for extra food for the hospital staff—a justifiable request, most agreed, since without a healthy cadre of doctors and nurses many more would have died—and he was close to his normal weight of 180 pounds. He looked with cold contempt at the three scarecrows who were almost speechless with fury and indignation.

"Look at you, you dumb bastards," he said. "You're starving to death and you're letting your parents starve to death because you're sentimentally attached to a damn dog. You make me sick. Get out of my way." And he bent back down to retrieve his scalpel and continue dissecting the dog. The three men flung themselves on the doctor. Bill Yankey got in one blow before he was thrown up against the barbed-wire fence. Hugo and Howard overwhelmed the doctor by sheer virtue of their long limbs. Polly and Margarete Mangels, Howard's fiancée, cried and yelled, "Hit him again!" Within a minute the fight was over, the bystanders having broken it up; the Japanese guards were coming, and soon they would all be in hot water. The doctor picked up his scalpel and his broken glasses, wiped his bloody nose with his sleeve, and stalked into the hospital. Hugo told Bill and Howard to stay with the dog—he knew how to fix Nance's wagon.

In a few minutes Hugo was back with a bar of Paris green. Hugo smeared the dog's bleeding carcass from one end to the other with the poison. He worked the bar of Paris green around in the steaming guts of the dead animal until it had thoroughly dissolved, while the other internees slowly drifted away. Dr. Nance did not reappear. When Hugo was done he wiped his arms on Poochie's dusty black hide and rolled her into a sheet that Polly had brought out from the hospital. Then he and Bill and Howard dug a deep hole under the barbed-wire fence and buried the dog—well beyond the reach of Dr. Nance and the cooking pots of the camp kitchen.

8

CAMP FREEDOM

Los Baños Internment Camp, January 5–13, 1945

I

Journalists and others whose task it is to make order out of chaos have always talked of the drama of war. The life and death of nations is an epic subject and justifies the division of the world into aptly named "theaters" of war. In the Pacific Theater there were countless dramas taking place, but many of those who were most intimately involved had to wonder whether their roles were as spectators or as participants.

Such was the position of the more than 2,000 internees at Los Baños. During the calamitous first act of the war in the Pacific, after Pearl Harbor and Corregidor and Bataan, they had been turned into pawns, or hostages to fortune. Forced to leave their homes and jobs, they lived in a limbo of fear and uncertainty for months—a situation that certainly had its moments of high drama. But then had followed the interminable second act so dreaded by dramatists—that period when themes are established, characters delineated, and antagonisms incited, but little action occurs. The audience grows restless. Get on with it, they mutter. Kill everyone, if necessary, but end the waiting.

Harold Bayley had been in the play from the beginning, going back to those weeks in Manila before the curtain had been raised. What was he now, he wondered, a participant in the drama that was unfolding as the Japanese struggled desperately to repel the oncoming Americans or merely a spectator? He stood beside his pig keeper's shack in the chill night air and watched the flames lick the sky over Manila. For three days now, and especially today, the sky had been crowded with American planes, and the ex-fighter pilot had felt a peculiar mixture of joy and jealousy as the war was carried at last, within sight, to the enemy. The first squadron of twenty-four planes, lumbering along at 30,000 feet directly over Los Baños en route to Manila, had sent the camp into hysterics of glee—an unseemly glee, it seemed to the Japanese, who issued stern orders that they were not to look upward. But Bayley had looked long enough to see that the bombers were flying without fighter escort, which could only mean that the Americans had virtual control of the skies. What a change from three years ago!

He had been having breakfast with Grace and Ralph Nash when the American bombers first appeared. The Nashes frequently asked bachelors like himself to join them, though they had little enough to share, and he usually brought along something for the common pot. Grace had laughed at the Japanese for firing their antiaircraft guns at the enemy planes, so obviously out of harm's reach, and the waste of ammunition had puzzled Bayley, too. Then it struck them both that the gunfire was too rhythmic. They listened more closely; it came from the American planes, not from the ground. The rhythm was somehow familiar. "Of course," Grace exclaimed. "It's Beethoven's Fifth Symphony." Bayley listened: Da-da-da-dum! the gunbursts sounded; da-da-da-dum! Morse code for the letter V; Beethoven's opening notes for the Fifth Symphony: Roman Numeral V—the victory symbol!

The flights had continued, incessant, glorious flights of planes so large that they must be based nearby, perhaps on Mindoro, a few hundred miles to the south—no longer did the Americans have to use carrier-based fighter planes to harass the enemy. Now the fighter planes—Vought-Sikorsky P38s, Bayley thought—were dodging and leaping across the hedgerows of the Philippine countryside, strafing Japanese columns, buzzing the camp so closely that once Bayley saw a pilot's sunburned, grinning face and a thumbs-up signal before he roared skyward.

The internees had been heartened not only to see the show of American power but the proof that their presence was known, for the Japanese had frequently taunted them by saying that the location of the internee camps was a well-kept secret. Equally satisfying to the internees were the obvious signs of panic among the Japanese guards. The commandant had vanished that afternoon in a camouflaged car, heading toward Manila. Moments later a P-38 had strafed the road, but shortly after that the commandant's car had skulked back into camp, undamaged. In the evening a dozen trucks had lined up in front of the gate, and scores of soldiers were observed loading them with food, ammunition, and guns.

Now, Bayley looked away from the flames over Manila toward the smaller fire behind the commandant's office. For hours the soldiers had been burning papers in the wire basket incinerators, and there was still an occasional flurry of burning paper floating into the air. Otherwise, though, all seemed quiet for the moment. The light from a full moon bathed the camp. The January chill was increasing and Bayley shivered slightly, but a trickle of nervous sweat tickled his spine. He started to rub his back against the side of his shack, then remembered that he was wearing his last shirt, a white broadcloth dress shirt that he had put on to celebrate the day's events, and he didn't want to rip it. But when would that crazy guard show up?

"You friend music ladies," the guard had said to Bayley earlier that day while the American was working in the camp garden. Bayley had tried to ignore the guard; Lieutenant Konishi punished infractions against the rule prohibiting any conversation between guards and internees by reducing rations for both parties. But the guard, a tiny man wearing ragged shorts, tennis shoes, and gartered dress socks, had persisted. His friend, the cello player, had told Grace Nash he could get her some food from the village if she gave him something to trade with. Grace had turned over everything she had of value, mostly jewelry and fountain pens. But the cellist had been shipped out unexpectedly that day. "Him very lucky, go home Japan," the little guard told Bayley. He was charged with carrying out the departed guard's promise to help Grace Nash and "nice piano lady"—Rosemary Parquette, Bayley guessed. He wanted Bayley to meet him beside his shack at nine o'clock. Bayley agreed—anything to get the guard out of his garden in broad daylight.

Shortly after nine the guard appeared and motioned to Bayley to follow. They were halfway across the compound when Bayley realized that not only was he out of his quarters after curfew but he was in the forbidden zone where the guards had orders to shoot any internee on sight—and he was wearing a shiny clean white shirt in a full moon. He grabbed the guard by the arm. "This is nuts," he said. "Okay," the guard said, "you right. Wait." And he vanished through the sawali fence into the surrounding jungle.

An hour later the guard was back, breathing hard and sweating, with a forty-pound sack of mungo beans. "Here food," he said, dumping the sack at Bayley's feet. "You wait, then give lady. Tell her Japanese friend keep promise."

Grace Nash's eyes filled with tears when she pulled her cubicle curtain aside and saw the food. She was expecting him, she said. The guard had just left. His pockets had been stuffed with eggs, and he had given them to her one by one as he explained how her musical admirer had been unable to keep his promise in person. He had been afraid to carry the bulky sack of beans through the middle of the camp himself, he told Grace, but said her friend from the pig shack would bring it for her. Bayley, exhausted from the nervous tension of the evening, left the Nashes' barracks with the kilo of beans she had insisted he take and tumbled into bed just before midnight. Not even the renewed signs of activity at Iwanaka's office could keep him going any longer.

On the other side of the camp, in the barracks where the members of the Executive Committee were housed, George Grey's night was just beginning. Blinking the sleep from his eyes and looking away from the glare of Corporal Ito's flashlight, he nodded as the guard gave him Lieutenant Konishi's message. Ito said something else he couldn't quite catch, something about shovels.

"Some shovels not yet turned in," Ito repeated impatiently. The Japanese had earlier ordered all camp shovels to be turned over to them. "Must have all shovels by one o'clock. You hurry now, get shovels, come to commandant's office."

Grey roused Murray Heichert, the head of the Executive Committee, and Pat Hell, the easygoing engineer from Arkansas who was in charge of the camp gardens and should know where the shovels were. A lot of irate internees had to be roused to give up their shovels in the middle of the night, but the three men found forty-seven more shovels to add to the twenty that had already been turned in. By the time they approached Iwanaka's office at one o'clock the camp was ablaze with light; nearly 100 Japanese guards milled around the dozen trucks, which stood half loaded near the main gate. The commandant's 1938 Oldsmobile, previously the property of the dean of arts and letters at the College of Los Baños, stood in front of his office with all four doors open. Grey and Heichert—Pat Hell had been ordered back to his quarters by the guards, as he was not a member of the committee— stood at the entrance uncertainly, then knocked, entered, and bowed to the Japanese officer behind the desk. It was Lieutenant Konishi, not Iwanaka. The supply officer looked even more disreputable than usual, with a hand towel wrapped around his head and a half-empty bottle of Johnny Walker Red in front of him.

"What's going on, Konishi?" Grey asked directly. "We've got a right to know."

Konishi ignored the Americans. He finished counting a pile of Japanese money—Mickey Mouse money, the Americans and Filipinos called it, because it was so devalued by this time that a handful of bills wouldn't buy a mango—and shoved it into a cardboard box. Then he pulled out the drawers of the desk and dumped their contents into a larger box. Grey asked his question again.

"Sit down. Shut up. You find out soon," was the reply.

Ten minutes later Major Iwanaka hurried into the office. His tunic was rumpled and unbuttoned and he needed a shave. His face was ashen. He barked an order—Grey assumed it was an order—at Konishi in a high, thin voice. Konishi nodded casually, his contempt for the doddering old man fully evident, and turned to the Americans.

"Major Iwanaka says I tell you we leave now soon. Executive Committee take charge as of five o'clock this morning. We leave enough food for two months. Keep all internees inside camp. Major Iwanaka says he not responsible for what happen if any people leave camp."

Grey tried to hide his elation and looked at Heichert to see if the chairman wanted to say anything. But Heichert was too exhausted—he was not a strong man, having suffered from a wasting disease as a child that left him with a withered left arm—and he merely nodded to Grey to ask the obvious question.

"Would it be permitted to ask the major," he said to Konishi, "how we are to protect ourselves if the need arises?"

Konishi did not even bother to translate. "That is all we have to say to you," he barked. "Now go!"

Five hours later the full moon was a pale disk in the western sky. In the predawn light nearly 2,000 people milled about noisily in the space before the commandant's office, shouting, laughing, crying, slapping each other on the shoulders, or simply standing quietly, struck by the enormity of the sudden transition from captivity to freedom. George Grey nodded to Paul Smith, who raised his trumpet and sounded reveille. As the last clear, piercing notes drifted away, Murray Heichert stood to address the crowd. "My friends," Heichert said, his soft voice booming above the amplifiers, "as you all know by now, the Japanese have gone . . ."

There was a deafening cheer, punctuated by shouts of "God be praised!" and "Good riddance!" until Heichert lifted his hand and pleaded for silence. ". . . and they have left us to our own devices. Before we continue, I think you will agree with me that it is appropriate for Bishop Binstead to lead us now in prayer for our long-awaited deliverance."

Bishop Binstead, the senior cleric of "Vatican City," stepped forward and looked silently at the throng before him. Then he spoke: "Our father, who art in heaven . . ." The entire camp—merchant seamen from Liverpool and San Francisco, Bataan widows, children who had spent half of their lives behind barbed wire, mining engineers, bank executives, Englishmen and Americans and Italians—all joined in reciting the Lord's Prayer. The aged priest then offered a short prayer for those who had died in the war, and concluded with a prayer of thanksgiving for their salvation.

When Bishop Binstead finished, the scratchy sound of a record rasped briefly and Bing Crosby's voice singing "The Star-Spangled Banner" brought tears to hundreds of eyes. It was followed by a rousing Royal Marine Band recording of "God Save the King." Then the American and British flags, faded and wrinkled from long years of being hidden in mattresses, were raised to the top of the bamboo flagpole just as the first rays of the morning sun touched the camp. The cub scouts whose last ceremony had been the funeral service for Burt Fonger served as the color guard.

"By common agreement of the Executive Committee, Murray Heichert announced, "This site is now renamed Camp Freedom!"

When the cheers had finally subsided, Heichert spoke again. "Now, if I may have your attention, there are some serious matters at hand. We must all recognize that our danger is not past. Indeed, this is the most potentially dangerous period of all. We are in a war zone, well behind enemy lines. Despite any rumors you may have heard, we do not know for sure that American forces have landed on Luzon. And the mere fact that the Japanese have left the camp does not mean that they are not still a threat to our safety. At this very moment there are two sentry guards from another Japanese unit stationed outside the south gate. We must do nothing to antagonize them. The flags we have just raised so joyfully must be lowered . . ." There was a loud groan of protest, but Heichert pressed on. ". . . and we must continue to act as we have before, for our own protection. This means that you must stay within the camp boundaries. No one is to leave the camp to seek food from the villagers. We have enough food for eight weeks"—cheers now from the internees—"but that period is calculated according to the previous stringent rations we were on before the departure of the Japanese.

"The stores of rice will be divided and distributed among you to supplement the food distributed by the camp kitchens, which will continue to function as before. But you must exercise self-discipline and put some of it aside for emergencies." Breathing deeply, Heichert pressed on with what he knew would be unwelcome news. "Because of the position in which we are placed now, in the middle of a war zone without protection of any kind, the committee feels it is necessary to continue the practice of a 10:00 P.M. curfew, and also a 10:00 P.M. roll call." Over the murmur of protest Heichert continued, with a slight smile. "Of course, it will no longer be necessary for you to bow during roll call." The crowd chuckled appreciatively. "In fact, you can stay in bed. But please do not forget the danger; continue to shield your lights as before, and turn them out by 11:00 P.M."

Concluding his remarks, Heichert noted that the only thing that had kept them well up to this point was their self-imposed discipline and order. A shadow crossed his face. Grey knew that he must be thinking of the reports of looting by internees already in the few hours that had elapsed since the departure of the Japanese. In their hasty departure the Japanese had left behind various supplies and personal effects; small boys were strutting through the crowd wearing Japanese garrison caps and empty cartridge belts, and the ragged pockets of adults who had never stolen anything in their lives bulged with Japanese coins, amulets, and diaries. Some hungry people had even raided the camp vegetable gardens, pulling up half-grown camotes and potatoes from the ground and eating them raw. But it was not the time for a lecture, Heichert realized as the crowd began to cheer and shout spontaneously. He thanked them for their attention as the scratchy recording of another Bing Crosby song began. The ex-prisoners wandered back to their barracks to prepare for their first real breakfast in many months, some of them singing along with the song: "Oh give me land, lots of land, and the starry skies above, don't fence me in. . . ."

II

For the next few days the citizens of Camp Freedom moved through a euphoric haze—all except the Executive Committee, which was busy setting up its headquarters in barracks Nos. 3 and 4, posting patrols around the camp perimeter to warn wandering internees against going into the village and trading with the natives for food, mostly extra Japanese rice for meat.

Food had been, first and last, the primary concern of all the internees, and it was the first problem addressed by the committee. Five kilos of rice were issued from the central stores to each family, with the repeated stern warning that it was to be saved for future emergencies. At the same time, Dr. Nance and the other members of the medical staff urged everyone to eat as much as possible of whatever else was given them to build up their depleted strength. The prisoners, only too happy to oblige, devoured with gusto the double rations that the hardworking kitchen staff prepared for them: fried mush for breakfast, boiled papaya, tea, and greens for lunch, and, on the first day, a magnificent feast for supper. Major Iwanaka's prize bull was slaughtered within eight hours of the commandant's departure, along with two carabao donated by the villagers and twenty pigs the Japanese had recently acquired for their own piggery. Instead of the ten or fifteen kilos of meat that had previously been stretched to feed 2,000 people, there were 800 kilos for that first meal. Knives and forks again had a use (most of what the internees had been served had been in the form of soup or stew, and could only be eaten with a spoon).

Moderation was too much to expect from people who had been hungry for so long. Shrunken stomachs rebelled against the sudden stretching of rich and plentiful food, and the lines to the latrines were images of agony. Some of the prisoners recklessly traded away their reserve rice and canned goods for perishable fruits. Others simply wandered through the village at will, gathering chickens and eggs, indifferent to the Executive Committee's warnings about straying from the camp. There was a hunger in many of the younger men simply for the freedom to move about as they chose, and it would be satisfied.

Sustenance of a different but equally nourishing kind came to the prisoners through the shortwave radio receiver left behind by the Japanese. With it the entire camp could listen to direct broadcasts from KGEX in San Francisco—the Voice of Freedom, as General MacArthur, with his flair for the dramatic, had aptly named it. The denial of news to the internees had been one of the cruelest deprivations visited upon them by the Japanese—that and the deliberate distortion of news that had been common earlier during the war. Japanese-planted stories that President Roosevelt had died from syphilis, that General MacArthur had not in fact escaped by PT boat from Corregidor but had been captured and shamefully hanged in Tokyo, that the war was expected to last until 1952, had been derided as absurd, but there had been no evidence to the contrary.

It was a great shock to hear the president's voice on Sunday afternoon, January 8, as his fourth State of the Union Address was being broadcast from the White House on Saturday evening. His audience was not entirely uncritical. Bob Kleinpell had always been convinced that FDR had plotted, schemed, and intrigued the United States into war, that he had deliberately set up the attack at Pearl Harbor in order to force a reluctant Congress finally to declare war against Germany and Japan. He despised FDR and considered him at least partly to blame for the very existence of Los Baños as an internment camp.

Other internees, while not so fiercely antagonistic to FDR, had hoped to see Wendell Wilkie defeat him for the presidency in 1940, believing that two terms were enough for any man, and particularly for a Democrat who seemed intent on changing the very structure of the nation. Engineers, business executives, and professional people made up a large proportion of the prisoners; they tended to be Republicans and held no great affection for Roosevelt's politics or personality.

Few of the internees had had the opportunity to understand how Roosevelt had led the country through its most difficult trials to imminent victory. But even those who were most hostile to FDR realized that they were listening to a man who was deathly tired, and who had somehow achieved a larger vision of the world than they had remembered him as having. The sarcastic wit and occasionally suspect eloquence had vanished, to be replaced by a more profound sense of resignation and acceptance, even in the face of victory. To the hundreds of internees standing in the dusty square in front of the commandant's office at Los Baños, the president's speech sounded like a valedictory, a summing up—and it would not come as a great surprise to them only ten weeks later to learn that FDR had died at Warm Springs, Georgia.

But what struck the listeners at Los Baños most was the president's obvious assumption that the war was all but over, even as they could hear the rumble of Japanese artillery and American bombs over Manila. Roosevelt's concern now was primarily with the problems the world would face after peace. He particularly feared a return to isolationism, Roosevelt said, and warned his listeners against such a path. "We delude ourselves if we believe that the surrender of the armies of our enemies will make the peace we long for. The immediate goal is unconditional surrender"—the term was a new one to the internees, and a puzzling one —"but it is only the first step." He went on to warn against quarreling among the victors, saying "the nearer we come to vanquishing our enemies, the more we inevitably become conscious of differences among the victors"—an allusion to increasing differences with the Russians over the division of power in Europe that, of course, was entirely lost on the Los Baños prisoners.

Roosevelt also warned against the folly of "perfectionism," the demand that the world reshape itself according to the wisdom of Washington into some kind of perfect order. "Let us not forget," he said, that it was the "alleged imperfection of the peace treaty at Versailles" after World War I that led to American withdrawal into its own fortress behind the two oceans and that in turn led to the present conflict because we were unprepared. It was a long and philosophical speech, lasting thirty-five minutes, short on details other than suggesting that the military draft be continued after the war so that World War III could be avoided. But it was just what most of the internees needed to hear to celebrate their newfound freedom, and they savored the president's concluding words nearly as much as they had Iwanaka's prize bull. The new year, Roosevelt said, "can be the greatest year of achievement in human history. 1945 can see the closing in of the forces of retribution against Japan. Most important of all, 1945 can see the substantial beginning of the organization for world peace."

On January 9 the internees were alerted by loudspeaker to stop whatever they were doing and listen to the following announcement from Radio KGEX: "This morning, January 9, 1945, General MacArthur led 68,000 men of the U.S. Sixth Army in a landing at Lingayen Gulf, 100 miles northwest of Manila. There was only light opposition from Japanese forces. The battle for Luzon has begun!"

Convinced that their liberation was now only a matter of days, the internees watched happily as American bombers droned overhead on their way to bomb the Japanese to the north and listened to rebroadcasts from KGEX of programs they had missed during the past years. They learned that the war in Europe was drawing to a close—the Americans were pushing toward the Rhine, having broken the back of the last frantic German assault at the Battle of the Bulge; that President Roosevelt's reelection had been a refutation of a strong movement in the United States to declare a negotiated peace with the Axis powers and turn their efforts toward a defeat of our erstwhile ally, Communist Russia; that General MacArthur had resisted efforts to promote him as a candidate to run against Roosevelt, declaring that his first and most important obligation was to liberate the Philippines, as he had promised to do; and that the invasion force now centered on the Philippines was second in size and power only to the D-Day invasion of Europe in June 1944. What they did not learn, because it was not yet known, was that the resistance the Japanese army would present would be of a ferocity unmatched in the history of warfare and that their own role in that final battle was by no means concluded.

Late on the night of January 12, George Grey sat in the hospital at Los Baños comforting an aged Negro known as Pinky. The old man had been too debilitated by malnutrition to be helped by the departure of the commandant and his men. One of the very few blacks in Los Baños, only a few weeks earlier he had been sitting in the gymnasium with half a dozen other men, watching the flames light the night sky over Manila. They could figure the approximate nearness of the bombs falling between them and the city less than forty miles away by working out the equation between the flash of the explosions and the sound, just as they had done when they were children with thunder and lightning storms. Somebody worried about the possibility that they could be killed by American bombs, but Pinky said, "Ah's not worried about a bomb dat's got mah name on it. If a bomb's got yo' name on it, it'll hit you and dat will be dat. But dah is one kind of bomb dat Ah is worried about, terrible worried, and dat's a bomb dat says "To Whom It May Concern'!"

Now Pinky was near death. His hands, swollen by beriberi, were like balloons stuck on the thin sticks of his arms. He looked at his fingers ruefully and shook his head. "Ain' gonna play no more piano with these fat hands," he said. Grey remembered the story he had heard about the old man being New York Mayor Jimmy

Walker's valet and entertainer back in the twenties. When the war started, Jimmy Walker and all his cronies were long dead and Pinky was playing honky-tonk piano in a Manila bordello.

All the cronies except one of the most famous, according to the story Grey had had from Les Yard. Judge Crater, a federal judge very close to Walker's machine, had vanished one day with his life's savings and a beautiful redhead. He was the most celebrated missing person of that generation, after Amelia Earhart, and was variously reported seen in South America, Switzerland, and Cuba. Many thought he was at the bottom of the East River, wearing concrete overshoes. Pinky had always thought otherwise; he had watched the judge play poker too many times to believe that either the law or the mob would catch him easily. But he wasn't prepared to see the familiar high-shouldered figure of the judge standing at the food line at Los Baños shortly after his arrival there in August 1944. The bushy white eyebrows were black now, the heavy jowls were covered with a curling white beard, and the bulky frame had shed some pounds, but Pinky knew him at once: "Judge Crater!" he cried with delight. The man looked at Pinky coolly and turned away. His name was McMasters and he was an exporter who had lived in Manila for thirty years, somebody told the crushed Pinky. The piano player remained unconvinced. An Asian country 10,000 miles from the United States where English was spoken and the Yankee dollar went a long way toward buying privacy, the Philippines was the perfect hiding place for people on the run the world over, and especially for American citizens.

Grey thought it might take Pinky's mind off his troubles to tell the story again. He had been hurt when the judge snubbed him, and he told his story over and over again to anyone who would listen. It seemed to be the one thing that he had left. But at that moment Grey heard a noise at the door. It was a Japanese soldier, a private who had been Konishi's supply clerk. He came inside as Grey opened the door, holding his arm in pain. The clerk spoke English well and had done what he could to mitigate Konishi's harsh policies concerning food for the internees. He explained that he had been left behind in the hurried departure and had spent the last week with an infantry company stationed at the rock quarry near Los Baños. He had an open wound in his upper arm, the result of stumbling into a thorn bush, and it had become infected.

The Japanese had little time even for troops wounded in action, Grey learned. There were stories of bedridden Japanese soldiers who were murdered by their own doctors when it appeared they might be captured. And it was not unusual for the American hospital staff to treat guards who were afraid to admit illness or injury to their own medical staff. Grey cleaned the wound with hydrochloric acid and sprinkled it with sulfa powder. He gave the guard a cigarette and asked him how he came to speak English so well. He had studied in the United States before the war, the soldier said. His father was a Christian minister in Honshu, and he had attended a small religious college in the Midwest in order to become a minister himself. Grey asked the soldier if he believed in the war, in what Japan had done. It was hard to explain, the soldier said. His family were respected and admired in his village, peaceful people who had not wanted war. But when war came and the call for volunteers went out, his father had called his son home and he had enlisted. There was no question, the soldier said, of right and wrong; it was simply his duty. He was happy that he had not had to kill anybody, and he was sad to see the innocent civilians at Los Baños suffer.

The soldier thanked Grey and got up to leave. He hesitated at the door. The Americans should not believe that their troubles were over, he said: it was likely that the commandant would return. It didn't matter, Grey said; the Japanese were through— a week, two weeks at the most, and they would be free. The soldier agreed but said there would be hard fighting before that happened and the internees would be in great danger. And what would he do when the American soldiers came, Grey asked the soldier. He would die, the soldier said simply, and vanished into the night.

At three o'clock on the morning of January 13, George Watty, who was sleeping in the more comfortable bed of the Japanese supply officer, Lieutenant Konishi, felt a rough hand on his shoulder. "Get out of here!" a rough voice said. He opened his eyes and saw Konishi standing over him with a flashlight in one hand and a pistol in the other. Frank Bennett had first learned of the abrupt departure of the Japanese from George Watty, the Scottish engineer. "Fr-r-rank! Fr-r-rank! Wake oop! Wake oop, mon! The Japs ar-r-re goon!" About an hour after the injured enemy soldier had left the infirmary, Bennett heard Watty's familiar rich burr again: Fr-r-rank! Fr-r-rank! Wake oop! The Japs ar-r-re bock!"

Camp Freedom was no more.

9

PLAIN MURDER

I

Los Baños Internment Camp: January 17–29, 1945

The Japanese murdered their first American civilian at Los Baños on January 17, the fourth day after their sudden return. The fact that, in retrospect, the death seemed almost inevitable did not make it any the less appalling.

The first signs of serious trouble between the guards and their "wards" appeared on the previous afternoon when a 2:00 P.M. roll call was announced over the recaptured public address system. All the internees, even the children and the elderly and the various work parties, were ordered to stand in front of their barracks, each group of ninety-eight faced by half a dozen armed guards. Masaki's clear voice over the loudspeaker sounded faintly apologetic, but the message, delivered in his flawless, barely accented English, was clear: the commandant had been displeased by the apparent reluctance of the internees to return the property unlawfully taken from Japanese quarters during their absence. Foodstuffs, supplies of bedding and clothing, and personal effects belonging to Japanese soldiers were still missing. A search of the barracks would now be conducted to retrieve Japanese property.

The internees gasped in surprise and indignation. The agreement struck by the Executive Committee with the Japanese more than three years ago at Santo Tomás, and tacitly understood at Los Baños, was that the committee would guarantee proper behavior, i.e., following Japanese-imposed rules and, in turn, the Japanese would stay out of their quarters. The internees milled about and muttered angrily as the barracks monitors were rudely pushed aside by the guards and the search began. George Grey caught Murray Heichert's eye. It was a dangerous moment for all of them for two reasons.

The first was that the Japanese had cause to feel abused, from their perspective. Judging from their physical condition when they returned, they had been using the shovels and tools collected before they left to dig trenches and foxholes for combat troops around Manila, where the American assault was expected to hit. Their clothes were ripped and muddy, their faces streaked with dirt and pale with fatigue beneath the grime. For the first day after their return, the Japanese had dragged themselves around the camp at half speed, reestablishing patrols and sentries. When they had had time to settle in, they were outraged that the Americans had apparently taken not only the food allotted to them but had broken open the Japanese storeroom and emptied it. The worst offense, though, was the theft of the commandant's radio and the return, not of that radio, but of another one.

Konishi had glared at Grey when the radio that the internees had been listening to was returned. "This not our radio!" he shouted. What had the Americans done with the commandant's radio, and where had this one come from? Grey pleaded ignorance, though he knew that the disappearance of Iwanaka's radio on the second day of Camp Freedom had caused Heichert great concern. It had apparently ended up in the village, traded for food. The substitute had been hidden in Chuck Woodin's mattress for the past two years; that explained, Isla Corfield noted later, why Bill Donald, the aide to Chiang Kai-shek, had always been so well informed about the progress of the war. Woodin contributed his radio when Iwanaka's disappeared, and the committee hoped it would satisfy their captors.

Konishi disdained Grey's explanation that the first radio was gone and the second one had been donated by a guerrilla unit that had passed through after the Japanese left. The commandant was missing two items of considerable importance to him, Konishi said. The first was the radio and the second was—here even Konishi seemed embarrassed—Major Iwanaka's personal rice bowl, hand-painted with the imperial flag. The major was deeply disappointed that the looters had taken something that meant so much to him.

The Japanese had lost face as a result of their departure; the loss was intensified by the discovery that the internees had profited by their absence and were furious at their return. This deep-seated anger against the Japanese was, Grey feared, even more dangerous to their chances of survival than the pique of their captors. Though, God knew, the anger was justified. Pinky, the piano player he had sat with the night before the return, had died at 3:00 A.M., when he heard the first soldiers stumbling off their trucks. Dana Nance's autopsy revealed that the old man had portions of a wool blanket and a leather belt in his stomach; it was small wonder that the six days of Camp Freedom had come too late for him. For those who had eaten well during Camp Freedom, the few days of good nutrition were not enough to offset the half rations ordered by Konishi on his first day back. Those like Grace Nash who had benefited from the week of good rations were now reduced to scavenging like street beggars—frying banana peels from the Japanese garbage, sifting through rotten coconut originally intended for Iwanaka's slaughtered pigs to find usable chunks of rancid meat for a coffee substitute, and being careful to pick out the rat manure and centipedes. And independent sorts such as Pat Hell, who had ignored the Executive Committee's warnings about trading for food in the village from the beginning, were now told to stand hungry behind the sawali fence when they knew food was available a few hundred yards away.

The immediate reaction to the return of the Japanese had been dismay, a heart-clutching nausea that would have made the job of the guards fairly simple. But the spirit of the internees was not crushed, as might have been expected. On the contrary, the taste of freedom, the obvious disorganization and low morale of the Japanese, and the constant overflights of American bombers and fighters had all combined to make the internees far less tractable than they had been before. And some of them, especially the younger men, were in no mood to roll over for the Japanese order to open their barracks for inspection.

Hank Mangels had been pegged as a troublemaker by the Japanese from the beginning, and under the eye of the Japanese guards he was housed in barracks No. 11 with a number of other similar types. There were dozens of young men in that barracks, including Ben Edwards and George Lewis, both Pan Am mechanics until their capture. Under ordinary circumstances they might have been marines or paratroopers—tough, combative, impatient men who were sure they were capable, even in their weakened state, of breaking their diminutive guards in half.

Hank suspected that he would have been put in the troublemakers' quarters in any event because of what the Japanese had done to his father. The elder Mangels, born in Germany but an American citizen, had been in the commercial import business in Manila, representing General Motors, General Electric, and other American firms. When the war began he was traveling in Davao, far to the south, for the Manila Cordage Company. A squad of Japanese soldiers had been ambushed and killed shortly before Mangels was captured, and the Japanese Kempetai suspected that he had something to do with the attack. The interrogators broke his left arm and his collarbone. For fourteen days he was forced to sit bolt upright in excruciating pain before he was released and sent to Santo Tomás. The tuberculosis that his father would later die from stemmed, Hank felt certain, from this period of privation and torture.

Hank himself had fared much better. His mother was Spanish and the family had spent a year in Madrid, so he spoke Spanish fluently; and, having grown up in Manila, he was intimately familiar with Filipino culture and also with Tagalog, the other dominant language, besides English, spoken in the Philippines. He was mentally sharp, having completed four years of high school coursework in advanced calculus, trigonometry, and physics in three after the family's return from Madrid. And he was physically tough from competition in basketball and track and field sports. His chances of survival when he entered the University of Santo Tomás Internment Camp in 1942 with his mother, two sisters, and a brother were the best one could hope for.

His first run-in with the Japanese after their return came about on the morning of January 13. He was walking across the compound toward Iwanaka's headquarters, carrying, as inconspicuously as possible, a record player that he had stolen the day the guards left. A soldier ordered him to stop and touched his chest with his bayonet. Why did he have the record player? the guard demanded. He didn't, Hank responded innocently. He was returning it. The guard lowered his rifle, snatched the machine from Hank and disappeared into Iwanaka's office. Hank waited for several minutes to see if he would be called in for questioning, but nobody came out.

He wandered back to his barracks. Two guards were just leaving, each carrying a fifty-pound sack of rice. One of the sacks had several small holes in it, and a light trail of rice appeared as the guards walked away. Floyd McCarthy, Hank's uncle though only a few years older than he, grinned in response to Hank's unspoken question. Floyd had just found the rice the evening before, he said, and hadn't noticed in the dark that one of the bags had a hole in it. The damn Japs had just followed the trail of rice to his door, Floyd said. They were so happy to get it back that they didn't even swat him.

By the time of the surprise inspection on January 16, Hank Mangels had had enough of being pushed around by the Japanese. The sergeant in charge of the search party was a ruggedly built and cordially hated man named Otashi. "You're not coming in here," Hank said, blocking the doorway. Otashi raised his rifle butt and Hank tensed to parry the blow and slug the sergeant; he was beyond caring about the consequences. Howard Curran spoke quickly: Iwanaka was coming, along with his interpreter. What was the problem, Iwanaka wanted to know. Curran explained, and Major Iwanaka gave his word that if the internees returned to their formation the search would be canceled.

It was a tense moment. At least fifty men had gathered around the lanky young American and the burly Japanese guard as they faced each other in front of the barracks entrance, and the other five or six guards all stood with their rifles at the ready. Curran looked at Iwanaka closely. "You give your word, no search if we get in line?" Yes, the major said testily, he gave his word.

The internees fell into formation. The guard at the nearby sentry post covered them with his machine gun, and Major Iwanaka walked away with Masaki. Sergeant Otashi and his men promptly entered the barracks and searched them for a half hour while the troublemakers steamed in the hot sun and considered the worth of a Japanese promise. When he reentered his cubicle, Howard Curran stood on his bed and reached into the thatched ceiling. Smiling with relief, he pulled out a small package wrapped in burlap. In the package was a .45 Colt revolver, shiny with protective grease against the tropical damp.

Pat Hell was, at thirty-eight, a much older man than Hank Mangels, and he had never been considered a troublemaker by the Japanese, even though he was there as the result of an earlier broken promise. Hell had left his wife of four months back in Arkansas with the understanding that she would join him after their baby was born. In the meantime, he had immersed himself in his work as a mining engineer in the mountains north of Manila. On his own time he set up a health clinic for the children of the mine laborers; he began a recreation center and worked with the local missionary doctors to show the natives how to improve their living conditions; and he did soil analyses for the farmers and showed them how to increase their crop yields.

When war began, Pat Hell had no trouble hiding from the Japanese. The grateful villagers would gladly have sheltered him for the duration of the war. But he was desperately eager to see his wife, who had never left Arkansas. When he got a letter signed by a Japanese general promising him repatriation if he surrendered immediately, Hell decided to take the chance of getting home rather than endure a freedom without his wife and new baby boy.

The SS *Gripsholm* left Manila in October 1943 with several hundred repatriated Americans on board, but Pat Hell was not one of them. By this time he had already been sent to Los Baños as one of the original 800. He started the garden there at once, in May, despite arguments from some that the work was not only tiring but useless: they would all be rescued before the crops were ready for harvest. But Hell persisted, and with the help of Harold Bayley, Dr. Curran, and half a dozen other volunteers he had planted and harvested two full crops by the beginning of 1945. The children of the camp knew the sound of the squeaky wooden wheels on Hell's little cart, and they would jump on top of the eggplant and potatoes that he gathered and delivered to the camp kitchens.

The job had its satisfactions, such as the children. And Pat Hell, a gregarious sort, liked working with interesting people like Bayley and Curran. Major Urabi, who had replaced Tanaka, enjoyed watching the two elderly men talk about the crops. The major seemed drawn to self-sufficient Americans such as Harry Fonger and Dr. Curran, and one day he sent the professor a box of cigars, "because you work so hard," the aide who brought them to the garden said. Curran accepted the gift graciously, and the aide left.

Curran gave the cigars to Pat Hell and Harold Bayley. Though he had been an inveterate smoker of Philippine cigars before the war and would have loved the taste of one now, he couldn't accept such a favor from a Japanese officer, not even one so kindly disposed as Major Urabi. He had accepted the cigars because he didn't want to hurt the major's feelings, but he couldn't smoke them.

But the old man shared the general fondness of the internees for their reluctant overseer, who reminded Harold Bayley a little of Ben Turpin, the silent screen comedian: the high-pitched voice, the bushy little mustache, and the stiff-legged walk all might have seemed amusing. But the walk was stiff because one leg was wooden, and the major's concern was real. On the day in July 1944 when he left the camp for another post—reassigned, some said, because he was too lenient—the internees lined the road through which his car passed and bowed, willingly and without shame. Professor Curran was among them.

Lieutenant Konishi, who had arrived shortly after Urabi's replacement, also took a great interest in the camp garden. But there were no leisurely chats between the American gardeners and the new Japanese order—just bitter resentment when the Japanese took the harvest for themselves, leaving the Americans to eat banana peels and leather belts. The mining engineer and the professor were at work on the morning of January 15, 1945, when Polly Yankey, Curran's daughter, rushed into the garden. She was quaking with fright. He had to come right now, she said. Bill and Hugo had just been caught by the Japs and she didn't know what was going to happen. The professor rushed away with his daughter.

Pat Hell lowered his sandy beard into his chest and grubbed up a few potatoes that the looters had missed last week. He knew that Bill Yankey and Hugo Curran had been out of the camp for three days now, from just before the Japs returned. They had gone up the hill to some Filipino friends to see if they could get the makings for a birthday cake for Mrs. Curran. Like hundreds of other internees—like Pat Hell himself—they had ignored the Executive Committee's warnings against leaving camp.

A few minutes later, as Hell was trundling his meager load of vegetables to the kitchen, he saw the professor walking with his arms wrapped around two tall, emaciated men—Bill Yankey, his son-in-law, and his son, Hugo. He walked with them to their quarters, where Polly and Mrs. Curran greeted them tearfully. What had happened, it seemed, was that Bill and Hugo had heard about the return of the Japanese and had decided that the safest time to return was in broad daylight, so there wouldn't be any doubt as to their honorable intentions. The guard at the gate had been astonished to see them, but he recovered himself soon enough and waved his rifle in their faces, ordering them to "march!" They marched smartly into the commandant's office, where a group of officers and men looked on them with eyes still glazed from fatigue.

About fifteen minutes of elaborate conversation among several officers followed—none of them Konishi, thank God, Howard said later—and when it was over one of the officers casually waved his hand in the direction of the door. They left without further discussion. It was sure as hell their last trip outside, Bill promised Polly; the natives weren't getting restless, but the Japs sure were. For a minute or two he'd had the feeling their number was up.

"We'd all better keep put," Bill said, looking significantly at Hell. Pat just smiled. "See you around," he said, and left.

Pat Hell was glad to see Bill and Hugo back safely, we can be sure. But it seems equally likely that he saw this latest episode as just one more instance of Japanese harassment. Urabi and Tanaka aside, they had broken every promise ever made to the Americans they were supposed to protect: to him specifically, beginning with the general's promise of repatriation and ending with the theft of his lovingly tended vegetables, and to the prisoners generally, who were supposed to be "protected" by these little bastards who were starving them to death.

Isla Corfield was feeding her two recently acquired chickens on the morning of January 17 when Pat Hell showed up at her door with a withered green pepper from his garden. She was glad to see him, of course—Higgledy and Piggledy, the fatter of her three chickens, were the result of a foraging party that Pat had taken her daughter Gill on a few nights earlier; and Gertrude, the scraw-nier hen, had been acquired somehow by Gill, along with a dozen coconuts, the next night. "You've trained my girl to be a scrounger," she said, laughing. "There's more chickens waiting," Pat said. Isla was worried by what she took to be a feverish gleam in Pat's eyes. He mustn't go out again, she said. It was too danger-ous. The Japs were too jumpy. He should worry about keeping himself fit instead of about everyone else.

Shortly before noon Pat Hell visited George Mora's mother with a small gift from his garden, an eggplant. He had always admired Mrs. Mora because despite her alabaster skin and frail constitution, she had insisted on working a regular two-hour shift in the garden, no matter how many blisters or broken fingernails it cost her. George Mora, who was visiting his parents and taking advantage of the free time to catch up with his diary, waved absentmindedly as Pat left. There was so much to record, even as he was writing, George thought. The committee had finally managed to get through to Iwanaka that something had to be done about letting them trade with the Filipinos. Watty and Grey and Heichert had simply sat down with the commandant and Masaki when all hell broke loose, George noted—a swarm of P-38s buzz-ing the camp sent the guards half out of their minds, hugging trees, diving into the trenches the internees had dug for themselves, scurrying like ants whose hill has been scuffed by a small boy's foot. No bullets actually hit the camp—the presence of the Ameri-can civilians was too well known—but that was small comfort to the Japs, George noted gleefully.

In the midafternoon hush after the American fighters had roared northward, the sound of a rifle shot seemed unusually loud; it was followed by three more shots in quick succession, then by a series of excited shouts from the Japanese sentries at the front gate. Harold Bayley, Professor Curran, and a dozen other internees rushed to the gate, where they were turned back by the sentries. But through the gate they saw Pat Hell, stretched flat on his back in the dusty road. He had been shot in the chest four times in broad daylight not 100 paces from the front gate. He had obviously been returning from a foraging expedition in the village. Beside him was a bag full of coconuts and bananas, and his right hand clutched a dead chicken.

II

Los Baños: January 27, 1945

Helen Espino did not hear the gentle tap on her door at first. It was ten o'clock in the evening, and she was napping on the couch in the living room. But the quiet tapping eventually cut through her sleep, and she sat up in alarm before she realized it couldn't be Captain Ohira or his men: their summons was always more emphatic. She turned off the lamp by the couch and cautiously opened the door. A tall, thin American of about twenty-eight leaned against the doorjamb, smiled crookedly, and said he was hungry. Could she give him something to eat?

Helen looked onto the street. It was empty. The village was asleep, and there were no Japanese patrols in sight. She motioned the American inside hastily, drew the curtains, and turned on the lamp. He shouldn't have come here, she said. The Japanese were patrolling the area closely since they had returned and especially since the man had been killed after getting food in the village. The American looked at her through glazed eyes. His complexion was blotchy, his ragged short-sleeved denim shirt and shorts hung loosely on his body, and she decided he was either sick or drunk, maybe both. He thanked her for the plate of rice she put before him and tried to tell her his name, but she cut him off abruptly: she didn't want to know. There was no telling when the Japanese would realize that her husband was the leader of a guerrilla band and pick her up for questioning. She had survived until now by being polite to the Japanese— they liked polite and pretty women—but they would be merciless if they learned that she had been taking jewelry smuggled out from the prisoners at the college and buying food for them in the village market. Her sex would not protect her: only last week they had murdered a Japanese woman who lived in the village—she was married to an American mestizo. The Japanese had made her leave her three children and her husband and live with a Japanese officer, but she had continued to send food to her husband at the camp and they had found out and killed her.

Helen had even been threatened by the youthful folly of her husband, Romeo. During the week in January when the Japanese had left, he and other guerrillas had visited the camp openly, chatting with the prisoners and collecting souvenirs that they had promptly brought back to the house for safekeeping. She had hidden the gas masks in the attic, along with the samurai sword, the bayonet, and the garrison cap, and she thought she had taken care of everything when Captain Ohira showed up one afternoon for tea. Her shock when she discovered a small packet of Japanese medals wrapped in oilskin at the bottom of the sugar canister was considerable; after the Japanese officer left she had tossed the medals into the septic tank.

Posing some days as a teacher at the local nursery school and a pliant, charming hostess to the Japanese, and others as a go-between for those internees with a few odd rings and watches and the villagers with extra food, Helen Espino lived from day to day, waiting for the long-delayed moment of liberation. In the meantime, her strong religious faith provided consolation, and she would not miss morning mass no matter what. Shortly before 5:00 A.M. she woke the American who, apparently exhausted, had fallen asleep on her couch, and told him that she had to leave— he himself would be wise to return to the camp soon. About an hour later, as she was leaving the church, she heard shots from the direction of the camp but thought little of them: there was so much shooting going on these days.

III

Los Baños Internment Camp: January 28, 1945

George Lewis had always been a hard-luck guy, Ben Edwards thought later, but he sure didn't deserve this. It was even worse than what happened to poor Pat Hell. They had never been particularly close, he and George, though they had arrived together a few months before the war to work as mechanics at the Pan Am hangars in Cavite; George had gone native while Ben was playing softball, choosing to play around instead with the girls in Manila. He'd gotten himself a good dose of clap within a month and had spent his time at Los Baños trying to scrounge enough penicillin to get cured. There had been talk, too, that he'd been a little closer to Konishi, another drug scrounger, than he should have been. But that probably wasn't true, given what had happened to him.

Like Pat Hell, George had apparently been out in the village looking for food when he tried to get through the fence shortly before dawn. George Grey had seen him, along with a few others, and whispered as loudly as they dared for him not to try to come in as there were guards waiting. But George had come on in, stumbling a little bit as if maybe he'd found something besides food to sustain him in the village and walked right into a sentry who shot him in the arm. He fell into the fence and lay there on the ground as the guards gathered around. Grey and Dr. Nance had rushed over to see what they could do. Nance could see that the wound wasn't serious, just a grazed arm or shoulder from the way Lewis was holding it, but Iwanaka came up and told them to back off. The guards faced the two Americans with bayonets while the officers chattered away. Finally, after an hour and a half, a couple of guards came up with a door and rolled Lewis onto it. They carried him off to the edge of the compound and shot him in the head.

It was time, Ben Edwards decided, to begin thinking about getting out of Los Baños.

George Grey wrote the vigorous protest that the Executive

Committee presented to Iwanaka. "You, as commandant of this camp," he said, "have no power to order the imposition of the death penalty upon any internee here for any offense whatsoever. We call your attention to Articles 60 to 67 of the Geneva Convention of 1920, which soon after the outbreak of the present war your government agreed with the government of the United States to follow in the treatment of civilian internees. Under these articles only a court may order the death penalty. The procedure is prescribed. In such cases notification must be given to the protecting power of the institution of the case. The right of the prisoner to defend himself is safeguarded as well as his right to have counsel and to appeal and these articles expressly provide that no death penalty may be executed until three months after the protecting power is notified of the imposition thereof. You have disregarded all these provisions in ordering the execution of Mr. George Lewis this morning.

"From no point of view was Mr. Lewis guilty of any offence involving the death penalty. At the worst he could only have been considered in the act of escaping when he was shot. The facts are to the contrary. He was actually returning to the camp and hence was not an escaping prisoner. In any case under Articles 47, 50, 51, and 52 of the Geneva Convention of 1929 an attempted escape is only an offense against discipline and the punishment thereof may not exceed thirty days' arrest. Moreover, there can be no doubt that the refusal to permit needed medical attention to be given Mr. Lewis after he was first shot, and the order for his execution within an hour and a half thereafter without any court action whatever, constitutes a record unlawful, inhumane, and shocking."

Isla Corfield wrote bitterly in her diary: "It is plain murder by the Bushido Japs. A man isn't shot coming into camp by a decent, civilized nation. He may be jailed, solitary confinement, etc. But if he's wounded they don't just murder him."

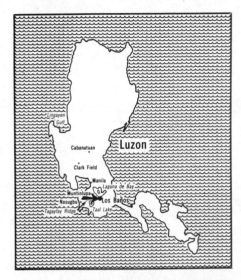

Los Baños, thirty miles southeast of Manila and well behind enemy lines on February 23, 1945, was accessible only by air and by water, across the large inland lake, Laguna de Bay. Map done for this book by George Doherty.

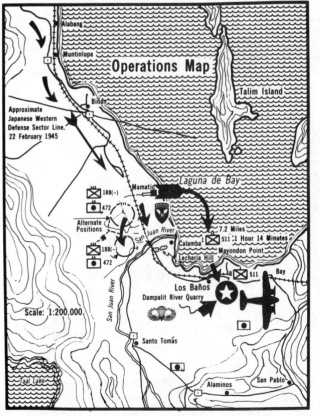

At 0700 hours, February 23, infantry and artillery units moved across the San Juan River to attack Japanese positions at Lecheria Hill; fifty-two amphibious tractors landed near Mayondong Point and moved toward Los Baños; and a company of paratroopers jumped onto a drop zone a few hundred yards from the Los Baños Internment Camp. Ironically, the only fatalities suffered by American forces occurred during the diversionary attack some fifteen miles from Los Baños. *(Courtesy George Doherty)*

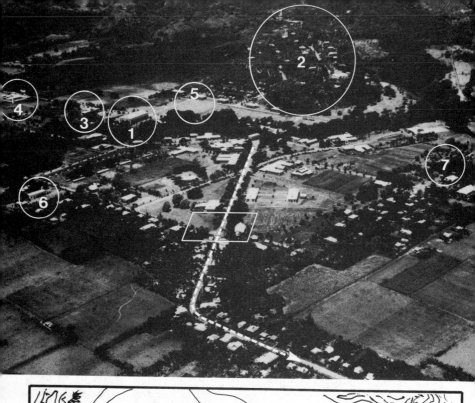

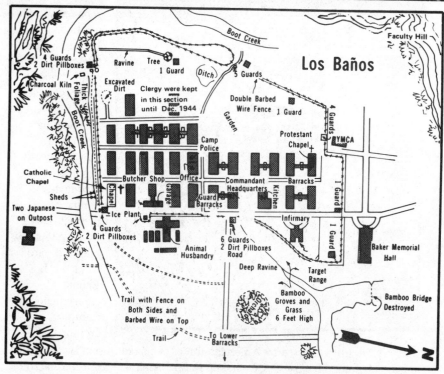

Boot Creek

Faculty Hill

Los Baños

4 Guards
2 Dirt Pillboxes

Charcoal Kiln

Ravine Tree
1 Guard

Ditch

5 Guards

Excavated
Dirt

Clergy were kept
in this section
until Dec. 1944

Double Barbed
Wire Fence 1 Guard

4 Guards

Garden

Thick Foliage

Boot Creek

Protestant
Chapel

YMCA

Camp
Police

1 Guard

Catholic
Chapel

Butcher Shop Office

Commandant
Headquarters

Barracks

Sheds

Chapel

Garage

Guard
Barracks

Kitchen

Two Japanese
on Outpost

Ice Plant

4 Guards
2 Dirt Pillboxes

Animal
Husbandry

6 Guards
2 Dirt Pillboxes
Road

Infirmary

1 Guard

Baker Memorial
Hall

Deep Ravine

Target
Range

Bamboo
Groves and
Grass
6 Feet High

Bamboo Bridge
Destroyed

Trail with Fence on
Both Sides and
Barbed Wire on Top

Trail

To Lower
Barracks

N

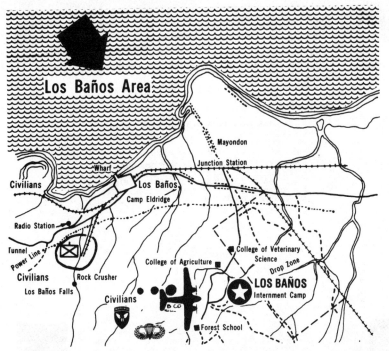

The Internment Camp occupied a corner of the College at Los Baños. See accompanying aerial photo and map. *(Courtesy George Doherty)*

OPPOSITE, ABOVE: Los Baños Agricultural College in 1938. See the following map of the Internment Camp for orientation. (1) is Baker Hall; (3) is the infirmary; (4) is the animal husbandry building; (5) is the athletic field where the internees were loaded into the amtracs; (6) is the Catholic church on the lower campus where civilians from Los Baños were murdered by the Japanese after the rescue of the internees; (2) is Faculty Hill, behind which is Mount Makiling; the dotted line represents the route taken by the amtracs from the college toward the beach. The boxed area on that route indicates where the road has since been closed off on the campus; (7) is the house where Tom Bousman, whose assistance in captioning these photos and the map of the camp was invaluable, lived with his family before they were interned. *(Courtesy Ben Edwards)*

OPPOSITE, BELOW: The original of this map was provided by Pete Miles and was done by him with the assistance of Ben Edwards. It was later adapted for *Combat Notes Number 7,* Assistant Chief of Staff, G-3, Headquarters, Sixth Army, May 1945, p. 37, and *After Action Report Mike 1 Operation,* U.S. Army Headquarters, XIV Corps, 29 July 1945, p. 163. The present version was done for this book by George Doherty.

U S P I F
HQ., RED LION DIVISION (25TH DIV. PQOG)
In the Field

21 February 45

To: Sgt. J. Fulton

Please transmit this communication upon receipt:

<u>URGENT</u>

ESPINO TO VANDERPOOL HAVE RECEIVED RELIABLE
INFORMATION THAT JAPS HAVE LOS BAÑOS SCHEDULED
FOR MASSACRE PD SUGGEST THAT ENEMY POSITIONS IN
LOS BAÑOS PROPER AS EXPLAINED MILLER BE BOMBED
AS SOON AS POSSIBLE PD

W. C. PRICE
Colónel, GSC (Guer)
Chief of Staff

Dear Johnny —
Please send this over as soon as possible.
Thanks.

YANDE
2. 11TH
ORDERS DELIVERED 1800 OCLOCK
FIFTEEN FEBRUARY : UMALI NOT
YET LOCATED. PREPARATIONS
IN FULL SWING. AMMUNITION
DELIVERED TO INGLES.

ESPINO
COLONEL

Radio operator Sergeant John Fulton had been sent by the planners of the raid on Los Baños to hide out with Romeo Espino and maintain radio contact with Eleventh Airborne headquarters. The urgency of the rescue mission was indicated by the message that "Col. Price" (Romeo Espino), a guerrilla leader, gave to Fulton. The note on the bottom says, "Dear Johnny—Please send this over as soon as possible. Thanks. WCP." It was never positively established that the massacre feared by Espino was in fact planned, but there had been a painful precedent at Palawan, where hundreds of POWs were killed. *(Courtesy John Fulton)*

Captain Donald G. Anderson flew lead C-47 over Los Baños. *(Courtesy Don Anderson)*

Baker Hall, one of the few permanent buildings used by the internees. Most of the pioneer 800 lived there for the first few months of their stay at Los Baños. *(Courtesy U.S. Signal Corps)*

Internee barracks as they begin to catch fire during the raid. So many of the prisoners were afraid to leave the only protection they knew that the soldiers had to fire the barracks in order to get them to leave. Baker Hall is in the upper left-hand corner. The large building on the right is the animal husbandry building. The infirmary, not visible here through the smoke and trees, is between them. *(Courtesy U.S. Signal Corps)*

The building on the lower right is the infirmary. Behind it is the ravine down which Ben Edwards, Pete Miles, and Freddy Zervoulakas escaped with information for the rescuing forces. *(Courtesy U.S. Signal Corps)*

Five amtracs move along the camp perimeter. Lightly armored, as ungainly on land as in the water, they nevertheless took hundreds of people to safety within hours. *(Courtesy U.S. Signal Corps)*

The infirmary at the top of the photo is marked with two red crosses. The small gate at the left is believed to have been near the Protestant Chapel. The circular structure was used for storing grain. Note how thoroughly the fire has consumed the end of the barracks, which were constructed in large part of highly flammable sawali and nipa. *(Courtesy U.S. Signal Corps)*

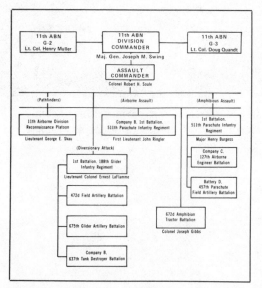

Table of Organization for the assault on Los Baños. *(Courtesy George Doherty)*

Out of range of Japanese guns, soldiers and internees are on deck, watching the approach to the beach at Mamatid, from where the amtracs had left earlier that morning. *(Courtesy U.S. Signal Corps)*

Once they were safe ashore, the prisoners were greeted, and the paratroopers began to leave their improbable transportation. *(Courtesy U.S. Signal Corps)*

Two elderly men wait to be placed in an ambulance.
(Courtesy U.S. Signal Corps)

BELOW: The more physically fit internees begin to load their few possessions into the trucks that would take them to New Bilibid. *(Courtesy U.S. Signal Corps)*

Two of the hospital trucks arrive at New Bilibid Prison, now a hospital and the new residence for several weeks for most of the internees. All agreed that the new jail was more to their taste. *(Courtesy U.S. Signal Corps)*

The desperate physical condition of some of the former internees is evident. Men generally seemed to suffer more from hunger and malnutrition, and especially older men, than women. *(Courtesy U.S. Signal Corps)*

The internees were permitted to take only one or two suitcases with them when they left Los Baños. Many were bankrupt, their homes and businesses long since destroyed. No government compensation was offered by the United States or by Japan after the war to private citizens for their losses. The elderly man at left may well be as poor in material possessions as the baby in the center, one of about fifteen born at Los Baños. *(Courtesy U.S. Signal Corps)*

Patrician, hard-driving, and demanding, Lieutenant General Joseph M. Swing was sometimes called the Patton of the Pacific, but he disdained bravado and showmanship as he led the Eleventh Airborne to a distinguished combat record. General MacArthur chose Swing to receive the surrender of the Japanese ground forces six months after Los Baños. *(Courtesy Glenn McGowan)*

Four of the key men who were involved in the planning of the rescue at Los Baños. From left, Lieutenant Colonel Glenn McGowan, Personnel and Administration; Lieutenant Colonel Roy Stout, Supply and Logistics; Lieutenant Colonel Henry Muller, Intelligence; Lieutenant Colonel Doug Quandt, Operations. *(Courtesy Glenn McGowan)*

Rescued internees meet with intelligence personnel to share their information about Los Baños. *(Courtesy Glenn McGowan)*

Glenn McGowan (right) and Frank Smith, war correspondent for the *Chicago Tribune,* with a Japanse flag taken during the raid on Los Baños. *(Courtesy Glenn McGowan)*

Less than a year after the rescue, Tom Bousman's father took these photographs of the camp site. "Jerry" Bousman, as everyone knew him, stands touching what is left of the ingenious stove that he built behind his family's cubicle. That stove, and a few isolated pieces of bed frame seen in the other photograph, are all that physically remain of the Los Baños Internment Camp. *(Courtesy Tom Bousman)*

10

A MEETING ON TAGAYTAY RIDGE

Tagaytay Ridge: February 3, 1945
I

On the morning that George Lewis died, a young Filipino received the order that would eventually lead him to make a unique contribution to end the suffering of the internees at Los Baños, as the only man to serve both as a guerrilla and as a member of the Eleventh Airborne Division. But then Bob Fletcher was an unusual Filipino. His grandfather, Joe Fletcher, was from Georgia. He had come with the American Army to the Philippines in 1898 and stayed to marry a girl from Cebu, Bob's grandmother. After a stint teaching English and Spanish, the ex-soldier had worked in the cold-storage business in Manila. When the Japanese marched into the city in January 1942, old Joe Fletcher was still on his feet, still hearty enough to be tossed into Santo Tomás, in March, with the other Americans, while his wife, as a Filipino, was allowed to remain outside in their home.

Short and slight, Bob Fletcher in 1942 looked even younger than his sixteen years, and his fevered attempt to join the Navy at Cavite on December 10, 1941, was rejected. He pleaded in vain to be taken into the service—surely his standing as a captain in the high school ROTC should account for something, he thought. But for the early months of the war he had to content himself with minor acts of sabotage, fueled by his increasing resentment of the Japanese presence in Manila. When the wealthy Americans who lived next door realized that their possessions would all disappear into the Japanese "treasure ships" after they left for Santo Tomás, they told their Filipino friends to come and take what they

147

wanted. Bob acquired a rubber stamp and fashioned with it a flyer that proclaimed "Long Live Freedom!" He ran off copies of the flyer and distributed it throughout the city, dodging Japanese patrols on his bike. He organized gangs of kids who would harass the soldiers who stood at every major intersection by passing in front of them singly, forcing the soldiers to return each bow, until finally the guards, sick of bowing themselves, would turn away and look at the wall. And he devised a means of disabling Japanese cars and trucks with native fruit; he would cut the top off a pomelo, stud it with nails, and sail it like a disk into the street. Passing vehicles would run over the fruit, pulverizing it beneath their wheels and thus destroying the evidence of his crime. Fletcher would wait hidden down the street and laugh as he watched the puzzled Japanese try to figure out why all their tires went flat at the same time.

One day early in March 1942, a squad of Japanese soldiers came to the Fletchers' house to tell Bob's grandfather he was to be taken to Santo Tomás. As they entered the living room, they saw on the floor the parts of an old GE radio that Bob had been working on. A sergeant took Bob onto the terrace, which was separated from the living room by glass-paned French doors, to question him about the radio. The boy's grandfather accompanied him, trying to explain that there was nothing illegal or unusual about a six-teen-year-old boy playing with a radio's insides. At that point the Japanese lieutenant in the living room motioned abruptly for the boy to return. As he moved toward the door, the boy found the bayonet of the sergeant poised at his chest—he was not to move. At the same time, the lieutenant on the other side of the glass raised his rifle threateningly toward Bob's head: he *was* to move, Bob understood. Furious at being presented with the choice of death by bayonet or bullet, he exploded at the guards—"Why don't you jerks make up your minds?" The tense moment passed without further incident, but Bob was convinced that it was time to get out of the city. He wasn't of any use here, and it was only a matter of time before bigger trouble with the enemy came.

He spent the next year working in the copper mines of northern Luzon. His job was to check and transcribe bills of lading, indicating how much ore came out of the mine and where it was sent.

He gave the Japanese supervisors the required five copies of each receipt. And he kept a sixth copy, which he placed under various rocks and bushes in the vicinity of his cabin near the mine. He had been frightened enough when he had learned from guerrilla intelligence what his assignment at the mine would be, and during his time there he grew even more apprehensive. What if someone was watching him, he wondered. The Japanese had *makapili* informants everywhere, and any one of his fellow workers could be following him as he left the mine each afternoon with his contraband copy of the day's activities. He decided to change the procedure for passing the information along, much to the distress of his angry contact, who called him on the phone to complain that the material was not where it should have been. From now on, Fletcher informed his contact coolly, he would leave the information where he chose, and when. But how would they know where it was, the contact complained. "You can call me and I'll tell you," Fletcher said.

He was right to be concerned, as things turned out. Fletcher had always distrusted the devil-may-care type who lived for the danger of the moment; at seventeen he had already learned that the only way to survive was to be silent and unobtrusive. And the only way to help your friends survive was to know as little as possible about what they were doing. One of his conditions for accepting his assignment had been that he be told nothing beyond his immediate task; it was only gradually, and almost by accident, that he had learned that all of the men in his cabin were working for guerrilla intelligence.

One of them was a barrel-chested, likable young would-be opera singer named Val. Emotionally extravagant by nature and by his training in opera, Val disdained the dusty, tedious recording of information deep in the bowels of the earth and longed to be fighting the enemy hand to hand out in the open. He constantly talked about finding some unit that would take the battle to the Japs instead of burrowing like moles in the ground. One day after work Fletcher was sluicing the caked dust from his body in the shower when a friend edged close and said, under the noise of the rushing water, "They've got Val!" Fletcher finished his shower and reflected as he toweled off. If the Kempetai—"they" could only be the secret police—had Val, it was only a matter of time before the singer talked. He had never shut up in the cabin—Fletcher had often left when he started to talk so he wouldn't have to learn things he didn't want to hear—and the Kempetai would squeeze him dry in a day or two. They were all in danger. Then he dropped his towel abruptly, as his heart raced; the first thing the Japs would do would be to search the cabin, and who knew what Val had hidden away in his trunk?

Still dripping wet, Fletcher ran back to the cabin, tore open Val's locker and found a box of 30.06 cartridges. The box was broken, so he scooped the shells into his straw hat and ran outside, where he scattered them in the thick elephant grass. Back inside, he found two more shells that had dropped out of the box. He picked them up and ran out of the cabin again, hiding in the thick grass as a Japanese truck with a squad of soldiers jerked to a stop. The soldiers ransacked the barracks for the next hour as Fletcher watched from his hiding place. They found nothing, he learned that evening, but he knew it was only a matter of time before he and the others would be turned in. He headed south.

After a year in the mines, Fletcher was ready for life in the open, and his next assignment agreed with him far more. His job was to record the movements of Japanese troop and supply trucks and vehicles, copying down the Japanese characters accurately even though he did not understand them and passing the information on to guerrilla headquarters. His chief was his old scoutmaster, Terry Adevozo, who had formed the unit called Terry's Hunters, or the Hunter ROTC group—a unit that, more than most of the other guerrilla groups, maintained the military order of command and procedure that Fletcher had come to admire while in high school.

During that time, in fact, Fletcher had been equally impressed by the murderous nature of both the declared enemy, the Japanese, and his supposed allies, various renegade bands of Filipino guerrillas. The worst of the renegades were the "Texans," so called because they looked like classic movie bad guys with their crisscrossed banderillas. The Texans would ride into a village, guns blazing, order up a feast that required slaughtering several carabao and disappear into the canebrakes with as many of the pretty young girls in the village as they could find. They had even stolen Fletcher's shoes one day as he was out on his rounds, mocking him for not bringing the shoes to them sooner. Whether or not they ever caused the Japs much trouble was debatable, Fletcher thought. Their occasional raids on Jap patrols probably got more villagers killed than anyone else. The Japanese had a policy of killing ten civilians for every soldier killed in a guerrilla attack, including young boys and old men—and frequently women and children as well. They made no distinctions between renegade guerrillas and legitimate patriots, and they adopted various means of trying to control them. Probably the most effective, and most detested, was the recruitment of Filipino sympathizers who would turn their countrymen over to the enemy for a price —either money or, in some cases, the lives of their own families.

One day early in 1944 Fletcher was passing through a village near Tagaytay Ridge with a guerrilla friend. They had been recruiting local citizens to help as spotters. A company of Japanese troops moved into the village and lined up all of the men of the village, including Fletcher and his friend, in the dusty square. Fletcher was afraid that he and the rest were going to be gunned down in retaliation for some guerrilla raid they had had nothing to do with. But when he saw the owl he knew that there wouldn't be a wholesale slaughter, just a selective one, maybe. The "owl" was a Filipino with a bag over his head and slits cut for him to see through—a local who understandably did not want to be identified. A Japanese soldier with a four-foot length of two-by-four walked behind the men who were lined up as the Japanese captain and the owl walked in front of them. When the owl stopped in front of a man and nodded, the soldier behind the unfortunate one brought the club down upon his head and beat him into the dust. When the owl stopped in front of him, Fletcher forced himself not to clench his fists, though he could feel the sweat dripping off his fingertips. He stared blankly at a spot between the slitted eyes of the owl. The bag remained motionless; then the owl moved on. Fletcher was beginning to release a careful sigh of shuddering relief when he heard the two-by-four come crashing down on the shoulder of the man next to him, the man who had been his recruiting partner. The last he saw of him, his partner was being trundled off in a caretella toward Manila and extended questioning by the Kempetai, his shoulder broken in two places.

Late in January 1945, Fletcher came in from a two-week stint in the field for a rest at Adevozo's headquarters in Laguna de Bay. His rest was a short one. The next morning he was summoned to Adevozo's headquarters, where he met Terry and Jay Vanderpool, the American major he had met once before. Operating behind enemy lines as the American liaison with the guerrillas, the broad-shouldered Oklahoman, a half-Cherokee, was, like Adevozo, soft-spoken but rugged. Gustavo Ingles, another guerrilla, told Fletcher that Vanderpool was the only American he had ever seen who could keep up with him in the mountains. Now Vanderpool and Terry handed Fletcher a new carbine, a pack of Lucky Strikes, and a wad of ten-peso notes—and an assignment. It was to go to Colonel Ocampo's Forty-Seventh Regimental Headquarters at Si-lang, between Parañaque and Tagaytay Ridge. En route he was to tell the local village headmen to get ready for the Americans in the Eleventh Airborne who would be landing at Nasugbu and marching northward toward Manila.

For the next five days Fletcher hiked along Route 17 with a young companion named Vicente. A survivor of the Bataan Death March, Vicente felt lucky to be alive, and he didn't mind the slight shuffle that a Japanese bayonet thrust through his left calf had left him with. Enteng Pilay was his nickname—the "Lame One." Fletcher and the Lame One doled out the Lucky Strikes to the lesser dignitaries along the way, smoking only four themselves, and impressed the more important figures with the ten-peso notes, which had VICTORY! printed on one side.

What most impressed the natives, though, was the shiny new semiautomatic carbine, and Fletcher kept tight hold of it until he arrived at Ocampo's headquarters. The colonel took Fletcher's report and his carbine and ordered him out the next morning to retrieve the machine guns from a downed American P-38 in the jungle, halfway down the other side of Tagaytay Ridge. When Fletcher protested that he needed to have a weapon for such a patrol, Ocampo scoffed. The only Japs on the ridge were at the Manila Hotel branch fifteen miles away, he said, and they were all recuperating pilots. Fletcher wouldn't need a weapon.

Ocampo had a twelve-year-old American boy with him who served as an aide and was a camp mascot; he was allowed to carry the colonel's .45 caliber automatic around his skinny waist. That night Fletcher tossed his bedroll down beside the boy and waited until he had gone to sleep. Then he stole the colonel's .45 and set out early on his mission to retrieve the American machine guns.

He found the plane, halfway down the slope toward Lake Taal, the icy blue lake that nestled in the extinct volcano crater behind Tagaytay Ridge. There was no sign of the pilot or of any guns—somebody had gotten to them first, probably the Japs, Fletcher thought. As he hit the crest of the ridge toward dusk the next day —at 3,000 feet from sea level, it was a day's climb down and back —a Japanese patrol spotted him and started shooting. Fletcher returned fire with his only weapon, the colonel's .45, ducked into the rocks along a stream leading down the mountain, and eventually escaped.

Early on the morning of February 3, Fletcher was padding nervously along the trails leading toward Route 17—he had only two rounds left in the .45, and for the past half hour, starting at about 7:30, there had been artillery fire and the chatter of machine guns from the area near the Manila Hotel Annex. There were sure to be Japs nearby, Fletcher thought; it was going to be unhealthy here very soon. But he wondered about Ocampo's reception when he returned to Forty-seventh Headquarters without the P-38 guns and no good explanation for taking the .45 from the boy other than the fact that it had probably saved his life.

It was at that point that the Eleventh Airborne literally dropped into Bob Fletcher's life.

II

Bob Fletcher was about to witness some 1,700 members of the Eleventh Airborne Division's 511th Parachute Infantry Regiment taking the high ground at Tagaytay Ridge. He could have no way of knowing that the next time part of the 511th jumped, he would be with them. But in a matter of days he would make the transition from guerrilla to combat infantry man, from being a behind-the-lines operative dependent on secrecy and stealth and solitude to becoming part of a group of tough, disciplined, and battle-tested combat troops. With the Eleventh Airborne, Bob Fletcher would soon be going home, to Manila.

A much more eminent former resident of Manila, Douglas MacArthur, had spent the past three years arranging for his own return; the fate of thousands of American prisoners, including those at Los Baños, depended upon his return being successful. For a time, it was a distinct possibility that the Philippines would be left to languish under the heel of the Japanese army until the war ended. MacArthur was called to a meeting with President Roosevelt and Admiral Chester Nimitz at Pearl Harbor in July 1944 and asked why the United States should not proceed with Admiral Nimitz's plan to bypass the Philippines entirely, attacking Formosa instead. Nimitz argued that the 400,000 enemy troops in the Philippines would thus be neutralized and that the home islands of Japan could be invaded by October 1945.

MacArthur was appalled by the Navy's plan. The Filipinos believed they had been betrayed once already by the United States, he said, when we failed to send men and matériel to Bataan and Corregidor in 1942. He had vowed to return to the Philippines in the name of his country, MacArthur said, "and promises must be kept." The Navy's plan to blockade the Philippines would result in the Japanese occupation troops appropriating whatever food was available and subjecting the people to even greater miseries. The Filipinos looked upon the United States as "the mother country," he said; to go back on his promise to rescue them would constitute a blot on American honor, making it impossible for the word of the country to be trusted again in Asia after the war was over.

The president wanted to know whether there would be heavy losses in life attacking Luzon—the toll in American lives in Europe and Asia included the sons of some eminent men, including those of Joseph P. Kennedy, Harry Hopkins, Roosevelt's senior aide, and Senator Leverett Saltonstall. Although there were fewer lives lost under MacArthur's command than under that of any other American general during the war, Roosevelt had to be concerned with the effect an extended and bloody campaign would have on American public opinion.

MacArthur responded that his plan would save lives. "The days of the frontal assault should be over," he said. "Modern infantry weapons are too deadly, and frontal assault is only for mediocre commanders." An attack on Formosa, he implied, would be a frontal assault upon a mountainous stronghold next door to Japan. It would make the earlier bloody assaults on the Pacific islands of Tarawa, Saipan, and dozens of others pale by comparison—assaults that, he did not need to add, were enormously costly to the United States in terms of lives lost and that were part of naval operations—not Army—in the Pacific. In any case, he said, it was impossible to encircle Luzon with a blockade as the Navy had suggested. The island was simply too big, even larger than Formosa itself, as a glance at the map would show. It would be an absurd misuse of naval power, requiring most of the Pacific Fleet to sit inactive while the war reached its climax.

MacArthur argued further that although the population of Formosa had no allegiance to the United States, many of the 17 million people in the Philippines had been fighting as guerrillas for the past three years, providing his headquarters with invaluable information about enemy troop movements and locations—and this intelligence would aid immensely in the attack on the Philippines.

MacArthur's original plan for the Pacific war had as its ultimate goal the Philippine archipelago, and he had approached it with the ingenious mix of lightning advances and cautious consolidation that had been the mark of his command from the early days of 1942. His plan, code-named Reno, called for the combined forward movement of ground, sea, and air forces on a single axis from Port Moresby in New Guinea to Manila, 3,000 miles to the north. By maintaining control of both sea and air, he had been able to launch major amphibious operations along the line of the axis. And during the months of fighting that preceded the battle for the Philippines he had moved from Port Moresby to Buna and Lae, through the Vitiaz Straits to the Admiralties, on to Hollandia and the Vogelkop, finally arriving at the springboard of Morotai, ready to jump to Mindanao.

The plan, he reminded the president, was based not on his emotional commitment to the people of the Philippines, nor on American honor, nor on his personal destiny, but on simple facts of geography: the Philippine Islands represented the keystone of Japan's island empire. They lay directly in the main sea routes from Japan to its sources of raw materials and oil in the Netherlands Indies, Malaya, and Indochina. Control of air and naval bases in the Philippines meant control of the main artery of supply to Japan's factories, its industrial heart. Sever the artery, MacArthur argued, and the lifeblood of Japan's war effort would cease to flow; the home islands would then be vulnerable to attack. But if nearly half a million Japanese troops were left unhindered in the Philippines and the sea-lanes from Japan to its supply sources in the south were not closed, the empire could fight on long after Formosa had been captured, and at a much higher cost in American lives.

MacArthur's eloquence and logic had prevailed, and by late fall his judgment seemed confirmed. The Navy had scored a stunning victory at Leyte Gulf in October 1944: in an epic battle that lasted for five days the United States Seventh Fleet had destroyed four aircraft carriers, three battleships, six heavy cruisers, four light cruisers, and nine destroyers. Ten thousand Japanese sailors and marines died, and the Japanese navy was no longer a fighting force.

On October 20, the day before the battle began, General MacArthur watched with satisfaction from the bridge of the cruiser *Nashville* as General Walter Kreuger's Sixth Army stormed ashore on the east coast of Leyte virtually unopposed. MacArthur then approached the beach with his staff in an LST that stopped in the shallow surf forty yards from shore. The harbor master, responsible for landing hundreds of small craft carrying provisions for Kreuger's forces, did not take kindly to an aide's request to provide a boat to take MacArthur to the beach. "Take a walk!" the harbor master barked. So the general and his staff waded through the surf. Water dripping down his legs, MacArthur announced to the people of the Philippines that he had returned.

But the battle for the island of Leyte was to prove far more difficult than the initial easy landing had suggested. MacArthur had been persuaded to violate his own rule of never committing ground forces without control of land and air. Assuming that the naval battle in the gulf would be a short one, he explained to Kreuger that he was to operate under the protection of carrier-based air power until he had secured the central valley of Leyte and built air-base facilities for two fighter groups, one night-fighter squadron, one medium-bomber group, and four patrols and reconnaissance squadrons. By early December Kreuger was supposed to have completed enough reinforced landing sites to allow heavy bombers to begin operating from the island, attacking northward toward Manila.

The Seventh Fleet had paid dearly for its success in the Battle of Leyte Gulf, though; the carrier pilots who survived were exhausted, and the Seventh was forced to withdraw for refitting. Most of Admiral Halsey's Third Fleet was busy off northern Luzon, and the best he could do was provide a few carrier-based squadrons of Navy fighters. At the same time the Sixth Army was trying to secure the central valley without benefit of air control, one of the heaviest monsoon seasons in the century hit Leyte with some thirty inches of rain in just a few weeks. Cousins of the typhoon that devastated Manila and Los Baños in November turned the already soggy marshes of the valley into quagmires. The Japanese, quick to realize that for once MacArthur was without adequate air defense, threw their remaining planes into the battle. General Yamashita was given sufficient time to send some 45,000 troops to reinforce the 50,000 soldiers who were already digging in for the American assault. The fight for Leyte was threatening to be a knockdown, drag-out battle by the time the Eleventh Airborne arrived late in November 1944 to join Kreuger's Sixth Army.

11

THE MUD RATS OF LEYTE

Leyte: November–December 1944
I

The 8,000 men of the Eleventh Airborne Division who hit the beaches at Tacloban had a lot going for them. They were young, the enlisted members averaging about nineteen. They were smart enough to have sixty percent of their number qualify for officer's training. They were tough—not big, for the most part, because airborne troopers were supposed to be under 6'2" and 185 pounds —but hardened by eighteen months of intensive training, the last five in New Guinea. And they were led by a hard-charging former cavalryman, a classmate of Eisenhower at West Point who had fought with Pershing in Mexico and in France during World War I: Lieutenant General Joseph M. Swing.

The men of the Eleventh Airborne had fought some good fights themselves before landing at Leyte, but most of them had been in bars near Camp Mackall and at Camp Polk in Louisiana, where the tankers in the armored division had the bad judgment to wear fake jump boots and had to be "de-booted" in order to learn their place. And they had seen their buddies die, not yet in the tropical jungles of the Philippines but in the swamps of North Carolina near Camp Mackall, where sixteen men lost their lives in two separate airplane accidents. They had even won a major though bloodless victory, along with their division commander—a victory without which there would have been no airborne divisions either in Europe or in the Pacific.

The antagonist in the Eleventh's first battle was none other than General Dwight D. Eisenhower. The losses suffered by the Eighty-second Airborne Division in the attack on Sicily during the spring and early summer of 1943, many of them through erratic communications between the air transport and paratroop commands, and faulty drops, had soured Ike on the concept and practice of airborne divisions. "I do not believe in the airborne division," he had written to General Marshall in mid-July 1943. It was not that Eisenhower doubted the effectiveness of paratroopers as combat troops but he felt they should be limited in size to regiments and separated into self-contained units of infantry, artillery, and special services. "The fact is," Eisenhower continued, "that at any given time and place only a reasonable number of planes will be available—not enough for a whole division of some 30,000 men to jump." Even if it could, Eisenhower said, "I seriously doubt that a division commander could regain control and operate the scattered forces as one unit. In any event, if these troops were organized in smaller, self-contained units, a senior commander, with a small staff and radio communications, could always be dropped in the area to ensure necessary coordination."

By a lucky stroke of coincidence, Eisenhower's airborne adviser for six weeks during the battle for North Africa and Sicily was General Joe Swing, on temporary reassignment from his duties as the commander of the new Eleventh Airborne Division at Camp Mackall. General George C. Marshall seldom questioned Ike's advice, but the decision to disband five airborne divisions—the 11th, 13th, 17th, 82nd, and 101st—could not be made hastily. Marshall called upon a man whose experience and probity he knew he could trust to head a board of investigation that would be charged with recommending future airborne operations. That man was General Swing.

The "Swing Board" consisted of Army Air Force and parachute glider infantry and artillery officers, and met at Camp Mackall during the month of September 1943. As the troops of the Eleventh Airborne roamed through the nearby pine barrens and marshes, their commander and his board hammered out a new set of operating procedures for the airborne that was designed to eliminate the kinds of errors that had plagued the operations in Sicily and North Africa. Chief among these was a detailed document that spelled out the mutual responsibilities of the Airborne and Troop Carrier Command as well as the various airborne units it would be transporting. Up to this time arrangements between the airborne and the transport commanders had been informal, even casual. Henceforth the procedures established by Swing's commission, not only for command coordination but for every phase of airborne training and discipline, would stand as the model for years to come.

In December 1943 Joe Swing took to the field under the eyes of General Marshall, War Secretary Henry Stimson, as well as assorted members of Congress and the military high command to show that his theories could be proved in practice. In one of the major military maneuvers of World War II, Swing's Eleventh Airborne Division, with the 501st Parachute Infantry Regiment attached, was to seize the Knollwood Airport from the "enemy" —represented by elements of the Seventeenth Airborne Division and the 541st Parachute Infantry Regiment. Swing opened the attack by launching assaults from four different airfields in North and South Carolina, approaching by roundabout routes that took them far over the Atlantic Ocean. Six days later, when the Knollwood maneuvers ended, Joe Swing followed the trucks that carried his men through a freezing rain back to Camp Mackall. They had all known—every young dogface private and West Point shavetail and NCO—the questions they were supposed to answer: Could a modified division-size force be transported over water (the Atlantic Ocean) by planes relying on instruments only and arrive at a selected drop zone precisely on time? Could gliders and paratroopers land without excessive casualties? Could the division engage in sustained combat once it was on the ground? And could the division be supplied by air alone?

Swing was satisfied in his own mind that his men had answered all of these questions with a resounding "Hell, yes!" On December 16 he heard from General Leslie McNair, the hard-bitten and skeptical commander of Army Ground Forces. After his initial enthusiasm, McNair had been sadly disillusioned by the airborne performance in Europe. He had been convinced before Knollwood, he wrote Swing, "of the impracticability of handling large airborne units," and he "was prepared to recommend to the War Department that airborne divisions be abandoned in our scheme

of organization and that the airborne effort be restricted to parachute units of battalion size or smaller. The successful performance of your division has convinced me that we were wrong,"
McNair generously conceded, "and I shall now recommend that
we continue our present schedule of activating, training, and committing airborne divisions."

The Eleventh had, then, accomplished a great deal since its
inauguration on February 23, 1943—a date that would later have
a particular significance. But in late November 1944, it had still
not been tested in battle. By the time it took Bob Fletcher under
its wing in late January it had not only been tested, it had begun
to record its own distinctive contributions to the American victory
in the Pacific, shaping its own vivid personality.

II

The Eleventh had won its spurs after being told to "relieve the
Seventh Infantry Division along the line Burauen-La Paz-Bugho
and destroy all Japs in that sector." General Kreuger's intention
was to split the Japanese positions in northern Leyte by crossing
the rugged mountains between Dagami and Jaro—a narrow, unmapped pass defended by two Japanese divisions. While the Seventh Infantry Division approached the Japanese from the rear
along the coast of the Bay of Ormoc, the Eleventh destroyed the
two enemy divisions, denied the Japanese the escape route to the
east that would have frustrated the attack of the Seventh, and
contributed significantly to the collapse of General Yamashita's
plan to make Leyte, not Luzon, the key battleground in the Philippines.

By comparison with regular Army divisions, Joe Swing's Eleventh was underarmed and undermanned—by design: its mission
was to move fast and hit hard. If it didn't move through the air,
then it was to move on foot: there were few transport vehicles. The
heart of the division consisted of two glider infantry regiments, the
187th and the 188th, with about 1,500 men each, or half the
strength of a standard infantry regiment, each containing two
battalions of three rifle companies. The 511th Parachute Infantry

contained about 2,000 men divided among three battalions, each of which contained three rifle companies rather than the normal quota of five. There were no heavy weapons, cannon, or antitank companies—division artillery consisted of two 175-mm pack howitzer battalions, a 105-mm howitzer battalion whose chief weapon was a short-barrelled howitzer that had nothing like the range of the 105s of a standard infantry division, and an airborne antiaircraft artillery battalion armed with 40-mm and .50 caliber guns.

Headquarters for the Eleventh during its Leyte operations were to be near Burauen, where Kreuger had seized three airfields and repaired them so that limited air operations were possible. The 187th Glider Regiment under Colonel Harry Hildebrand was assigned to protect the Twenty-fourth Corps' rear installations near Bito Beach, where the division had landed. The 188th Glider Infantry, under Colonel Robert "Shorty" Soule, was to patrol the area between Bugho and La Paz, drawing what Japanese forces it could flush out into battle. The 511th Parachute Infantry Regiment was given the toughest mission, that of cutting through the mountains to Ormoc on the western coast of Leyte.

Every organization derives its personality from its leader. Joe Swing, who looked like Hollywood's idea of a general with his patrician profile, piercing blue eyes, and square jaw, had a low regard for flamboyance and even less for public relations: no pearl-handled revolvers for him, or quiet dinners with the gentlemen from The New York Times. He distrusted men who talked too much and were not fit—he transferred dozens of good officers who couldn't keep up with him on the ten- and fifteen-mile training runs he had led through the scrub and the swamps of North Carolina.

Swing chose men in his own steely image for his command and told them to do likewise. One of his first and key appointments was a taciturn Alabaman named Orin Haugen, West Point Class of 1930. Haugen had gained a reputation at Camp Toccoa, Georgia, as the toughest man in the regiment he created for the twenty-five-mile runs he regularly led up and down Curahee Mountain. An austere man not given to casual or informal associations, he was nevertheless widely known by his nickname, "Hardrock"—shortened, by the time the regiment hit Leyte, to the slightly more affectionate "Rock."

Haugen opened his attack on November 28 by sending the First and Third Battalions before him on parallel trails about ten miles apart. The distance by air from Bito to Ormoc, almost due west on the opposite coast, was less than twenty-five miles; from Buraven, less than twenty. But between the 511th and its destination loomed the central mountain range of Leyte, crawling with 6,000 Japanese troops who had been ordered to hold or die.

It took six days for the First Battalion, under Colonel La-Flamme, to reach the halfway point to Ormoc—a tiny village known by the natives as Mahonag. To the troopers it looked like Shangri-La, and it was indeed a kind of oasis of flat rock, a tabletop rising 150 feet above the surrounding jungle. Though less than the length of two football fields and only 200 feet wide, the cleared plateau was good enough to become the headquarters for the 511th for the next two weeks, housing not only the command post but a supply depot, a signal center, a parachute supply drop zone and cemetery, a herd of wandering carabao—and enough of a runway for Cub scout planes to take off and land.

Some indication of the difficulty of the terrain through which the First Battalion slogged is provided by the fact that they had not yet encountered effective enemy resistance. The Japanese had hit Bito Beach and ambushed the First Battalion's C Company, which was approaching the same destination via a different route. But it had not fallen to the men in either of the advancing battalions to claim the first reported kill of an enemy soldier. That honor went to George Skau, the leader of the Reconnaissance Patrol, a gruff, muscular immigrant's son from Poughkeepsie whose social manner made Rock Haugen look like Pearl Mesta. All of the men in the Recon Platoon—the Killer Platoon, as it came to be known—had been selected because they were loners, cunning, and capable of being ruthless. They also had to be capable of operating far behind enemy lines; of reporting the movements of the Japanese without giving themselves away; of making accurate rough maps of terrain that, twisted by earthquakes and ancient volcanic upheavals, seemed to have no logical configurations; and of getting back through their own lines without getting shot by their comrades. Skau seemed born to his work; it was as natural as breathing for him to shoot the Japanese soldier who stepped in front of his jeep as he was being taken to report to the 188th regimental command post. It was one of the many ironies of war that the Japanese soldier was far behind American lines and may well have been attempting to surrender. Skau shrugged the suggestion off as irrelevant when someone made it to him.

But LaFlamme's main antagonist up to the time the First Battalion arrived at Manarawat was one he shared with the Japanese: the jungle. The men had had plenty of exposure to the jungle on New Guinea during the months they spent there. They weren't surprised by the incredible tangle of wrist-thick vines and creepers that clutched at them, by the distorted, nightmarish shapes of mahogany, banyan, and eucalyptus trees that obscured the sky during those rare moments when it was visible through the incessant pouring rain, by the black flies and the mosquitoes that crawled into their eyes and ears and mouths, by the tarantulas and cobras that lurked underfoot, nor by the pythons that hovered above their heads. But there is a big difference between slogging through the tropical jungle of Leyte with limited supplies—one meal a day, usually K rations—and knowing that the next day, and the next after that, will be the same, if you're still alive, and coming back to camp in New Guinea after five days in the bush for a USO show with Jack Benny or Judith Anderson; between trying to apprehend "The Thing," presumably a local citizen, who crept among the camp at New Guinea stealing boots and food, and waiting for the rustle in the jungle grass to be followed by a banzai charge.

A great deal of the time the Eleventh spent in New Guinea was not in jungle training but in doing what they had signed up to do —and what some actually enjoyed doing: jumping out of planes. Joe Swing had exercised his influence in Washington to get a full-scale jump school established at their camp in New Guinea. He was determined that every man in his command who could be would be qualified to wear the wings of a jumper, including the glider troops; by the time the Eleventh embarked for Leyte some seventy-five percent of the enlisted men and eighty-five percent of the officers had made their required jumps, and Swing had achieved his stated goal of qualifying virtually the entire division.

But it took very little time to discover that if the jungles of Leyte were hard to pass through on foot, they were virtually inaccessible to paratrooper attack. One of the last remaining untouched rain forests of the world, the northern half of Leyte was unmined, unlogged, unfarmed, uninhabited except for a few scattered tribes, and virtually unmapped. There were few places among its festering jungles and deeply etched gorges where even small craft could land, let alone L-5s and C-47s. Except for occasional individual jumps from Cub scout planes flying out of the Rock, most of the Eleventh would finish their first campaign—and by general consensus the toughest—without ever feeling the jump sergeant's boot on their butts.

As it turned out, it was not the infantry but the field artillery that made the major American combat jump on Leyte. The 511th had been supported during its initial phase by Corps artillery, thunderous 155-mm howitzers positioned near the east coast. From the Rock westward, though, it would be beyond the reach of the Corps' big guns. It needed its own smaller guns, but they were ten miles down the mountain, and there was no way they could be brought up the narrow footpaths. Until the 511th had its artillery to cover its advance to Ormoc, it would be stalled. They would have to airlift their guns.

But an army is much like a state government: each part of it wants more than is available and has to function on a make-do, catch-as-catch-can basis. The dozen C-47s the Eleventh needed to drop the 457th Field Artillery Battalion's A Company and its equipment were busy dropping supplies to the 185,000 men under Kreuger, spread over 11,000 square miles. Colonel Stadtherr, the resourceful commander of the 457th, managed to find a sympathetic pilot named Myers at San Pablo who said he'd be willing to help out: the name of his place was "Rescue." Within two days "Rescue," never sleek, had her doors ripped off and her belly festooned with half a dozen racks designed to hold the barrels, plates, and wheels of the artillery pieces that would be reassembled on the ground at Manarawat.

Colonel Stadtherr had Myers fly him on a dry run over the drop site at Manarawat, a half mile from the Rock. The engineers had cleared an area about 500 feet by 150 feet, which was adequate if he made the drop from about 300 feet. However, the drop zone was ringed on three sides by high cliffs and could only be approached by following a deep canyon to the site. Then the pilot had to make a sharp right turn—blind—make the drop, and bank sharply up and left to avoid running into a mountain. Stadtherr got permission to try it once; he jumped the five men who flew with the equipment himself. The drop was perfect. He and Rescue then returned for twelve more trips, all flawless and a marvel of timing and coordination that would not be matched for some time —until February 23 over Los Baños.

However, the major parachute assault on Leyte would be made not by the Americans but by the Japanese. General Yamashita, seeing that Leyte would be lost unless he could neutralize American air power, ordered two divisions to attack and seize the three airfields east of Burauen during the first week of December. The spearhead of the attack was to be the 300 handpicked men of the Katori Shimpei Force, which was to jump on the night of December 6 on San Pablo—less than half a mile from General Swing's division headquarters.

At six o'clock on the evening of December 6, General Swing was standing outside his headquarters when seven Japanese bombers made a bombing run on San Pablo. Minutes later he heard the familiar offbeat engines of more Japaneses planes and saw the skies filled with enemy paratroopers. By their daring thrust the Japanese had achieved complete surprise. Even worse, the airstrip they were after was only lightly defended, and not by infantry but by one of the 127th Engineers, a signal company, and Headquarters Battery of the Division Artillery. Company clerks left their typewriters and joined the engineers, radio men, and liaison pilots as the Japanese paratroopers raced through the area, torching supply depots, destroying planes, and digging in. It took two days for Swing and his men to repulse the attack.

They were aided by the confusion and ineptitude of the Japanese. Many died without firing a shot, the result of defective quick-release harnesses that dropped them like rocks to the ground from fifty feet up. Others were drunk on Japanese whiskey: empty bottles were found on their bodies, bearing labels that instructed them not to touch a drop until they were airborne. Some of the enemy carried cards with phrases in English apparently meant to demoralize the Americans: "Go to hell beast!" and, more elaborately, "I am chief commander of Japanese descent paratrooper army. All the airdrome has been taken tonight by the Japanese army. It is resistless, so you must surrender. All the Japanese army has done great attack." Fortified by what they apparently regarded as a profound insight into American psychology and their whiskey, some of the Japanese dashed heedlessly through the battle zone, making a terrific din with whistles and horns and bells, shouting, "Surrender, surrender! Everything is useless!" until they were gunned down. The ground units that were supposed to be the main strength of the Japanese attack, behind their paratroopers, never got their efforts properly coordinated, and the airfields were secure after a week of nasty fighting —what General MacArthur, to the constant dismay of his men, liked to call "mopping up."

The failure of the Japanese forces, and their quaint notions of inspiring fear in the hearts of their enemy with slogans and sake, did not make them appear comical—their determination not to be moved out of their mountain strongholds was too intense for that. But many of the Americans on Leyte were struck by the diminutive size of the Japanese soldier. They seemed even smaller to Captain Tom Mesereau from the perspective of his 6'4" and 225 pounds.

Early in December Mesereau surprised three enemy soldiers splashing water over themselves in a streambed. For some reason the streambed was nearly empty despite the heavy rains Mesereau's C Company had only recently been slogging through (he was part of the contingent that was to go with Hardrock Haugen and the other 511th Regimental command personnel along the so-called "Middle Trail" up the mountains, toward Manarawat). It was very odd, Mesereau thought. Not half a mile back the lead scout had signaled "enemy in sight" and killed two soldiers with a burst of light machine-gun fire. Yet here were these soldiers splashing their scrawny brown torsos with water, like street kids he'd seen in Harlem playing in the fire hydrants, as though they hadn't a care in the world. Probably the heavy canopy of leaves and the dense thicket that lined the streambed had deadened the sound of the shots.

Sergeant Stamm, beside Mesereau, opened fire and killed the three Japanese soldiers as they bathed. The Filipino scout, a pig hunter they had picked up a few miles back, smiled nervously and motioned to the Americans to follow him along the creek bed. As they rounded a bend in the creek the guide disappeared into the jungle and the roof fell in on C Company and the regimental command: they had been led into an ambush by the guide. Volleys of shots sprayed from the bushes along the stream. Sergeant Stamm dropped in front of Mesereau, dead, his eyes still staring open—the first dead American soldier Mesereau had seen. A grenade landed near his feet and his men dived for cover. Mesereau picked it up and side-armed it back in the direction from which it had come, a few seconds later there was a muffled explosion, followed by anguished moans of pain. He flipped two or three more grenades back in this manner before the company managed to find some high ground and repel the Japanese attack. They would sit there for four days, beating off attacks from the surrounding Japanese. On the second day a Japanese officer walked over with the treacherous guide under a flag of truce. He demanded the surrender of the Americans. Haugen told him to go to hell and shot the guide between the eyes.

The Japanese could watch and prevent the movement of any group larger than a platoon through the jungle, but they couldn't hope to seal the company off entirely—a few men could get out and bring back help. The men to go were those who were most vital to the success of the division's mission—Hardrock Haugen and several of his staff. There were no sentimental farewells: Haugen knew he was leaving the command in the hands of his most capable officer when he turned it over to Mesereau, and Mesereau knew that Haugen would get him out if it could be done.

From his first days at West Point Tom Mesereau had impressed his superiors as a man with special qualities; not the least of these was his own acceptance of what he regarded as in some sense a protective star that guided him, though it would fade frequently and disappear entirely on occasion. With uncommon maturity for a man of only twenty-three years, Mesereau was capable of regarding his unusual gifts with a detached objectivity that shielded him from egotism. The most valuable of these gifts were uncommon strength and a stamina that allowed him, alone of all Haugen's men, to not only keep up with the Rock but surpass him in endurance. He had played guard for three years at West Point, and during the 1942 season had averaged fifty-nine minutes of playing time per game. It was in that year that he was named an All American.

Ruggedly handsome, athletically gifted, and apparently fearless —his exploits with the grenades in the ditch would become part of the lore of the Eleventh—Mesereau had early on caught General Swing's eye, and that of one of his daughters as well. But there was a reflective side to his nature as well. Though he managed to survive the heavy concentration of engineering, math, and science that West Point required, his favorite subjects were English, history, and psychology. And his pleasure reading was unlike that of most of his classmates—not biographies of Stonewall Jackson and Napoleon but fiction, narratives not of great men recognized as such by the world but of sensitive, trammeled, misunderstood men caught in the prison of their own personalities or in prisons made by other men. Early in high school he had been vividly impressed by Stephen Vincent Benet's "John Brown's Body" and its account of the notorious Confederate prison camp called Andersonville. He was deeply moved by the suffering of the 30,000 Union soldiers who fell into the hands of Captain Wirtz, the Swiss-born prison commandant, "half brute, half fool, and wholly clod" whose incompetence and malice had cost thousands of men their lives.

And he had been drawn as well to the story of a boy in some respects like himself: the outsized Eugene Gant of Thomas Wolfe's *Look Homeward, Angel,* like Mesereau the eldest in a large family. The differences between Eugene Gant and Tom Mesereau were as notable as their great physical size. Tom's father, a gentle man, had nothing of the manic, self-destructive qualities of the half-crazy stonemason who drove Eugene to excesses of love and hate. And the morbidly sensitive poet of *Look Homeward, Angel* seemed to have little in common with the West Point athlete. But Mesereau was drawn to the story of the boy who struggled with the isolation that went with his special sense of being different from those around him, with his desire to leave a mark on his world, to be a part of something grand and glorious.

On Leyte, Tom Mesereau became more and more impressed with the fickleness of fate. Often tragic, as in the case of Sergeant Stamm, and in that of the trooper who had been killed in his tent when the base plate for his own howitzer had crashed from the sky during a supply drop and killed him, it could be comic too: there was no other word for the grotesque accident that had happened to one of his own men, a corporal, on top of the hill when the heavy cloud cover had finally lifted and the L-5s had been able to drop them some food.

Under anesthetic while a medic stitched up a gash in his buttock caused by shrapnel, the soldier had been lying there unconscious with his arms outstretched when a misguided parachute bearing a box of chocolate landed on his right arm, breaking it neatly below the elbow. The medic, without missing a beat, finished stitching up the injured man's wound and promptly splinted his arm for him while he was still unconscious. When the corporal awoke the medic was gone and the stretcher bearers thought he was crazy because he kept asking how come he was wearing an arm splint for a piece of iron in his ass.

It wasn't the kind of thing paratroopers talked about easily with their buddies, but by the time Mesereau had spent a few days sitting on top of his hill on Leyte he thought that he might have found his own destiny in the midst of war. He still had the sense of his star, of being immune from danger. On their way up the hill he and two of his men had approached a large log that blocked their path. The first man had crawled over the log and been shot in the head. Mesereau was next, and he emerged safely on the other side. The third man was killed just as the first had been. There was simply no explanation why some men lived and some men died except luck, though it was probably true that chance did favor the well prepared. It was, he came to feel, his destiny to be the kind of commander men would choose to follow: a man who was not only gifted with the ability to lead but with the luck to stay alive, and to keep his men alive, too.

He'd seen them, many of them, arrive at the train station in Taccoa, a gray town mired in red clay—brash, cocky kids whose idea of danger just a year or two ago was stuffing Limburger cheese into the high school ventilating system; who thought they were fighters because they played football and that they were tough because they could walk up a flight of barracks steps on their hands; who had grown up watching the selfless heroism of *Gunga Din* and *Lives of a Bengal Lancer* and *Charge of the Light Brigade;* who had badgered their parents when they were sixteen and the Japs had bombed Pearl Harbor to let them quit high school and enlist, in anything, anywhere—the Royal Canadian Air Force, the Marines, the Navy—anything but the Army, because who wanted to be a lousy foot soldier? Then they had turned eighteen and enlisted in the airborne because they had seen a movie in which the guys yelled "Geronimo!" as they leaped into the blue, and they wondered if they'd have the guts to do that— or they had been drafted at twenty-one or twenty-two and liked the idea of the extra $50.00 a month. They all wanted the glory they knew would be theirs, and the adoring appreciation of the American public that would be part of that glory.

But there hadn't been any bands to welcome the trains that pulled into Taccoa through the morning mists from San Diego and Chicago and Pittsburgh and Philadelphia. No small boys stepped off of Norman Rockwell's *Saturday Evening Post* covers to gaze wonderingly at the heroes as they stumbled off the train —only a sergeant who stood with his hands on his hips and eyed them with contempt as they fell into something approximating a formation, bedraggled and exhausted after days on the train.

The sergeant would scan the ranks of the unshaven recruits and laugh. "Who's the toughest hombre here?" he would demand. There was seldom a response—the kids weren't stupid, just green. Then the sergeant would grab one and say "Gimme twenty-five," and the recruits would watch as the sacrificial goat labored through fifteen push-ups, then twenty, not quite making twenty-five without the help of the sergeant's forefinger raising him by the belt loop on the back of his pants.

"You think you're tough guys," he would say then. "You listen to me: a year ago I made a living as a stunt man, crashing cars through flaming walls in county fairs, fighting the biggest bastard in six counties with bare knuckles for seventy-five bucks, winner take all, jumping off a fifty-foot platform into a bucket of spit. I was one tough sonuvabitch, I tell you. Or I thought I was until I landed right here where you are a year ago and proceeded to learn what tough really means."

And they *had* learned, Mesereau thought. It wasn't that the training was physically beyond their reach—he'd been pushed nearly as hard at the Point, and despite what the sergeant had said many of these kids were as tough when they arrived as when they left. It was the idea of doing things as a team that the training was intended to drive home. One man alone might find it damn near impossible to make that three-mile run up Curahee with the red clay sticking to his boots like five-pound weights, each weight at each step having to be yanked loose from the slimy, sucking clay with a sound like a plunger in a plugged toilet. It was ten times worse than the football training he had put himself through at the Jersey shore, Mesereau thought, running through the knee-high surf because the red clay slid underfoot, unlike the sand; a mile, half a mile of Curahee was plenty. But they had all run up that mountain and back down it together, driven by Haugen and the stunt-man sergeant until by the time they shipped out to Mackall three weeks later they were sure that no jungle hell could be worse than the red clay of Georgia.

Mesereau, too, was amazed at how the Army had taken these young men—thousands of them, from all over the country, barbers and firemen and bank tellers and college students—and turned them into a highly trained and disciplined unit within a year. He had been a cadet at West Point for four years training to be an officer; other men in his unit had been in the Army for much longer—General Swing forever, it seemed, though he was only forty-nine; Haugen since '31, Ed Lahti since '37. It took a long time to get adjusted to the military, Mesereau knew. But these young men had done it. They had become a team by the time they took their next long train ride across the country, in cars with narrowly slitted windows that kept curious eyes from peering in as the division crossed the nation on its way to Camp Stoneman, near Sacramento, and eventually, for twenty-eight endless days, the trip to New Guinea.

But for all their training, both in the States and in New Guinea, the men and many of their officers—including Mesereau himself —had not yet had to kill or be killed in battle. Mesereau would emerge from his hilltop with those of his company who were still alive—sixteen would be carried out and buried in the small cemetery at Mahonag—convinced that his men had stood the test well and would acquit themselves well.

But even more important to Mesereau than the evidence that his men were fit and he was lucky was his growing conviction that the hardships of war, even the horror of it, brought out the best qualities in men, not the worst: they were nobler and better, by and large, than they were in ordinary circumstances—a truth that was vividly brought home to him a few days after his company had been rescued by a relief column sent out by Haugen. Elmer Fryar was the last man Mesereau would have thought of as heroic: a small-town boy from the deep South, Fryar had been the company barber, a quiet, respectful man, at thirty-two no longer young, who shunned the horseplay and profanity of his buddies and talked mostly about going back to live in Denver after his tour was up and opening his own shop.

On December 8, after a fierce clash near Mahonag, the company barber deliberately stepped in front of his platoon leader and took a burst of automatic weapon fire in the chest; his last act as he crumpled to the ground was to lob a hand grenade in the direction of the sniper who had shot him—it was the twenty-seventh man he had killed that morning. The quiet company barber would become one of two men in the Eleventh to receive the Medal of Honor.

By the time the division left Leyte the Eleventh would earn, in addition to Elmer Fryar's Medal of Honor, 96 Silver Stars, 6 Soldier's Medals, 423 Bronze Stars, 90 Air Medals, and hundreds of Purple Hearts for wounds received in action. About 130 paratroopers would rest in rude graves until their bodies could be reinterred in the American cemetery in Manila after the war was over.

There was one aspect of the Leyte campaign that rankled the men of the Eleventh: they were not sure that anybody knew or cared what they had done. Some thought it was because General Kreuger favored the First Cavalry Division and had it in for the

Eleventh; others thought it was because General Swing believed deeds, not words, were what counted and neglected to see that their actions received the press coverage they deserved; others blamed General MacArthur himself for failing to tell the world of their exploits. One day in the middle of December two privates from H Company of the 511th who had been wounded, Feuereisen and Merisiecki, were on light duty at Tacloban, helping to load supplies on C-47s. They decided to find out for themselves, from the top, why MacArthur had been slighting them in his communiqués. The privates marched up the steps of the villa where the general had his headquarters and asked a one-star general standing there if they could see MacArthur for just a minute. The general smiled indulgently: sorry, he said, not possible. The general was a very busy man. But MacArthur heard them through the open window of his office and called them in.

The two privates sat down in cushioned bamboo peacock chairs and told the commander in chief of the Allied Forces in the Pacific why they thought they were getting a raw deal. MacArthur heard them out, then showed them the operations map of Leyte. He explained that the Japanese had apparently been stunned by the daring and ingenious attack of the 511th, including the unprecedented artillery drop, in large part because they had not considered such a forceful assault in impassable terrain possible (the Japanese liked to flatter themselves that they were the only army capable of jungle warfare). He obviously knew every move of every unit of the Eleventh. But their mission would be jeopardized if it became public knowledge in the press—the Japanese could read the newspapers, too. In the meantime, he gave the men a message for General Swing and his division: when the time was right, the world would know the fine job they had done on Leyte. General MacArthur courteously escorted the two privates to the door, concluding the interview and one of the more unusual exploits of the 511th.

12

DEATH IN MANILA

I

Neither the intrepid privates of the 511th nor MacArthur himself knew on the day of their impromptu visit how great a disaster Leyte would be for the Japanese, one of whom would say, after the war, that losing Leyte "was tantamount to losing the Philippines." In addition to the backbone of their fleet and their air force, 65,000 Japanese soldiers had been wiped out by the 185,000 men under Kreuger's command. The Japanese supply lines to the Dutch East Indies had, as MacArthur predicted, been severed. American losses—2,888 men killed, 10,000 wounded—had not seriously jeopardized the effectiveness of the Sixth Army.

Now, General Yamashita, forced to make a last-ditch stand on Luzon, waited for them with 275,000 men, the largest enemy force of the entire Pacific campaign. Both the American commander and the Japanese knew there was only one feasible route of attack on northern Luzon: it was by means of the Lingayen Gulf, the same route the Japanese had taken three years earlier. Like MacArthur also, Yamashita knew that the city of Manila was strategically worthless and began to withdraw his armies to the north into the high mountains near Baguio, the summer capital of the Philippines. The largest part of Yamashita's forces, comprising some 152,000 men, was the Shobu Group, under his own command; it was responsible for defending the northern half of Luzon. The Kembu Group, consisting of 30,000 men, was positioned from Clark Field south to Bataan. The Shimbu

Group, 60,000 strong, was responsible for the central and southern parts of Luzon, including Manila and Los Baños. General Yokoyama, commander of the Shimbu Group, had been ordered by Yamashita not to try to defend Manila: his mission was to delay the Americans long enough by blowing bridges and fighting delaying actions for the massive supply depots in the capital to be moved north. Some 20,000 of the men under Yokoyama's command were naval marines, the Thirty-first Naval Special Base Force, under the command of Admiral Iwabuchi.

The bulk of MacArthur's enormous invasion force of 280,000 men—more than Eisenhower had commanded in the campaigns in North Africa, Italy, and southern France—would land at Lingayen Gulf and forge southward through the long central valley. But MacArthur had earlier made a decision that was to have a profound effect on the Luzon campaign and on the Eleventh Airborne. Midway through the battle for Leyte, against the advice of his own staff and despite objections from Washington that his idea was "too daring in scope, too risky in execution," MacArthur decided to invade the island of Mindoro. Mindoro was 300 miles northwest of Leyte and, at its northern tip, less than 100 miles south of Manila. MacArthur's intuition had told him that Mindoro would be lightly defended, that Yamashita would have withdrawn his forces there for the more important battles to come. On December 15 the Americans found Mindoro virtually empty of Japanese troops, and MacArthur had four sandy airfields from which to attack northward—flights the internees at Los Baños watched eagerly.

On January 30 the 511th landed on Mindoro while the rest of the Eleventh hit the beaches at Nasugbu, sixty-seven miles south of Manila on the west coast of Luzon. Once again, as on Leyte, its mission was to cut the Japanese lines, separating the Shimbu force from its supply lines to the north. In addition, driving northward, it was to act as the bottom half of a pincers movement on Manila. Part of that attack was the drop of the 511th, which had taken off from Mindoro, on to Tagaytay Ridge—the drop that the young Filipino with the American name had witnessed.

II

Douglas MacArthur would, much later, be characterized as an "American Caesar" by a biographer, and he was indeed an imperial presence who could seem remote from the fears of ordinary men. But one of the less appreciated aspects of MacArthur's character was his strong emotional commitment to the safety of those whose lives were in his charge—those of his own soldiers as well as those of the civilians who had the bad luck to be caught in the field of battle. His policy of leaving strongly held enemy positions like Truk to "wither on the vine" instead of attacking them had spared countless lives, while his daring and ingenious assaults had routinely surprised and steadily pushed back the Japanese forces from the lands they had conquered.

Certain as MacArthur was that he was shaping not only the outcome of the present war but the destiny of Southeast Asia for centuries to come, it would not be surprising to find him indifferent to the fate of individuals during the heat of battle. But such was not the case, as his patience with Privates Feuereisen and Merisiecki indicates. He was indeed concerned about the fate of his men, particularly the 30,000 he had had to leave behind on Bataan and Corregidor in 1942. In 1942 many of these men—7,000 Americans and as many Filipinos—had been imprisoned at Cabanatuan, fifty miles northeast of Manila. By February 1, 1945, there were fewer than 500, all sick or crippled. Some had been shipped to POW camps in Manchuria and Japan. A few had, in December 1944, been sent to New Bilibid Prison. But most had died of neglect or maltreatment at the hands of their Japanese captors. Only later would the grim truth be known: that of the 26,000 American military men held prisoner by the Japanese during World War II, more than 10,000 would die; by contrast, all but 1,000 of the 46,000 American military held by the Germans would survive.

The appalling barbarism of the Japanese toward their military prisoners had been demonstrated early in December on the island of Palawan, where some 150 Americans were murdered by the Japanese, who had promised them that they would be killed if

American forces landed on the island. On December 15, 1944, the prisoners were ordered into their tiny air-raid shelters because, the guards said, American planes were approaching (the shelters were tiny boxes with narrow entrances, less than five feet high). The guards then poured gasoline into and around the shelters and lit them with torches. As the Americans staggered out, their clothes and hair in flames, they were clubbed and bayoneted. A few men got as far as the barbed-wire fence before they were shot. About forty, faced with certain death by fire and bayonet, leaped from a fifty-foot cliff to the beach below. Four lived; most were injured too badly to move and lay there until a Japanese patrol buried them alive. One prisoner was caught just as he entered the water. The Japanese poured gasoline over his left foot and lighted it. Then, jeering and hooting, they set fire to his other foot, to each of his hands in turn, and finally to his body. Making sure that he was still conscious and avoiding mortal wounds for as long as possible, they plunged their bayonets into his charred body until he was dead.

The American command was understandably sickened and outraged by the massacre at Palawan—5 of 150 men escaped to tell the tale—but what particularly alarmed them was their suspicion that such atrocities did not seem to be maniacal departures from ordinary procedure by a few soldiers crazed with bloodlust. Rather, they were part of a deliberate, calculated policy. Their suspicion would later be confirmed by the Japanese War Ministry's policy statement. The policy for "handling prisoners of war in these times, when the situation is becoming more pressing, and the evils of war extend to the Imperial Domain, Manchuria, and other places," the ministry said, was to make every effort and to spare no pains "to prevent prisoners of war from falling into the enemy's hands." Individual units were left, as the war diary of a camp on Formosa revealed, to devise the specifics of the ministry's order: "Whether they are destroyed individually or in groups, or however it is done, with mass bombing, gas, poison, drowning, decapitation, et cetera, [we must] dispose of the prisoners as the situation dictates. In any case, the object is not to allow the escape of a single one, to annihilate them all and to leave no trace."

Nobody knew how many of the original 26,000 American military prisoners who had fallen into the hands of the Japanese were still alive; neither did they know if the enemy thought of the 7,000 civilians supposedly in its protective custody in Manila and Los Baños as "prisoners," and therefore to be executed. But it was obvious to MacArthur that the lives of all Americans in Japanese hands were in jeopardy.

The first of a series of raids designed to save American prisoners occurred on January 31 when 121 members of the Twenty-sixth U.S. Ranger battalion and 286 Filipino guerrillas attacked the Japanese at Cabanatuan, twenty-five miles behind Japanese lines north of Manila. Most of the 200 prisoners were barely able to walk, and a Japanese tank force overtook them before they could reach American lines. The Rangers destroyed twelve tanks and lost twenty-five men before breaking free; the surviving rescuers were personally decorated by MacArthur for what he called one of the most daring and successful raids of the war.

MacArthur was heartened by the success of the Cabanatuan rescue but appalled by the condition of the men who were brought out. He called in Major General Vernon Mudge, the commander of the First Cavalry Division, then still seventy miles north of the city. "Go to Manila," he told Mudge. "Go around the Nips, bounce off the Nips, but go to Manila. Free the internees at Santo Tomás." Mudge turned the operation over to Brigadier General William Chase; two "Flying Columns," each consisting of a cavalry squadron of 700 men, a tank company, a battalion of 105-mm howitzers and enough vehicles to carry the men and supplies, left within hours of MacArthur's order. Hitting speeds of up to thirty miles an hour, the Flying Columns raced down the eastern edge of the Luzon plain, fording streams where the bridges had been destroyed but mostly roaring across them before Japanese demolition teams could blow them up, they bore down on Manila. Marine fighter pilots guarded their advance; one of them flew over Santo Tomás, waggled his wings at the gaping internees below, and dropped a small package into the main yard of the university. It was a pair of pilot's goggles with a note attached: "Roll out the barrel," it said. "Santa Claus is coming today!"

On Sunday evening, February 3, the first Flying Column, guided by Filipino guerrillas, rumbled down Rizal Avenue and through the city to Santo Tomás, where they crashed through the main gate. The first American troops to enter the heart of the capital city, they rescued the largest number of American civilians held in one place by the Japanese—more than 4,000 men, women, and children. The ordeal at Santo Tomás was over—almost.

III

"We saw and heard the battle to the north for the first time last night, the third of February," George Mora recorded in his diary on Monday morning. "Every few seconds the horizon to the north, just east of Manila, would be lit up by red and orange flashes. Right now, at 8:00 A.M., the rumbling still goes on, not as often as during the night but still one a minute and considerably louder—more than rumblings. Everyone is very heartened by the sounds—it's a big thing to be able to hear the battle and know that it is coming our way."

There was much activity among the guards in camp, too, George noted happily—trucks moving in and out so that it looked as though the Japanese might be getting ready to leave again. "I did a little spying on the Nips' activity last night, and it was considerable. I am really feeling good about all this, and I pep myself up with the observation that one of three things is bound to happen: one, our forces arrive from the north; two, the Nips pull out and leave us to our own resources; three, a landing in Batangas and a quick delivery by our army."

Not until February 26 is there an entry in George's diary indicating that the internees at Los Baños knew that their friends and relatives thirty miles away had been rescued on the night of February 3. It was probably just as well that the truth of what was happening in Manila was not known to them. For the flames leaping into the sky were coming less from American artillery than from fires deliberately set by the Japanese, and they were consuming the city. The Japanese had elected to blow up everything that they defined as a military installation, including everything in the port area, every bridge, and every building capable of being fortified by an enemy force. Included within the broad Japanese definition of military installations were the city's water supply and its electrical power system. The flames seen by George Mora were mainly from burning installations around the harbor and the northern half of the city, filled with combustible bamboo shacks and teeming with people.

Some thirty miles to the southwest of the city, and almost an equal distance due east from Los Baños, the Eleventh Airborne watched from Tagaytay Ridge on the morning of February 3 as the Pearl of the Orient lay basking in the sun. It was the first city they had seen for more than a year, since leaving San Francisco. But as they watched they saw tall columns of smoke begin to rise from the Japanese destruction. A young lieutenant on the ridge named "Fly" Flanagan would later write the military history of the Eleventh, and note wryly that they had not fully appreciated the depravity of their enemy until that day. "First we learned that the Japs had destroyed the Coca Cola plant and the largest brewery. This maddened us. Then we learned that they had demolished the city's largest nightclub. This infuriated us. No wonder we developed an un-Christian hate for the Japs as we discovered their vicious, criminal methods of fighting."

Fly Flanagan's characterization of the Japanese turned out, tragically, to be no joke. Admiral Iwabushi, the rear admiral who commanded the large force of sailors and marines, had taken it upon himself, despite Yamashita's orders to evacuate Manila, to fight to the death—and the death of everyone else within reach. It was Iwabushi who had torched the city, and it was Iwabushi who had further fortified the city in preparation for his own version of Götterdämmerung. The city had long been well fortified against the possibility of an American return; even though Yamashita had realized it was indefensible, his predecessors had built a last redoubt called the Genko Line, a series of 1,200 concrete pillboxes and connecting tunnels winding more than four miles through the heart of the city, from Manila Bay on the west to Laguna de Bay on the east—the large inland lake shaped like a clumsy three-fingered mitten, at the base of which was the village of Los Baños.

Within these massive pillboxes, some two and three stories

deep, were set five- and six-inch guns and 150mm mortars, facing south—the expected main route of attack by the Americans when they were built and the present route of the Eleventh. Many also contained 20, 40, and 90mm antiaircraft guns. The Japanese had apparently copied the German technique of scattering concrete and steel pillboxes in depth, but some of the small forts were made of stone, with dome-shaped roofs thickly covered with dirt—and sometimes, an indication of how long they had been lying in wait, with dense bushes and small trees. Each pillbox was occupied by one or two soldiers who stayed there until they died.

The pillboxes were augmented by forty-four heavy artillery pieces (120mm coastal defense and dual purpose antiaircraft guns), 164 antiaircraft guns (single-, double-, and triple-barrel up to 40mm), and innumerable 13-caliber machine guns. Outside the line were buried 245 100-pound bombs and thirty-five antisubmarine depth charges, rigged as land mines, and every road approaching the line was lined with 500-pound bombs armed with low-pressure detonators. In what was apparently a more recent addition to the line, judging from the rawness of the dirt around them, sat more than 100 tanks, buried up to their gun turrets—additional pillboxes, deadly corpses whose graves, or some of them, may well have been dug by Lieutenant Konishi's men with the shovels so hastily rounded up a few weeks before at Los Baños.

Around, through, and beyond the Genko Line was a tangle of barbed wire and barricades of overturned trucks and trolley cars. Apartment houses and office buildings had been converted into machine-gun nests, their entrances sandbagged, their staircases barricaded, and their walls ripped open in narrow gouges for firing slits. The big guns had been removed from the Japanese ships in the harbor and positioned at street corners.

It was this formidable defensive line that the Eleventh would now hurl itself against. It had taken them only four days to roll 169 miles from Nasugbu, where they landed on January 31, to Parañaque. The next 4,000 yards would take them nearly three weeks. During that time more than sixty men of the 511th would be killed, including Hardrock Haugen, and more than 200 wounded, including Haugen's replacement, Ed Lahti, who would take a four-pound piece of shrapnel in his arm. The 187th and

188th together would lose 100 men killed and more than 500 wounded. In the process they would destroy the Third Naval Battalion and isolate the Abe Battalion, accounting for some 3,000 Japanese lives. And they would see the final contribution of the Japanese Co-Prosperity Sphere to the citizens of Manila.

The full extent of the carnage wrought by the Japanese upon the innocent civilians in Manila would not be revealed until weeks later. The bare figures alone—100,000 people killed—could only suggest the horror. It would later be argued by some that the majority of civilian deaths were the inevitable consequence of their city having been turned into a battlefield—even that MacArthur had to share the blame for forcing the fight. It was said that what happened was, in any event, the result of a kind of mass temporary insanity on the part of the Japanese, who saw their world tumbling around them and determined to take as many people with them to their doom as they could. But documents captured afterward revealed what their own eyes told them as the Americans fought to control the city, and what they heard from the Filipinos who sought out their protection: the savage massacres were the result of specific and explicit directives—orders that, moreover, were in place as early as December 1944. Points four and five of the key document taken from the files of the "Manila Navy Defense Force and South-Western Area Fleet Operation Order" said, "When killing Filipinos, assemble them together in one place, as far as possible, thereby saving ammunition and labor. The disposal of dead bodies will be troublesome, so either collect them in houses scheduled to be burned or throw them into the river." That this order was widely distributed and understood is evident from the diary of a Japanese warrant officer: "We are ordered to kill all the males we find," he wrote. "Mopping up the bandits from now on will be a sight indeed . . . Our aim is to kill or wound all the men and collect information. Women who attempt to escape are to be killed. All in all, our aim is extermination."

The Japanese employed both direct and indirect fiendishly ingenious methods of murder, but they preferred the latter, generally under the guise of protecting the people they intended to kill. The scores of people who had hidden beneath the German Club for protection from the battle received the direct treatment: the Japanese surrounded the building with paper and wood and set fire to it. The men who ran out were shot, the women raped, after which the Japanese poured gasoline on their hair and lit it. A more clever method of murder was employed at St. Paul's College, where 250 people were confined in a large room with the doors and windows barred. Some of the prisoners noticed that the three chandeliers had been wrapped in black paper and that wires ran from the light fixtures to the window and outside the building. Nothing happened for an hour. Then the Japanese returned, smiling and reassuring, with trays full of biscuits and pastries and pots of tea. As they left, the Japanese said they hoped their friends would appreciate the trouble they had gone to to protect and feed them. The hungry Filipinos clustered around the long tables underneath the chandeliers. Outside, a soldier touched a detonator and the chandeliers, packed with explosives, blew up and killed most of the people under them. The few who survived and ran through the hole in the wall blown out by the dynamite were cut down by machine guns.

There were no safe havens. Nuns were raped in the Manila Cathedral, hospital patients strapped to their beds and set afire, nurses and doctors at the Filipino Red Cross building killed along with some sixty people who thought the Red Cross would protect them. A Japanese soldier kept a tally: "7 Feb. 45, 150 guerrillas were disposed of last night. I stabbed 10. 9 Feb. 45, Burned 1,000 guerrillas tonight. 13 Feb. 45, I am now on guard duty at the Guerrilla Internment Camp. While I was on duty 10 guerrillas tried to escape. They were all recaptured and bayoneted. Later all the guerrillas were burned to death."

Another showed some remorse: "Feb. 6. Every day is spent in hunting guerrillas or natives. I have already killed over 100. The innocence I possessed at the time of leaving the homeland has long since disappeared. Now I am a hardened sinner and my sword is always stained with blood. Although it is for my country's sake, it is sheer brutality. May God forgive me. May my mother forgive me."

Coolly or remorsefully, directly or deviously, but always brutally, the Japanese would kill nearly 100,000 citizens of Manila while the Eleventh was fighting there. By the time they had cracked the Genko Line and reached Nichols Field in the third week of February, the brash young troopers of the Eleventh had long since lost whatever innocence had been left them after Leyte. For some of them, their next mission, that of saving lives rather than taking them, would have a significance far beyond what it might have had just a few weeks earlier.

13

BREAKING CAMP

I

Very few of the Filipinos murdered in Manila were "bandits" or guerrillas; most of the guerrillas were safely away from the city, engaged in their own activities. High on their list of priorities, especially as news of what the Japanese were doing in Manila became known, was the rescue of the internees at Los Baños.

Terry Adevozo, who had recently sent Bob Fletcher to Ocampo's headquarters with instructions from himself and Jay Vanderpool to alert the natives along the way to the coming assault by American forces, had been alarmed by the impetuous plans of other guerrilla units to storm the camp at Los Baños. On February 7, he and Vanderpool sent a young lieutenant, Gustavo "Tavo" Ingles, to Nanghaya; his instructions were to scout around the internment camp and to discuss plans with Lieutenant Colonel Honore "Naning" Guerrero, commanding the Forty-fifth Hunters Regiment, for rescuing the prisoners and coordinating their efforts with the Eleventh Airborne.

Both the urgent need to do something at Los Baños and the difficulties of coordinating actions so that the internees would not be killed at the moment of rescue were dramatically illustrated at a meeting in Dayap on February 13. Terry had managed to get all the various guerrilla groups to attend—the swashbuckling Markings, the PQOGs (President Quezon's Own Guerrillas), represented by Helen Espino's husband, under his nom de guerre of Colonel Price, the Fil-Americans, and, of course, the Hunters. Also present, perhaps invited to keep order by the weight of his venerable presence, was General Juan Cailles, a veteran of the Philippine Revolution of half a century ago and a former governor of Laguna Province.

But the center of attention in the schoolhouse where the guerrillas met was not the old governor but the three men who had slipped out of the Los Baños camp the night before and been brought by guerrillas to the meeting. Gaunt, tired, and dirty, they were Robert Schaeffer, an American, Pete Newsome, a British sailor, and Pete Miles. Miles was the leader of the group and their spokesman. With his light blond beard and Arrow-shirt-ad profile, the Los Baños snake tamer was the least visibly affected by the night's journey. The guerrillas listened intently to Miles' description of the decline in camp rations and the increase in Japanese hostility.

Bob Schaeffer added an emotional plea for weapons, though Miles shook his head. The guerrillas pointed out the difficulty of smuggling weapons into the camp and the likelihood that few of the internees, many of whom were nuns and priests, would be able or willing to use them. In any case, most of the guerrillas themselves were armed only with old Enfield and Springfield rifles, relics of World War I. The guerrillas' suggestions were, unfortunately, not much more practical. The main problem was not overpowering the small Japanese guard contingent—there were some 3,000 guerrillas who could be mustered for that task—but doing it without getting the internees killed. There was also the considerable problem of what to do with the prisoners once they were rescued, miles behind enemy lines and within a day's easy march of 8,000 Japanese troops to the south.

Late that same evening, February 13, the three Americans made it safely back through the double fence around the camp and found George Grey, who was just returning from a frustrating meeting with Konishi (the Japanese had spent the evening confiscating all the internees' electrical equipment, including wire, light bulbs, and a small portable generator kept at the hospital for emergencies, and the Executive Committee had demanded to know the reason). That interview had ended as had all the others with Konishi—abrupt dismissal.

Grey felt that by rights he should have reprimanded the men

for risking their lives, especially after the death of Pat Hell and George Louis, but he was so heartened by their news that he couldn't bring himself to do it. However, he was unsure exactly what use he was to make of what they told him. Grey was right to be cautious. The lack of effective communication among the guerrillas made it difficult for them to coordinate their movements with one another, even with members of the same units. While the three Americans had been meeting in Nanghaya, Tavo Ingles was passing a message to an internee named Freddy Zervoulakas, who happened to be the brother of a Hunters guerrilla. It was in fact a more direct and useful contact than the one with the assembled guerrillas had been. What Ingles wanted to pass along was the letter of instructions from Major Vanderpool. Those orders included making contact with the internees. It was essential that Ingles meet with someone responsible from the camp. George Grey, the youngest and fittest member of the Executive Committee, was the natural selection. On the night of February 15, Grey followed Freddy through the camp fence, which by now was beginning to show some signs of wear and tear, and met with Ingles at the home of a professor, Dr. Sandana.

Tavo Ingles had just come from a long and difficult day in Nanghaya. It was the first time the American Army had been present—in the person of Major Vanderpool—at one of the guerrilla conferences and the meeting was almost a disaster. Surprisingly the Hukbalahaps—sons and grandsons of the same fierce Huks who had fought the Yankees in 1900, who would fight anybody who tried to establish control over them, and who were reportedly riddled with Communists—had been quiet and agreeable. But the Markings and the Fil-Americans had challenged the young officer's authority. By what right, they asked, did he claim to be MacArthur's personal representative? By no right, Ingles replied—his only association with the U.S. Army was through Major Vanderpool. The quiet American nodded in agreement. Well, then, how did he expect them to provide support for the rescue when they didn't have any good rifles? Everybody knew that the 457th Hunters were the only ones who got carbines from the Americans. They might be more cooperative, the dissidents implied, if the Hunters would be a little more generous.

Jay Vanderpool listened without comment as the guerrillas talked and talked. One of the reasons he got along so well with them, he had decided long ago, was that he kept his mouth shut. He admired the guerrillas for their fiery courage, and he understood how eager they were, after years of hiding in the jungle, to take the battle to the enemy. But he had known, even before he sent Tavo Ingles on his mission to Guerrero on February 7 that there were limits to what the guerrillas could do by themselves. He hadn't seen Ingles again by the evening of February 8, when he joined General Eichelberger and General Swing in the officers' mess at Parañaque, but he knew enough about the situation to be able to respond to Eichelberger's direct question: MacArthur had asked him again about his plans for rescuing the internees at Los Baños, Eichelberger said. Could the guerrillas do it alone?

Vanderpool shook his head. He understood that Eichelberger and Swing were reluctant to pull any troops out of the ongoing battle for Manila, for each day it was prolonged was costing thousands of lives. But the guerrillas could not do the job themselves, he said. They were too lightly armed; coordination among the various groups was hindered by old rivalries and political infighting; and he doubted that the sick and hungry internees would want to entrust their lives to the guerrillas if they had to run a gauntlet of Japanese troops to reach safety. American support in the form of amphibious attack would have to be very large in order to be effective, involving several thousand troops. It would probably succeed only in drawing the Japanese Eighth Division, twenty miles to the south, into battle. The prisoners would be caught in the middle, and their survival would be at risk.

There was only one way to proceed, Vanderpool suggested: the rescue had to be under the direction of the Americans, with the guerrillas in support. He thought the Hunters were the best organized and most reliable group, and he would be willing to act as liaison between the two forces.

Now, a week after that meeting with the American commanders, Vanderpool held his peace until the guerrillas were once again balked by the intractable problem of how to rescue the internees alive. The one thing that would end the bickering, he knew, was the information he brought about the plan developed by Doug

Quandt and his staff during the past few days. It was a plan, he said diplomatically, that could only succeed with the help of all the guerrillas. The plan called for a "vertical assault" of the 511th by Company B. The date was tentatively set for February 19, early in the morning. More than that he could not tell them at the moment. But as he received more details from Lieutenant Skau, who was constantly in contact with the Eleventh AB headquarters in Parañaque, he would let them know what they needed to know for their plans.

The guerrillas cheered Vanderpool's news enthusiastically. During the next few hours they agreed to divide their forces into three main parts, each further subdivided into smaller units and all coordinated to support the drop of Company B. There were to be some 500 guerrillas involved, according to the plan, which required hitting the camp guard posts and bursting through the fences at precisely 7:00 A.M.—the exact moment, according to reports by Pete Miles and others, that the guards were doing their morning calisthenics.

Vanderpool and Ingles left the meeting convinced that the plan of attack was indeed feasible. But there was still the nagging problem of how to transport the internees and where to take them. They were less than an hour by road from Manila, less than that to American lines, and the truck convoy that had been planned for their evacuation should be able to do the job, provided it could get through Japanese lines. If it could not, the internees would have to hike to Nanghaya, a distance of ten miles, under guerrilla protection. The 100 men of Company B would have to walk with them. Nothing was said at this meeting about an amphibious attack by the Eleventh Airborne.

Now George Grey, exuberant at having gotten out of the camp safely and happy to meet the guerrillas who proposed to help them, shook Ingles' hand warmly when they met. The Filipino winced and withdrew his hand; the nails were a mottled blue and yellow—the result, Ingles explained, of bamboo slivers driven under them by the Japanese when they suspected—rightly—that he could tell them some things they would like to know. He had not told them, he said, smiling thinly.

Ingles introduced the two or three young men who had accompanied him and asked Grey for the names of the members of the Executive Committee at the camp and the person in charge. Grey told him. Ingles then explained in outline the plan for attacking the camp and rescuing the prisoners. Grey was disturbed by two aspects of the plan: first, very few of them were capable of walking any distance, he said. But his real reservation lay with Ingles' suggestion that the internees be armed after their rescue, and some of them before, in order to help out, just as he understood Mr. Schaeffer had proposed. That would be a violation of international law, Grey said. And they were entitled to protection only so long as they were legitimate noncombatants. Ingles was aghast. Did Grey have any idea what was happening to noncombatant civilians in Manila right now? Had the Japanese abided by international law in starving them nearly to death, in shooting two of his friends at Los Baños? Grey was adamant: he would see that the internees cooperated in every way possible, but he would not arm them. Practically, he said, the little bit they could do to defend themselves was only enough to goad the enemy into killing them. And besides, it was wrong.

Ingles was disgusted. The attack is on for February 19, he said. "Be ready. You better go now." Then, softening, he told the American to wait a minute and pressed two newly minted American dimes into his hand. "For good luck."

A day in the life of a diplomat, George Grey sighed as he crept back toward camp behind Freddy—dismissed by Konishi as a nuisance and by Ingles as an impractical idealist.

Heichert and the other members of the Los Baños Executive Committee held a meeting in the hospital while they waited anxiously for Grey to return from his dangerous meeting with the guerrillas. Bob Cecil said the book bindery had closed because there was no more glue, and the musical program scheduled to be put on three days before had been canceled because two of the priests in the chorus were too ill to sing. Dana Nance said they had more serious problems—Walter Shaw had died that morning. John Edwards had died two days earlier, and he was certain that Stanley Mosk would be dead within a day—all from starvation. There was also a birth to be reported: a girl, Elizabeth, born to Mr.

and Mrs. Joseph Louis Francisco, on February 14.

Frank Bennett said the food would be gone by February 19 and reported on the visit of Bishops Binstead and Jurgens, the Episcopal and Catholic leaders in the camp, to Mr. Ito to ask for more food, even if it amounted to only a few extra bags of rice or coconuts. Mr. Ito had replied that he would place their request before the commandant but that they should understand the desperate situation outside the camp with regard to the needs of the Japanese army. He assured the bishops that the Japanese recognized their responsibility to feed the internees and that food would be forthcoming.

Heichert then gave the details of the order issued the day before by Lieutenant Kaseno. From now on there would be a 7:00 P.M curfew, except on Wednesdays and Sundays, when it would be extended to 7:30 P.M. Even moving from one barracks to another after curfew was forbidden: violators would be subject to being shot on the spot. The same penalty held for anyone caught trading. Internees were also forbidden to stage any kind of demonstration, including gathering in groups, when American planes flew overhead or when firing was heard near the camp. The Japanese reminded the internees that anyone not showing "proper respect and courtesy to the military" would be dealt with severely. And they still wanted their radio back.

The committee discussed Kaseno's order and agreed that it would be wise to tell the internees to stay out of open areas, moving through the barracks as much as possible. Alex Calhoun reported that the problem of thievery was increasing, and DeWitt noted that "it is becoming increasingly difficult to persuade people to do their share of work in the camp—most of the necessary work was being done by a very few people."

George Grey came in shortly after ten o'clock and told the committee members about his meeting with Ingles. They agreed that the situation was exceedingly dangerous. The fact that they were still alive was due in great part to the generosity of the Filipinos who lived near the camp, they realized, and they were grateful beyond words that the guerrillas were anxious to work for their rescue. But they felt frustrated by their inability to communicate directly with the American Army, which they knew would bear the primary responsibility for their survival. They needed to send someone to talk face to face with the planners of the operation at the Eleventh Airborne headquarters, which, according to Ingles, was in Parañaque. Then, too, there were details that only someone who had lived in the camp could give the planners about the condition of the internees and about the ability of the Japanese garrison to deal with an attack, including the location of their sentry towers, machine-gun nests, pillboxes, and their normal patterns of operation. The problem now was that of deciding who should go.

II

Los Baños Internment Camp: February 18

Violating both the blackout and the curfew regulations—it was nearly ten o'clock—Ben Edwards carried a kerosene lantern in one hand and supported Pete Miles with the other. It would be obvious to even the nervous Japanese guards that they were not trying to avoid being seen; the two men were clearly on their way to the hospital so that the one with the injured leg could get treatment.

It was not all show. Pete Miles had indeed twisted his ankle two days ago. But merely being inside the hospital seemed to have a miraculously restorative effect on his health. Where was Freddy? he asked quickly, peering through the window toward the fence behind the hospital. It was clear, he said. They had to get moving. The door opened and Freddy Zervoulakas slipped in quickly. He had watched the two men from his barracks to be sure they made it, then lit his own lantern and crossed to the hospital. The three men left with warm hugs and thumbs-up signs from the nurses and made their way quickly through the barbed-wire and sawali fence.

Freddy led the way down the path he had established earlier that evening toward the rendezvous point with the guerrillas. The three escapees crept down the steep gully toward a rocky creek some fifty feet below. There was no sound except the crickets and the tree frogs, and the slight rasp of their breathing in the heavy, humid night air. It was so still that when Ben kicked a tin can its progress down the rocks to the creek seemed as long as a sermon and as loud as a clash of cymbals. They froze in the shadows of the bushes lining the creek for what seemed an eternity; high above them they could see the outline of the hospital against the moonlit sky, and beyond it—within earshot they were sure—the nearest of the four sentry posts. After a few seconds the sounds of the night resumed: a baby wailed in a house in the village; flashes of light from the north, where the battle for Manila raged again after a few hours of respite, were followed by distant rumblings. They moved on.

A few hundred yards down the gully waited two young guerrillas, boys no more than seventeen, Ben thought. They walked silently through coconut groves and deserted plantations for an hour, when they arrived at Barrio Tranca, at the headquarters of "Colonel Price," Romeo Espino. It was then about 11:00 P.M. He would be happy to help them, Espino said, and explained that he would provide them with an escort to Pila on the west side of the inland lake. As they were talking, what looked to Ben like a tall, strongly built German soldier wearing a helmet walked by and said, "Hiya, Mac!" It was an Eleventh Airborne radio man, part of the 511th Signal Company, the first American soldier any of the three had seen since 1941. Since that time the shallow World War I helmets that were the only ones they knew had been replaced by ones that looked to Ben like the coal scuttles worn by the German army.

They had no time to talk to the American sergeant; Espino hustled them out of his camp by 1:30 A.M. so they could reach the safe part of the lake by dawn. The moon that had lighted their way through the plantations and coconut groves earlier was now obscured by clouds—"Blacker than the inside of a cow," Ben grumbled to Pete Miles—but the young guerrillas set a stiff pace across country. Midway through the night Ben took off his shoes to keep them dry as they crossed a stream. He sat down to dry his feet and to put his shoes back on; the guerrillas passed him silently and disappeared into the jungle. Within seconds they were out of sight, leaving Ben alone with his dry shoes. "Hell and damn," he muttered, tying his shoes together and draping them around his neck

as he hurried to catch up. The guerrillas didn't stop until they reached the National Highway; while they scouted the road and the open fields beyond for signs of the enemy Ben pulled a nettle from his heel and put his shoes back on. His feet didn't stay dry for very long. The next leg of their journey was across the rice paddies on the other side of the road, and he promptly slipped off the narrow mud bridge that the young guerrillas knew by heart into the waist-deep mud. A guerrilla stopped to give him a hand, chuckling softly.

An hour later the guerrillas stopped at a small nipa hut and woke a middle-aged Filipino woman to ask her if there were any Japanese in the area. The woman was frightened, and her hands shook as she lit a coconut-oil lamp. No, she said, her voice quavering, she hadn't seen any Japanese. Then her gaze settled on the mud-caked internees. "Americans!" she said, the relief in her eyes and voice assuring them and the guerrillas that she was obviously not one of the *makapili*.

They reached the shore of the lake at dawn. Several fishermen were there, about to set out for the day in their bancas, heavy sailboats that the guerrillas quickly commandeered. The Americans washed off the mud in the warm waters of the lake and the boats pushed off for Pila. Exhausted after the long night, Ben fell asleep as the fresh morning wind took them out onto the lake. He was rudely awakened some time later by the sound of shots and a sharp burning pain on his neck. Opening his eyes, he saw a boy holding a carbine and happily pointing to two dead ducks in the water ahead. Ben looked glumly at the boy and plucked the ejected carbine shell from beneath his shirt collar. As his heart gradually stopped pounding he dozed off again.

Shortly after noon the bancas landed at Barrio San Roque, where they were met by a guerrilla colonel named Abdinago Ortiz. He listened to their story and agreed to take them to General Swing's headquarters at Parañaque. But it was not a simple matter, Ortiz explained. To reach Parañaque they would have to travel at least ten miles by boat and then another ten miles through both enemy and American lines. First they should rest and have something to eat.

It was the best beach picnic Ben Edwards had ever known. As

the three escaped internees sat and discussed their plans, the guerrillas brought them fried duck eggs, fried rice, pork, fish filets, —all served on banana leaves—and a bowl of fruit. Freddy had been in and out of the camp several times and had always been fed by the guerrillas, but it was Ben Edwards' first decent meal in months, and one he would remember for years.

But the hazards of the journey Colonel Ortiz had described gave them pause. If all three of them continued, their eggs would all be in one basket, they decided. One of them should go on, leaving the other two behind. If the first one didn't make it, then the second man should try; if he was killed, then the mission would fall to the third man. Pete Miles, they agreed, would go first, with a map of the camp that he and Ben sketched. Ben would go next, if necessary, then Freddy.

Late that afternoon, when the evening breeze was picking up, Pete Miles set out for Parañaque.

14

DECISIONS AT PARAÑAQUE

Eleventh Airborne Headquarters, Parañaque: Monday, February 19, 1:00 P.M.

Two long white fans that looked like propeller blades turned slowly in what had once been the formal dining room of an old Spanish villa. French doors opened onto a wide veranda with a finely detailed fleur-de-lis wrought-iron railing. The remains of a formal garden were dimly discernible through the ruinous explosion of giant pigweeds and sawali, volunteer banyans and palm trees, the result of three years of neglect. Barely five miles away explosions of a more destructive nature signaled the ongoing demolition of the oldest part of the city of Manila, Intramuros. Here, though, in the temporary headquarters of the Eleventh Airborne Division in Parañaque, Butch Muller—Lieutenant Colonel Henry Muller, division intelligence officer—could think about the raid on Los Baños with some degree of comfort and security.

Muller had not been as surprised as Swing's other officers when he and Doug Quandt were told in mid-February to start thinking about getting the prisoners out of Los Baños. Late in December, before the Eleventh left the beach at Dulag for Nasugbu, a Filipino was brought into his tent for questioning—as Divisional G-2, Muller was, at twenty-six, responsible for gathering and sifting intelligence from whatever sources were available. Some of his information came from captured Japanese soldiers. Some of it came from photographs taken by a soldier from a hand-held camera as he leaned over the side of a Piper Cub—Muller suspected 197 that the soldier was always airsick because the photographs were taken at such an oblique angle that they looked like modern art. But much of the most valuable information, beginning on Leyte and continuing through to the end of the war, would come from Filipino guerrillas and ordinary citizens.

The middle-aged man who was shown into Muller's tent was, it turned out, a wealthy landowner from Mindanao whose wife had been sick. He had traveled all the way to Manila to get medicine for her, then made his slow, tortuous way south, through Luzon, and across the Visayan straits, by banca, by oxcart, and by foot. Muller was quickly satisfied that the man was not a Japanese sympathizer; the information that he willingly communicated to the G-2 confirmed too precisely what Muller knew to be true from other sources. But what most piqued the American officer's curiosity was the Filipino's casual reference to the prison camp full of American civilians south of Manila. What camp? Muller had asked, startled: it was the first he had heard of such a camp.

Muller was uncomfortable as well as surprised. General Swing firmly believed in Napoleon's axiom that "the character of a unit is a reflection of the commanding officer's character." His own gifts were extraordinary, and he did his men the honor of assuming that they shared his fierce and zealous dedication to duty. He rewarded them for good performance and punished them quickly and efficiently for failure. When the general pointed to a map indicating that a Japanese artillery battalion was here, or an infantry regiment was there, somewhere in the Texas-sized expanse of Luzon, Muller had damned well better be ready to give the precise number and disposition of all enemy troops—including names of officers and noncoms, in many cases, which American intelligence had as the result of a lucky break early in the war.

Swing's attitude toward intelligence seemed to be a mix of distrust and grudging admiration. Maybe it was part of what seemed to Muller his technique of always keeping you off balance. His own introduction to Swing had been unsettling. It was back at Mackall when the general arrived and saw a couple of men under Muller's command who were not properly in uniform. Swing had called the young captain into his office. A warm smile creased his handsome face as he waved Muller into a seat. The general put the captain at his ease; they chatted about Los Angeles and Santa Barbara, where Muller had grown up. His father, the grandson of a Swiss immigrant who had founded a brewery in Philadelphia, had moved west during the 1920s, and his son had graduated with a degree in geology from UCLA in 1938, and with an ROTC commission as a second lieutenant in the Army. The general had looked benignly at the dapper, slender young captain, who bore a slight resemblance to the movie actor William Powell, then said mildly that he would appreciate it if the captain saw to it that his men were in uniform henceforth. Muller smiled and said that he certainly would try his best, then got up to leave. Swing returned his salute and continued in the same mild voice: "Oh captain, by the way . . ." "Yes, sir?" Muller replied. "That wasn't a suggestion I just made to you!" the general shouted. "That was a goddam order!"

Since that time Muller had seen young officers summarily dismissed because they lacked stamina and had to fall out of a Swing Session run, or because they couldn't point to the precise location of one of their units on the map during an operation, or for any one of a dozen reasons. He had gradually come to realize that Joe Swing's division was probably the most tightly disciplined in the Pacific, maybe even tougher than Patton's Third Army. And he approved, because with discipline they all stood a better chance of staying alive. But he'd learned to be wary of the general, even though Swing now called him Butch—a nickname Muller would just as soon have gone without, the remnant of college fraternity high jinks after a night at a Jimmy Cagney gangster movie when he and his gang had all returned, half loaded, pretending they were hoods named "Butch" and "Spike."

Part of being an intelligence officer, Muller had learned, was dealing with the strong and sometimes erratic personalities who had risen to become generals. MacArthur's chief of intelligence, General Willoughby, was a case in point. Charles Willoughby had been born Karl Widenback in his native Germany, and his manner, size, and political philosophy seemed more consistent with Bismarck than with the armies of democracy. A gigantic man, six inches over six feet, weighing well over 240 pounds, Willoughby stared intently at a point well above his listener's head—like a man always looking over a high board fence, as one of his many enemies put it. Willoughby, the self-made immigrant from the wrong side of the tracks, hated Swing, the polo-playing West Pointer, the aristocrat who seemed to regard him as a presumptuous peasant. But, like Swing, he was a gifted man in his own way. It was part of MacArthur's own genius for command that he could value two such different men as highly as he did.

Muller had met Willoughby in April of 1944 shortly after he had assumed the important role of G-2. The burly general had been surprised by the youthful appearance of the slim lieutenant colonel, several times asking how old he was and shaking his head in wonder. Well, he seemed to say, there was no help for it. Did Muller understand how to use a two-way pad? Yes, Muller did—the two-way pad was the most secure form of secret communication between two persons. Very good, Willoughby said. Now the young G-2 should listen carefully to what he would say, because he did not like to repeat himself. Sometime in the future he would get a message identified as a "crystal ball" report. The information contained in such a report would be absolutely reliable. But it must be conveyed to the responsible officer without indicating its source. "This is absolutely vital!" Willoughby said, the slight Teutonic accent emerging more than it did in ordinary conversation. "You must swear never to reveal the source of the crystal ball information, which will be me!" Muller agreed. He put the precious two-way pad in a safe, where it sat unused for six months —until he was in the middle of the Leyte campaign on December 6, 1944.

It was late in the afternoon of December 5 when Muller received a "crystal ball" message that required the use of the two-way pad, and the young officer's heart pounded as he put it together: the following day, December 6, at 1800 hours, the Japanese would launch an airborne attack on the American airstrip at Burauen. Only an officer as well schooled as Muller would recognize the dilemma posed by Willoughby's message. The proper function of an intelligence officer, he had learned at Leavenworth, is to gather information and use it to make an estimate of enemy capabilities. But you must never predict enemy action as an intelligence officer. No ambiguity, no doubts about that part of the job: NEVER PREDICT. Fair enough. But Willoughby had also sworn him to absolute secrecy. He was to tell no one what his source was. Not even General Swing? Muller had asked. "You haff not been listening!" Willoughby had roared. "Nobody is to know!"

What this meant was that Muller had to overstep the requirements of his post and make a prediction of enemy action without citing any source—or he had to reveal his source and break his word. He had foreseen the difficulty and queried Willoughby about it. You are an intelligence officer, had been the response. Be intelligent. "You will find a way."

Muller had included the information buried at the end of his day's report. He noted that the next day was the anniversary eve of Pearl Harbor, that there were reports of Japanese paratroop activity in southern Luzon, and that there were few American combat troops stationed at Burauen airfield. It was clearly within the capability of the enemy, and consistent with his past activities on the anniversary of Pearl Harbor, to launch a surprise attack. Burauen seemed a likely candidate for such an attack. Muller concluded by noting that the majority of such attacks came either at dawn or at dusk. His estimate of enemy capabilities suggested dusk.

The clerk to whom Muller was dictating this message looked up quizzically. "Do it," Muller said shortly. The clerk shrugged.

Two hours later General Swing coldly thrust Muller's report under the G-2s nose. Where did he get off saying that "this was in no sense a prediction, just a statement of fact"? Who told him there would be an attack? Muller saw the futility of persuading the general that his report was anything other than a prediction. He was torn between his oath to Willoughby and his duty to Swing. He said that he had received the information in a crystal ball message from Willoughby. "I might have known he was behind this!" Swing had exploded. How many of those periodic reports had been circulated? he demanded to know. Only a few, Muller said, not quite truthfully; he thought the rest were still in the message center. Swing ordered him out to destroy the remaining reports and to compose a corrected copy, omitting the Burauen prediction.

Promptly at 6:00 P.M. on December 6 the general and his staff emerged from their mess tent to see Japanese parachutes floating through the tropical dusk. The Americans were caught completely by surprise; fortunately, the attack was poorly coordinated and executed by the Japanese, and disaster was averted. General Swing had never again mentioned the Willoughby affair or Muller's report, for which the young officer was grateful. He had, after all, broken his oath, and even though he had done it to save lives he was troubled. But he realized that General Swing, the only man who knew he had done so, was not likely to acknowledge that fact to Willoughby. In any event, Muller thought he detected the general looking at him with a new degree of interest and that he seemed to ask for Muller's opinion rather more frequently than he had in the past.

In fact, as the word about his uncanny, though unappreciated, ability to predict the future in the case of the Burauen raid began to get around, Muller found himself regarded as something of a wizard—an impression that, of course, he was not at liberty to dispel. It was not until well after the end of the war that he learned why Willoughby's information had been so accurate: the Japanese secret code had been broken years before. The information about the Burauen raid might as well have come directly from General Yamashita to General Willoughby.

So for Muller to learn about Los Baños casually in December had been slightly disconcerting, though consistent with the way things happened in war. He had pumped the Filipino for more information about the prison, but the man had been passing through the Los Baños area as quickly as he could, and he could offer him little more except the assurance that there were indeed at least 2,000 Americans being held by the Japanese at the old college near the village. Muller had duly made his report and filed the information in the back of his mind. It would be a problem for somebody to handle, but probably not him. The Eleventh's mission was to move up the west coast of southern Luzon from Nasugbu to Manila, taking Tagaytay Ridge and tying up Japanese forces in central Luzon so they couldn't interfere with the Sixth Army's advance on Manila from the north. Los Baños lay more than fifty miles from the nearest point of the Eleventh's planned route north, across steep mountain ranges infested with Japanese troops. Any rescuing force would have to come south from Manila, not from the west.

Now, less than six weeks later, Muller needed to learn much more about Los Baños. The Eleventh had accomplished its mission in time to participate in the battle for Manila, moving somewhat hastily into the old house in Parañaque—hastily because it was close enough to the battle lines for Japanese snipers to fire on observers who stood on the third-floor cupola to watch the battle for Corregidor. The house had been deserted and stripped of furniture. The garden in the large backyard that fronted on the bay was rank with untended weeds, and the swimming pool was empty. Doug Quandt promptly set up his operational sand tables in the pool. Quandt, a shambling politely soft-spoken West Point graduate who was part of what Muller thought of as Swing's Royal Circle but never abused his influence, had always struck Muller as the ideal G-3. And one of the many things he had to give Swing credit for, Muller knew, was the encouragement he had given to his intelligence and planning staffs to work together. Throughout the campaigns so far Quandt and Muller had established their offices only a few feet away from each other; now Muller had taken over the tiled grand foyer of the house, and Quandt had the dining room.

The house in Parañaque was always crowded, even at the best of times, with scores of soldiers reporting. Their heavy boots and loud voices in the uncarpeted halls and rooms made quiet contemplation impossible for Quandt and Muller, though the problem Quandt in particular faced was both troubling and complex: how were they going to rescue 2,000 people from behind enemy lines without losing a number of them in the process, even assuming they were successful? Muller was charged with getting and coordinating every possible scrap of information about Los Baños. Most of it would come from the Filipinos, who responded, when the call for intelligence went out, in overwhelming numbers. Muller had a dozen men taking reports in the crowded foyer, including Jay Vanderpool.

Late in the morning of Tuesday, February 20, Hank Burgess stood by the open window and looked across the smoking city, toward Laguna de Bay, where his men were waiting for him to come and tell them what was going on. They had all thought they were slated for a rest when they were pulled out of the fighting for McKinley and moved to downtown Manila. God knows they were ready for it, after three weeks on the Genko Line. But his men had had exactly twenty hours of rest on Monday morning when he told Bud Ewing to load them on the trucks and set out for Mamatid, on the western shore of Laguna de Bay.

At twenty-six, Burgess was young to be a major and in charge of his own battalion. The son of a Wyoming rancher, he had graduated from Harvard and left the University of Michigan Law School to enter active duty with the National Guard Cavalry in 1941. He was independent and confident of his abilities, and smart enough to realize that his first impressions of things and men were usually accurate. He had seen clearly enough during his Wanderjahr summer in Germany, in 1937, that war was coming, and he had joined the Wyoming National Guard as soon as he got home in order to be ready for it. When war did come he hadn't minded the switch from horseback to airborne; the hell-for-leather cavalry types like Joe Swing and the men who jumped from planes into the middle of battles were cut from the same cloth: direct, uncomplicated, and often short on tact.

Burgess' first reaction to Doug Quandt's information about the coming mission had been characteristically blunt: "Why us?" Because, Quandt replied, Ed Lahti had said so. MacArthur had been worried about the possibility of failure of the raid when he and Swing had discussed it earlier. "Just be sure you do it right," he had told Swing. "Do it right." General Swing had sent Lieutenant Colonel Glenn "Mac" McGowan to bring Ed Lahti, the new 511th regimental commander, to Parañaque. They were all shocked when Lahti came in, his arm in a sling and his face yellow with jaundice. Orin Haugen, the redoubtable "Hardrock" who had led his men through those long runs in the Georgia mud, had not, after all, been immortal—though it had taken a 20mm artillery shell through his chest to kill him. His replacement had almost lost his arm himself just days earlier when a four-pound shell fragment buried itself in it during the battle for Fort McKinley. Lahti had refused evacuation to a field hospital; the medics could patch him up, he growled. The wound required twenty-six stitches. When he developed jaundice a few days after that, Lahti could hardly walk but refused to be relieved of duty. He could still do his job, he said.

And truth to tell, the planners could see no evidence that Lahti's wound, pallor, and exhaustion were affecting his judgment. He had picked up quickly on every detail of the plan that Muller and Quandt outlined for him and wasted no time in designating Burgess' First Battalion the least affected by casualties. Lahti spent the next two hours testing, probing, and quizzing Quandt's plan. When he left he was satisfied that the reserve was in good hands; he regretted that he couldn't participate himself, but he had some unfinished work to do at Fort McKinley.

Considering the time and the materials that Quandt had to work with, it was surprising that he was able to put together a workable plan of any kind. It had only been a little more than a week, after all, since the top-secret message from XIVth Corps headquarters was handed to the duty officer, Glenn McGowan, in the middle of the night. "Imperative you move on Los Baños ASAP," the message had said; it was 3:00 A.M., February 8. McGowan took the message to Swing's chief of staff, Mike Williams, who rubbed the sleep from his eyes. "Let's get Doug Quandt," he said. They had roused the operations officer and the three men sat around in the dimly lit kitchen drinking coffee for an hour, piecing together the little they knew about Los Baños.

It was later that day that Eichelberger and Swing asked Jay Vanderpool about taking the camp with only guerrilla forces. When he learned that American troops would have to bear the burden of responsibility, Swing began working with Quandt and Muller on plans for rescuing the internees. There were some things that made the planning easier than it might have been: there were plenty of aerial photographs of the Los Baños Agricultural College from before the war, and the frequent overflights of bombers en route from Mindoro to Manila had resulted in a great many more high-resolution pictures. These eight-by-ten glossies were placed around the edge of the sand table. Few people were evident in the photographs, however, either in uniform or out. The camp looked almost unoccupied.

Muller and his staff knew that such was not the case, though, from Vanderpool's intelligence. But the reports from the Filipino guerrillas had not been confirmed by direct American observation (Vanderpool's was second hand). Muller, Burgess, Quandt and the others had no real idea of the terrain in which they would be operating, the strength and mood of the garrison they would be attacking, or the physical ability of the people they were hoping to rescue to help themselves. All of these questions had to be answered before their ingenious and complicated plan could work.

The first phase of the rescue operation had been set in motion on February 12 and was designed to answer the questions concerning terrain and enemy strength. George Skau, the rugged leader of the Reconnaissance Platoon, had been sent across Laguna de Bay in a banca to make contact with the guerrillas and to map the terrain. With him was Lieutenant Haggerty; the two men had been back and forth half a dozen times since that first jaunt, Muller had just explained. Haggerty was there now, scouting out the appropriate landing places for Burgess' amtracs. Muller had no idea where Skau was.

The amtracs: Burgess had grimaced when he heard about that part of the mission. It was bad enough to walk instead of jump; it would be even worse to spend nearly two hours grinding through the shallow waters of the Laguna de Bay with his men. He had seen amtracs before. Amphibious tractors, properly called, but usually known as alligators. On land they looked, at a distance, like tanks. Lightly armored, noisier than a New York garbage truck, with hatch doors aft that flopped down to let small vehicles and artillery pieces enter its cavernous hold, the vehicle was an ingenious invention, born of wartime need. But carrying attack troops was not its primary role. It moved through the water at a geriatric pace, less than four miles per hour. Even if the night remained calm, the noise of fifty-four amtracs would be heard halfway to Tokyo. Every Jap within 100 miles would be waking up and grabbing the nearest mortar to lob a few at the crazy Americans sitting out there in the starlight.

The fifty-four amtracs would be under the command of a lieutenant colonel named Gibbs; he would be responsible for shepherding the machines from Parañaque some ten miles to the jumping-off point at Mamatid. Muller, Quandt, Burgess—everyone involved with the operation—tried to calm their fears about breaking security: the city was still thronged with Japanese soldiers and Filipino sympathizers who would be curious about the destination and intent of such a large convoy. But there was not enough time to send the amtracs in small groups that would be less likely to attract attention. If Japanese intelligence was functioning at all the movement of enough amtracs to carry hundreds of people, poised on the shore not seven miles from Los Baños, might well trigger a response from the Japanese around Los Baños. They would just have to trust their luck. The departure time from Mamatid would be a couple of hours before dawn. They would travel a course of 7.2 miles, on an arc across the lake from Mamatid to Mayondong Point. There would be no lights, artificial or otherwise: the moon would have set by the time they left, and the drivers under Colonel Gibbs' command would have to develop some nautical skills quickly, operating by hand-held compasses.

After the amtracs hit the beach they would keep crawling toward Los Baños, two miles away. They should be able to see Company B jumping from the nine C-47s just as the alligators hit the beach, Muller said. What time would that be? Burgess asked. They hadn't settled that precisely just yet, was the reply: sometime around dawn.

If it worked, Quandt concluded, this would be the first triphibious operation of its kind—airborne troops approaching by water! —in military history. But it was only fair that they knew it was an operation that violated some of the basic rules of warfare. First, Los Baños had no strategic meaning whatsoever. The primary goal of any military operation is to seize and hold territory, or to destroy an enemy force, and they would have to relinquish any ground they captured. Second, there was no way to prepare for this mission. There were no books to explain how it should be done, and there was no time to practice. They had to do it all perfectly the first time—the only time.

Two days later, on Tuesday, John Ringler was taken through the operations plan by Quandt. He figured the chances of sustaining heavy casualties for Company B were pretty good: from North Africa and Sicily through Normandy every drop made by American paratroopers behind enemy lines had resulted in heavy loss of life, and this seemed no different. Particularly with that high-tension line adjoining the drop zone and with the height of their drop set at 500 feet, barely enough time to let the chutes open and slow the descent of the men, even though they were carrying much less than their usual sixty-plus pounds of gear.

The heavy responsibility of overall command for the mission would fall to a stocky, crew-cut career Army officer, Colonel Robert Soule, commander of the 188th Parachute Infantry Regiment. Only ten men in the Eleventh Airborne Division would win the Distinguished Service Cross, second only to the Medal of Honor, during the war, five of these posthumously. The sawed-off "Shorty" Soule was one of those decorated survivors, for his actions during the fighting on Tagaytay Ridge. Soule was to have command of the mission and would accompany the commander of his First Battalion, Lieutenant Colonel Edward LaFlamme, as it pressed south via the main road from Manila to Los Baños. The 188th would have with it the 675th and 472nd Field Artillery Battalions and Company B of the 637th Tank Destroyer Battalion. They were to provide a diversion from the other activities at Los Baños by attacking Japanese positions at La Lecheria Hill, then moving toward the rock quarry a few miles north of Los Baños.

The Americans had to contend with knotty problems of logistics and timing in their effort to rescue the internees. Their overriding concern was that as many internees as possible be brought out safely and that as few soldiers be killed as possible. But how could they expect to herd some 2,600 people, counting internees and soldiers together, around, behind, and through Japanese-held territory and not lose a number of lives in the process? Their only chance for a relatively bloodless and successful raid lay in surprise. But there had already been three surprise attacks of a similar kind, all within the past twenty days: Santo Tomás, Cabanatuan, and Old Bilibid Prison. How many times a month could the Japanese be surprised?

If the enemy had not been so hard-pressed, surprise would probably have been all but impossible. But the very heart of Japanese resistance was being destroyed as the planners met with the men of the Los Baños mission. It would have been incomprehensible to the Japanese commanders, even if they had stopped to think of it, that the Americans would pull hundreds of their finest troops out of the climactic battle for Manila in order to rescue a group of old men, women, and children.

The Los Baños mission had, in fact, been set back four days from its original date of February 19 because it was not certain that there would be enough planes ready for Ringler's men: on the morning of February 16, the first of more than 2,000 men of the 503rd Parachute Infantry Regiment jumped over Corregidor. The scene of America's greatest military humiliation and defeat three years earlier, Corregidor held enormous strategic and emotional significance for both the Japanese and the Americans. Admiral Iwabushi had mined the beaches of the tiny island, and he had crammed enough food and ammunition into the tunnels that MacArthur had once occupied to keep his army of 5,000 men going for months. It had taken General Homma from December 1941 to May 1942 to bring Corregidor to its knees, and Wainwright had had fewer than 1,300 fighting men at his disposal. When Wainwright surrendered, he did so because his defenses had been pulverized by extensive pounding from Japanese gun batteries on Bataan. He had to surrender or let the thousands of people on the island die in the tunnels the Japanese threatened to seal with rock.

MacArthur had neither the time nor the inclination for a lengthy bombardment of Corregidor. He directed the 503rd, commanded by Colonel George M. Jones, to land on top of the Rock, secure the artillery positions there that guarded the beaches, and cover the landing of the Thirty-fourth Infantry Regiment, Twenty-fourth Division. The Japanese were holed up in the tunnels with a cache of ammunition meticulously recorded by their supply officers: 35,000 artillery shells, two million rounds of rifle and machine-gun bullets, 80,000 mortar shells, nearly 93,000 hand grenades, and uncounted tons of TNT. The Japanese refused to surrender, and the Americans could not evict them from the tunnels, so they tried to seal them in, just as the Japanese had threatened to do to Wainwright. Each day for nearly a week the tunnel entrances were blasted shut, and each night the Japanese dug them open. Then they ran up the hills, charging the American positions, until they were slaughtered: "It was like a massacre in a lunatic asylum," said one American later.

Even as the battle for Corregidor raged, the last act of the battle for Manila was beginning. By February 18, when Quandt started calling in Burgess, Ringler, and Soule, the Japanese had been driven into their last redoubt, the ancient walled city of Intramuros. The narrower the confines of the fighting, it seemed to the Americans, the nastier it got. It took a week to blast the Japanese out of the two-story concrete police station that blocked the entrance to Intramuros, and similar battles had to be fought for the city hall, the post office, the Manila Club, and the University of the Philippines. MacArthur himself had been in the thick of the fight for the Manila Hotel. He had watched his penthouse go up in flames. He fought his way with a patrol up the stairs and found a dead Japanese colonel lying on the floor by his bookshelf, next to the smoldering grand piano. At his feet were the remains of a Japanese vase that his wife had left behind when they fled the city in 1941. The room had evidently been used by the Japanese until that very morning, then fire-bombed when it appeared that MacArthur would return to claim it once again. As MacArthur stood amid the havoc, silent and grim, an aide ran his finger down the spines of some of the 3,000 volumes of military history, philosophy and literature that lined the walls—Gibbon, Macaulay, Caesar's *Gallic Wars*, Toynbee, the heart and soul of Western civilization. They crumbled into ashes when touched.

The walls of Intramuros had been built four centuries before by the Spanish. Forty feet thick at the base in places, and sixteen feet high, they enclosed the notorious Santiago Prison, home of the Kempetai, two sturdy stone churches, and a warren of tunnels dug by the Japanese beneath its 160 acres. Nearly 2,000 Japanese soldiers and naval marines were holed up in Intramuros, with 4,000 Filipinos as hostages. On February 17 General Griswold had pleaded over a loudspeaker for the enemy to surrender and release the hostages: "Your situation is hopeless, your defeat inevitable. I offer you honorable surrender. If you decide to accept, raise a large Filipino flag . . . If you do not accept, I exhort you that in the spirit of Bushido and the code of the samurai you permit all civilians to evacuate the Intramuros by the Victoria

Gate without delay in order that no innocent blood be shed."

The Japanese did not respond, and Griswold began a massive shelling that would continue for six days. It took that long for the modern technology of war to demolish the medieval fortress built by the Spanish, but by the morning of February 23 tank-sized holes had been blasted through the walls with point-blank assaults by howitzers and 75mm guns. The Japanese soldiers who retreated to the dungeons where the Kempetai kept their prisoners were incinerated by flame throwers; burned with them were the corpses of most of the 1,000 males, men and boys, who had been murdered and stacked like cordwood by the Japanese in the same cells where they met their own death.

Muller could be fairly certain, then, that the Japanese commanders in and near Manila were unlikely to concern themselves with the disappearance of several units of the Eleventh Airborne Division from the battle. Even so, steps had been taken to ensure secrecy: Ringler's men had been shut up in the New Bilibid jail and held incommunicado, knowing nothing of the coming raid, and Burgess' First Battalion was left similarly uninformed.

Muller knew that American strategy after Manila called for the Eighth Army to move southward, to the Visayan straits that lay 200 miles south of the capital. From there a series of amphibious operations would be launched to clear the smaller islands of Japanese troops before tackling the last remaining strongholds in Mindanao. U.S. intelligence indicated that Colonel Fujishige had concentrated an estimated 8,000 to 10,000 men of his force on a line extending from Los Baños to a road junction some twenty-five miles southwest of Los Baños. Stretching across several high peaks, Fujishige's line would stand between the advance of the Eleventh Airborne and other American units toward the Visayan straits. But judging from the disposition of the Japanese forces, it seemed likely that Fujishige's primary mission would be to keep the Americans from rounding the eastern shore of Laguna de Bay.

What would Fujishige do if he learned that the Eleventh Airborne, which had already humiliated him once, was about to snatch 2,000 hostages from Los Baños? Not just from under the lion's nose, so to speak, but out of his mouth, for the key to the Japanese defense of the southern sector lay not twenty miles away from Los Baños. There was little doubt in Muller's mind that the internees would be executed before they would be rescued. Or that Fujishige would give anything to annihilate the rescue team if he could. Yet it would be almost as dangerous if Fujishige knew nothing of the raid until it occurred. For he might reasonably assume that the main attack of the Eighth Army that he had been told to repel at all costs had begun, and launch a counterattack himself. He could move several thousand men to Los Baños within hours. If the attacking force did not get in and out within the same day, preferably half a day, all might be lost.

But coming back to the more immediate concerns, Muller explained to the officers that he just didn't have all the answers to the main questions: How many guards were there? What were their routines, their schedules? How good were they? Where were the internees likely to be when they jumped? Were the sick and the elderly kept separate? How many were in the hospital? How many would be able to walk if necessary? And, most important, what would be the best time to go in? Cabanatuan had been hit in the middle of the night, Santo Tomás in the later afternoon. Dawn was the traditional hour for surprise attacks, which was as good a reason as any to avoid it, though that was the time he now had in mind. Presumably, because of the P-38 strafing missions, the enemy would have become accustomed to their presence at all hours. If surprise were to be gained, then, the time of the day might be of relatively little importance.

Quandt told the officers that there were other complicating factors to remember. This was not a military POW camp they were liberating, full of young men who were accustomed to react quickly and decisively in an emergency, to receive and follow orders—men who were trained fighters and would quickly become valuable comrades-in-arms as soon as they had weapons in their hands again. To the contrary; many of the civilians they would rescue (and they were all civilians, according to reliable reports) were missionaries, nuns, and priests, and many others were women, children, and old men. There might be as many as 500 who were bedridden and would have to be carried out on stretchers.

The psychological reaction of civilians to a sudden clash of armies was likely to be frozen panic. They will dive for cover if they are especially alert, Quandt said, but most will simply stand and stare as bullets past by their heads. When they do move, after you've convinced them that you are there to take them away, the G-3 continued, they are likely to want to carry all their belongings with them, everything they have accumulated, though it won't be much, over the past several years. The men would have to be ruthless in getting the people aboard the amtracs. There would be no time for souvenir collecting or small talk.

It was shortly after noon on Tuesday, February 20 when the answer to some of Henry Muller's questions arrived, in the form of Pete Miles, the snake tamer, barroom bouncer, and mining engineer with the Arrow-shirt-ad profile. With him was the gruff, silent Lieutenant Skau of the Recon Platoon, who reported with a casual salute to Muller. He'd followed Mr. Miles from Nang-haya after learning from Colonel Ortiz and Ben Edwards that Miles was being taken to Parañaque, he said. He had wanted to make sure Miles arrived safely because he was sure G-2 would be interested in what the internee had to say.

Miles had been awake since leaving Edwards and Freddy Z. the evening before, and there were dark circles beneath his pale blue eyes. But he walked lightly over to the map table and placed on it the crumpled map that he and Ben had drawn on the beach. Done with an engineer's precision, it marked not only the precise location of the barracks occupied by the internees but told which ones held the nuns, the elderly, and, closest to the guards' quarters, the troublemakers like Ben Edwards, Hank Mangles, and himself. By the time Miles finished correcting the map put together by Muller based on aerial photographs and guerrilla reports, the planners knew the layout of the camp as precisely as if they themselves had spent a year and a half living there.

But beyond question, the most valuable information brought by Miles concerned the locations of the Japanese and their pattern of movement. Miles' information was based on what he knew from firsthand observation, some of it determined after he had received guerrilla reports and insisted upon confirming them himself. The guerrillas had been extremely accurate, he told the planners, and he would stake his life on the figures he was about to give them.

First, he said, only about eighty guards were actually present within the camp. They were hungry and dispirited, and they had no faith in their leadership, neither Major Iwanaka nor Konishi. Perhaps familiarity had bred contempt, but they did not appear to him to be warriors in the samurai tradition but rejects, for one reason or another, from the regular army.

Outside and around the camp it was a different story. There was an infantry company stationed at the rock quarry about two miles west of the camp, with two 105mm guns and four machine guns; there were at least twenty soldiers at Mayondong, where the amtracs were scheduled to land. There were also two three-inch guns on the wharf at Los Baños, trained on the lake. And there was a roadblock in the path of Colonel LaFlamme's 188th; some eighty enemy soldiers were positioned at the roadblock, and they were supported by two 75mm guns from La Lecheria hill nearby.

Though Muller had already had reports of most of what Miles brought him, he was now able to pinpoint precisely the location of the machine-gun nests and pillboxes in the camp and the drop-zone areas. What did surprise him was Miles' startling information about the exercise habits of the guards. Like their American "wards," or prisoners, the Japanese understood the need for adherence to a regular routine no matter how frenzied their lives became. The Americans had kept on with their church services, their classes, and their basketball and softball games—though the latter ended when the players, weak from lack of food, seemed to be moving in a dreamlike trance, and when the Executive Committee realized that their moral leverage on Konishi in pleading for more food was weakened by the sight of enthusiastic, though slow, games.

The Japanese held to their own routines too, Miles said, and one of these routines was morning calisthenics. Every morning that he had been in the camp, for more than eighteen months, the troops who were not on duty in the four guard posts—two men each—would gather in the open space about fifty yards from the guards' barracks. Their exercises began promptly at 6:45 and ended at 7:15. During that time all their guns were stacked and locked in the connecting room between the two barracks, in front of the lavatories.

It was almost too neat, Muller thought, too easy. If Skau and his men hit the guard posts and cracked the fences while the Japs were doing their push-ups, the attack should be over in ten minutes. He and the other men questioned Miles closely for another half-hour. There was nothing in the engineer's manner or his information to give them pause: he was confident without being arrogant, and everything he said corresponded with information they had previously received through Skau and Vanderpool. Finally Quandt nodded. It was set, he said: Skau and his men would hit the camp with the guerrillas, and Ringler's B Company would jump at exactly 7:00 A.M. Everything from now on would be keyed to that time.

Skau turned to leave, and Miles started to join him. Laughing, Muller stopped him. Even snake tamers had to rest, he said. Skau knew the way by himself. Miles protested: he hadn't left Los Baños with the intention of running for safety and cover but to bring the information he had brought and then to return. The Japanese didn't like it when people failed to show up for roll call and took it out on the ones left behind. He would go back and take his chances with the others. Muller explained that Miles had to stay put. He knew too much about their plans to be out running around in the jungle, even with Skau. If the Japs caught him now there's no telling what they would do to him to get the information they would be sure he had, and no assurance that he, or anyone, could keep it from them. Besides, Muller was sure that Miles could tell them much more about the camp than he had in such a short time. He would do much more for his fellow prisoners by staying at the headquarters of the Eleventh than by going back.

Miles grudgingly agreed. But, he insisted, Skau had to stop at Nanghaya on his way back and pick up Ben Edwards and Freddy Zervoulakas. Freddy had valuable contacts with the guerrillas through his brother, and Ben probably knew the lay of the land around the camp better than anyone else because he had been in charge of wood-gathering details for the past three months. Skau looked at Muller, who nodded his agreement. The lieutenant left, and Muller told Miles to get a couple of hours' sleep. They had a lot more questions they wanted to ask him.

15

MAKING READY

I

Los Baños Internment Camp: Wednesday, February 21, 6:30 P.M.

A half dozen men were gathered in Dana Nance's infirmary. It was time for the weekly meeting of the Executive Committee, and Murray Heichert was asking for the attention of Nance, Frank Bennett, Clyde DeWitt, George Watty, George Grey, and Alex Calhoun. It was important that they agree on the accuracy of the particular part of the minutes he was going to read, he said. The minutes recorded a meeting of three days earlier, on February 18, with Lieutenant Konishi:

Mr. Konishi was asked what food could be expected through the gate in the future. He replied that he could not permit any such inquiries, nor could he promise anything. He could only say that he would do what he could. He was then asked if he could be prepared to make up the serious shortage in weight issued. [The internees were referring to the short-weighted provisions they were receiving; they were sure the Japanese were stealing from their allotted supplies.] He replied that the issue would have to do for four days. It was pointed out that actually the issue was only sufficient for three days' supply. Mr. Konishi stated it would have to do for four days, as that was all he could secure. Mr. Heichert, chairman of the committee, said to Mr. Konishi that he could not understand the position at all. He could not believe that the Japanese could treat men, women, children, and old people in this manner. They had promised to feed the camp. They now give us what we cannot eat, and in addition give us short weight. It was something that completely passed his comprehension. Mr. Konishi replied that it was futile to talk to him on this kind of thing, that he has no wish to discuss the matter further.

The members agreed that the account was correct, though restrained, and approved the minutes. In fact, Konishi had shouted his answers, not simply "replied," and had glared threateningly at Bennett and Dr. Nance in particular. He still suspected Bennett of "stealing" food and seemed to regret that he hadn't gone ahead and shot him that afternoon when Pat Hell died, as he had been threatening to do. As for Dr. Nance, he had pushed his luck a little too far.

The Japanese were wrong in blaming the internees for stealing their radio, as it turned out. But they were quite right in suspecting that there was a radio in the camp. There was. It was a small set that had been smuggled in to Dr. Nance with his medical supplies early in the fall of 1944, and he listened with great satisfaction to the news of the American advances through the Philippines. For safety's sake, only a few people knew of the radio, including Bill Donald, the former aide to Chiang Kai-shek, George Grey, and Frank Bennett. When the power went out at the camp early in February, after the local generating plant was hit by American bombs, the doctor was desperate for news. Nance had used all his ingenuity and called in some past debts in the form of medical services to overcome this problem: Bob Jackson, who could make a radio out of piano wire and light bulbs, was handed a few tubes and condensers through the fence by a helpful villager, and he promptly put together a small receiver. Somebody managed to steal a stationary exercise bicycle from Baker Hall. Dr. Nance contributed the motor from the centrifuge in his hospital, and Bob Hughes in the camp shop had Radio Freedom on the air in a matter of hours.

There were five men in the shop after curfew when two guards opened the door and demanded to know what they were doing. The radio was under cover and Nance had arranged an alibi if they were caught: he was trying to see if they could generate electricity for his operating room. The guards took each of the five men, starting with Nance, in to see Konishi. The Japanese lieutenant had once seemed friendly to the doctor, hoping perhaps to get some drugs from him, Nance supposed. But his uncompromising report on George Lewis' death and his insistence on recording the death of other internees as due to starvation had infuriated Koni-shi. If the other men did not convince him that Nance was telling the truth, he said, the doctor would find himself in deep trouble.

Nance left the lieutenant's office sweating heavily. Bill Donald, Grey, and Jackson had been briefed on their cover story, but Bennett had not been there and he had not yet had time to fill in Bob Hughes. What would Hughes say? When the shop foreman finally walked out of the Japanese headquarters it was nearly 3:00 A.M. The guard with him indicated that the other four men, each of whom had been forced to sit in silence while they waited for Konishi's decision, could return to their quarters. Nance spent a sleepless night, waiting to see Hughes the next day, but it was late afternoon before he was able to find the time. "What in the world did you tell him?" he was finally able to ask.

The only thing that made any sense, Hughes had responded. He had told him they needed the electricity to power the operating room in the hospital. It was a lucky guess. The radio stayed silent after that. But Konishi was still suspicious, and he had spent little time with the Executive Committee when they asked for more food. In fact, Nance noted after the minutes were approved, the situation today, February 21, was much worse than it was a few days ago. He and Bennett had learned only that afternoon that the supply of rice was exhausted, according to Konishi. There were several dozen sacks, however, of unhusked rice, or palay, which Konishi said they could have. The rice has to be husked first, Nance reminded Konishi. Each kernel was protected by a tough husk with razor-sharp edges. The internees might as well eat ground glass as unhusked rice, which would slice through the walls of their intestines. Konishi laughed shortly. The Americans first asked for food, then complained when he gave it to them. They could husk the rice the same way the peasants did in Japan and here in the Philippines: by rubbing it between sticks. Konishi knew, of course, Nance told the committee, that we would burn up more calories than the food contained trying to husk it without proper equipment. Don't forget to put that in the minutes of this meeting, he barked to Heichert as the committee chairman left. One way or another, it didn't seem possible that there would be many more meetings of the committee.

Late in the afternoon of February 21, Tom Bousman was tending the evening cooking fire in the small portable fireplace that his father had constructed from a piece of tile pipe. His father, he reflected, was an ingenious and compassionate man, but Tom could hardly bring himself to understand his reluctance to condemn the Japanese for their behavior. The elder Bousman had reminded the boy of the visit they had made to Japan in 1937 and again in 1938 on brief holidays from their Presbyterian mission in Los Baños. Even as a young boy—he was only seventeen now— Tom had been impressed by the grace and subtlety of Japanese art, the exquisite harmony of the gardens, the sensitivity and courtesy of their hosts. Had he forgotten all of that, Tom's father asked. Could he really believe that the Japanese were by nature the brutal conquerors they now seemed to be? No, his father insisted. What was happening now was an aberration; Tojo and his war machine had captured and enslaved the people of Japan. The guard whose boots they heard on the hard clay outside their door would rather be home tending his garden than keeping watch over a group of hungry Americans who had done him no harm. He was as much a prisoner as they, as were the Japanese people. Forgiveness, not anger, was called for.

Fine, Tom thought. But would Donald Rounds, a boy about his own age, be able to forgive the Japanese for beheading his missionary parents on the island of Panay—and his eight-year-old brother? Closer to home, maybe the Japanese were not directly to blame for Burt Fonger's death—though they certainly created the conditions that led to it. But the two men who had been shot for trying to get more food, George Lewis and Pat Hell—should that be forgiven, too? Tom sighed as he stirred the twigs that fed the tiny fire and tried to emulate his father's large-minded understanding. But it was something deeper within him than compassion for the Japanese that responded to the deep, throaty roar of the P-38 that suddenly burst out of the evening sky.

They weren't supposed to look up at the passing American

planes, Tom knew. Not long before, three young brothers had climbed a tree to wave and cheer as a flight of American bombers passed overhead. Two guards had chased the boys out of the tree and marched them to an area behind the Japanese guards barracks, despite the anxious protests of the parents. A few minutes later there were shots. The parents were frantic, but the boys soon reappeared. The shots had come from the front gate. They had been fired into the gardener, Pat Hell.

So it wasn't safe, and it probably wasn't even very Christian, for Tom to feel such an intensely satisfying excitement as the P-38 roared between the barracks, wings perpendicular to the ground not thirty feet below. Through the open canopy the boy could see the pilot's white teeth flash a grin. He could swear that the pilot was looking right at him as he gave a thumbs-up sign—though it was at most a matter of seconds before the plane roared into the early-evening sky.

II

Barrio San Roque: Wednesday, February 21, 9:00 P.M.

Ben Edwards watched sleepily as the pretty young schoolteacher sighed in mock protest and began to play, for the fifth time, "My Rose of San Antone." Tom Rounceville, a big-footed Texan who had come into Colonel Ortiz's camp that morning grinning broadly, pushed his Australian-style bush ranger's hat to the back of his curly red hair and sang along in a high tenor. The Cherokee Indian who was with him watched, relaxed but alert. They were Alamo scouts, part of a team of behind-the-lines operatives on their way south to Mindanao sent by MacArthur to make contact with Wendell Fertig and his guerrilla units there. They would be on their way in the morning, Skau had told Ben. Ben thought that tomorrow would be none too soon for Skau, who watched the young Texan narrowly. Though they were safely within an area that the guerrillas had claimed to be free of Jap troops, there was only one way to stay alive behind enemy lines, and that was to keep your damn mouth shut. That included, his dour expression said clearly, singing asshole songs like "My Rose of San Antone."

There was no nonsense about Skau, Ben had learned the day before. He and Freddy Z. had just learned from the boatmen who took Pete Miles to Parañaque that Pete had made it safely. They had both settled back for a midday nap on Colonel Ortiz's floor, relieved and happy that the pressure to follow Pete was off them, when the big lieutenant arrived, along with the slender young Lieutenant Haggerty. They were leaving in an hour for Los Baños, Skau told the two internees; he wanted to see the lay of the land there. By midnight the four men were standing in the creek bed at the southeast corner of the camp. It was so quiet that they could hear the low voices of two women from the nearest barracks—the nuns' quarters, Ben said softly.

But Skau knew that already, Ben realized: they'd been around the camp twice in the past two hours. Every footpath, every trail through the heavy scrub and what was left of the timber that Ben's crews had gathered for firewood, had been noted and marked by Skau with the stubby pencil and small sweat-stained notebook he carried in his shirt pocket. They had started at the deserted lower camp, near which B Company would drop, and where Skau had told Haggerty to mark two positions for the phosphorous grenades to be placed. Then they had scrambled and clawed their way through the hilly terrain north of the camp, toward the slopes of Mount Makiling.

Looking at the camp now, for the first time, as an objective to be attacked, Ben was struck by its vulnerability, especially on the northeast side, where there was a stand of bamboo more than six feet high. A hundred men could creep through such a thicket, follow the deep ravine behind the infirmary, where he had kicked that damned can only a few days before, and ease through the barbed-wire fence, past the infirmary and the kitchen to the Jap command barracks. The west-facing fence, in the middle of which was the main gate, would be the toughest: there were four guards in each of the corner posts and five in the middle, at the gates.

However, the camp was not really designed to keep a strong attacking force out but to keep unarmed civilians in. The pillboxes at the southwest corner, near which they now stood, were made of dirt, not concrete, Skau had noted with satisfaction: instant graves, he whispered to Ben. The whole thing would be a piece of cake. Even so, Ben noted that Skau and Haggerty moved with great care as they circled the camp, and that their senses seemed to be unusually acute—as were his own. The sharp blue spurt of a match struck by a guard leaving his post startled the Americans as they stood listening to the nuns. Within an instant, they all had their faces in the dirt. Ben was not unhappy when Skau said he had seen enough.

Now, as the rendition of "My Rose of San Antone" came to an end, Skau had apparently had enough of the festivities. He got up to leave, motioning to Haggerty to follow. The schoolteacher, much taken by the dashing Alamo scouts, offered to play another song, but Skau held up his hand for silence. In the distance, maybe two miles away, there was shooting—small-arms and machine-gun fire, Ben thought. Haggerty turned the lights out and the men grabbed their carbines and waited. Fifteen minutes later Rudy Fuentes, one of the guerrillas Ben had gotten to know, came in. They had caught a Jap patrol, some twenty men, he said. All were dead except two. Colonel Ortiz had ordered him to take the two by banca to Parañaque for questioning, and he was leaving with them now.

Ben thought he noticed a wolfish gleam in Rudy's eyes. All of the guerrillas hated the Japanese with a fierceness that made Ben's deep resentment of them pale by comparison. He had heard stories of calculated Japanese brutality toward Filipinos that were almost beyond belief: of school principals bayoneted before their students' eyes, of priests crucified on their church doors, of a concert violinist forced to play for his captors before they beheaded him. Rudy had his own grudge against the enemy.

When the war started, Fuentes had been at home, on leave from the military academy in Baguio. The Japanese had come into the village and ordered everyone to assemble in the marketplace. An officer had given a little speech calling attention to the similarity of skin color between the Japanese and the Filipinos and had smilingly invited a young woman carrying a baby to stand beside him on the picnic table he had mounted to address the crowd.

"See?" he said, baring his slender arm and placing it beside the young mother's face. "We are the same color! Your white oppressors, the Americans, are being expelled, and you are now free to join the Greater Asia Co-Prosperity Sphere. From now on Asia will be for the Asian, and all will be free!"

It was a pretty good speech, Fuentes said. The young officer seemed sincerely to believe what he was saying. Nobody in the village felt that they had been oppressed by the Americans, but of course they knew better than to say so, and the officer left in good spirits. Later that afternoon the sergeants he had left behind undid whatever good work the officer had begun when they made everyone fill out residency cards. They reprimanded an old woman, a palsied old man, and several others who were too slow by slapping them briskly across the face.

Fuentes had left the village that evening to join the Hunters guerrillas then forming under Terry Adevozo. Two weeks later his mother was bayoneted for calling a Japanese sergeant a pig. A month after that he was captured and held for questioning for three weeks by the Kempetai before a raid freed him and a dozen others so that they could rejoin the guerrillas.

Ben told Skau he had his doubts about the wisdom of letting Fuentes take the two Japanese soldiers to Parañaque, especially in a sailboat. Skau said it didn't matter—the Japs couldn't tell them anything they didn't already know. He laughed. If Ben thought Fuentes was a bad ass, he said, just wait until tomorrow, when the whole gang of guerrillas showed up for the last briefing in the pretty schoolteacher's classroom a mile away.

III

Nichols Field, Manila: Thursday, February 22, 3:00 P.M.

The men of John Ringler's Company B who would leap over Los Baños had been sent directly to jail without passing Go on Monday afternoon, February 19. Filing down the dank corridors of

New Bilibid Prison, they passed a locked cell, where a bearded prisoner, a Filipino, rattled the bars and greeted them joyously. "I bin waiting for you guys! Lemme out!" he shouted.

"Sorry, pal," they responded. They didn't know why they were there themselves, or how long they'd be there. But at least, they noted to themselves, their doors weren't locked. That was probably because Ringler had told them to take Bob Fletcher and the other two Filipinos out in the yard and show them how to jump out of a plane.

Burt and George Marshall, two brothers from San Diego, and big Tom Zaharias, a sergeant from Colorado, took Fletcher into the yard behind their cell and put him on a platform. Another survival lesson, Fletcher thought: he had already had a few since he'd signed on with the Eleventh. Zaharias was his first tutor. "You got no weapon, kid, and you need a helmet," he noticed on Tagaytay Ridge. A wounded soldier was being carried past them on a litter. He grabbed the soldier's helmet and patted him lightly on the shoulder, saying, "You won't be needing this where you're going," and clapped the helmet on Fletcher's head. It promptly descended around his ears, so Zaharias showed him how to adjust the helmet liner. Then he flagged down a passing ammo truck and appropriated an M-1. "You got eight rounds for sighting it in, kid," he said. "After that you fire for effect."

His second tutor was Bob Samsell, the bazooka man for B Company. Sharing a foxhole with Samsell during the battle for McKinley Field, he woke from a restless sleep shortly before dawn to find Samsell's calloused, horny hand over his mouth. He quit struggling when Samsell whispered fiercely in his ear, "Shut up and listen!"

Fletcher listened and heard rustling sounds in the dry grass. Yes, he nodded, he heard them. "Okay," Samsell said, removing his hand. "Lemme show you how to throw a grenade." He took four grenades from his belt and handed two to Fletcher, motioning him to do as he did. Then, holding a grenade in each hand, he crooked each index finger and pulled the pin of the grenade in the opposite hand, counted to seven, and looped them both in the direction of the rustling grass. Two seconds later there were muffled explosions and loud cries of anguish. Fletcher did the same, resisting the temptation to get rid of the little bombs as soon as he pulled the pins, while Samsell looked on approvingly, then repeated the process. The next morning they counted seventeen dead bodies around their foxhole.

Fletcher's next lesson was administered at McKinley Field by a rangy electrician from New Jersey named John Ciereck. It was Ciereck's turn for watch, and he was out like a light, so Fletcher gave his shoulder a rough shake. As he did so, he felt a hand clamp against his throat and another clutch his shirt. His feet left the ground and he flew through the air, landing against the side of the ditch. Dazed, Fletcher looked up in time to see Ciereck's tall figure outlined against the stars, with his rifle raised high above his head. He was swinging it by the barrel and it was poised above Fletcher's skull. "Lost wallet!" Fletcher screamed. "Lost wallet!" That day's password, like Lillian Russell, Lady Luck, and Lillibullero, was hard for the Japanese to say. The American grunted, lowered his rifle, and went back to sleep.

The young Filipino had been vividly impressed by the Americans—most of the Japanese soldiers he had seen were about his size or smaller, maybe 120 pounds and slightly built. The GIs all seemed to be as tough and as strong as Zaharias and Ciereck, who had tossed him through the air as easily as if he were a two-year-old. They even talked tough—every other word was a curse. But they could be gentle too, like the machine gunner in the Second Platoon, Jim Holzem, who had taken Oscar under his wing at Parañaque. Oscar, a sixteen-year-old from the Manila slums, told Fletcher later about what happened. He and his kid brother had appeared one afternoon while Holzem was digging a foxhole underneath a house. They'd give a T-shirt and an infantry knife, the Americans said, if the boys would dig the hole for them. When they were done, Oscar said, Holzem, who was eating lunch, was opening a can of milk for himself. His sister had just had a baby, Oscar said, and the baby was dying because it didn't have any milk; could he have some milk instead of the T-shirt and the knife? Holzem told him to wait a minute and disappeared. An hour later he was back with a case of milk, donated by A and B Companies.

The next day, Oscar said, his parents returned with him to

thank Holzem for the gift of the milk. They wanted to give him something in return. That wasn't necessary, Holzem said. No, they insisted: they gave him Oscar. "Oh shit," Holzem said under his breath. He was a machine gunner, not a big brother. But the parents pleaded: he will do whatever you tell him to, for as long as you want, they said. The American finally gave in. Nobody wants to carry the ammo for all these damn machine guns, Holzem had said. Oscar could be the ammo bearer. He would end up following Holzem all the way to southern Luzon, through many months of heavy fighting. But first he would get a good case of malaria, right during the middle of the battle for Manila, and Holzem would sit up with him for a couple of nights covering him with wet sheets until the fever broke.

The Americans weren't soft; Fletcher had seen them kill the enemy with flamethrowers and grenades and bayonets, even with their bare hands, and the more they saw of the atrocities in Manila, the more ruthless they became. "The veneer of Japanese civilization is like the lacquer on a woman's fingernails," one GI with a literary flair had told him. "The Japs are lice," said another. And they weren't emotional about each other, not on the surface, though the quiet bond of affection between soldiers like the Marshall brothers was obvious. It was said that their mother, at their request, had made a special plea to Eleanor Roosevelt to allow them to be in the same unit together, side-stepping a rule intended to keep families from losing more than one son at a time in battle.

Fletcher had been very touched himself when Lieutenant Ringler returned from Division HQ Thursday afternoon with the final word on the mission. "Troopers, gather around me," Ringler had said. The soldiers were curious—they had been locked up in the jail for three days, waiting to hear what was afoot. What was the big deal about security? The prisoner who had greeted them, out of his cell now, followed the soldiers into the yard. Ringler looked up sharply and said, "No Filipinos!" Fletcher, standing on the edge of the group with Zaharias, started to move away. "Get back here, Fletcher!" the sergeant said. "You're one of us."

Ringler drew a rough map in the dirt with a pointer. He told them they were going in at 7:00 A.M. the next morning in nine C-47s, three V formations, dropping from about 500 feet. They were to hit the ground, shuck their chutes, and run for the camp. The drop would be a little tricky because of the high-tension line that adjoined it—"If you hit it, it'll kill you." He did not add that he expected their casualties, once they hit the ground, to be high, but the men knew they might be in for a rough time when he said they would be given three days' D rations—concentrated chocolate. There was no way, some of the soldiers figured, for them to stay alive for three days with all the Japs there were around south of Manila.

They would get their chutes at Nichols Field that afternoon, Ringler said, and sleep under the wings of the planes. "One more thing," he said as the men started back to their cells to gather their gear. They were to keep those big chocolate bars in their packs. "When we hit the camp those people are going to be half nuts. They've been locked up for two or three years, and they're all starving. They'll be all over you, trying to thank you and tell you what great guys you are, but there won't be any time for that. Get them together and get them moving. And don't give them any of your rations. We're going to save those people, not kill them with kindness and concentrated chocolate."

Later that afternoon the men lined up at Nichols Field beside a C-47 that had just flown in from Leyte with a fresh batch of parachutes. Fletcher was looking his over when Zaharias walked up to give him a hand. The young guerrilla was disappointed to see that his, unlike the others, was not a brilliant, shiny white but a dull, blotchy green and brown. Zaharias generously offered to trade Bob his chute, showed him how the thing worked, and strolled away. Fletcher, gratified that he wouldn't have to make his first jump with such an ugly chute, turned and saw Fred Salzbach grinning broadly. "Nice guy, huh?" Fletcher offered. A great guy, Salzbach said; he had just swindled his good pal out of the only camouflage parachute in the shipment. If it was him, he'd go get it back. Fletcher smiled wanly. A deal was a deal, he said. Zaharias could keep the chute.

IV

Los Baños Internment Camp: Thursday, February 22, 3:30 P.M.

Bob Kleinpell, the oil geologist, and Darley Downs, the missionary and Japanese linguist, had disagreed fundamentally about the change that had overtaken Japan during the past forty years. For Downs, the rise of Japanese militarism had been an unqualified disaster, destroying the gentle, sensitive people he had known during his many years there. The genie of fascism had been released from the bottle 10,000 miles away in Europe and had floated across the world to find a willing new master, he said. Kleinpell had scoffed. He was unembarrassed by the fact that he had come to Manila in 1939 after the agreement at Munich that gave Hitler dominance in Europe. He had come not to escape but because he honestly felt that Japan and Germany were the two forces for stability in the world in the face of Russian communism. *That* was the real danger, he had assured Downs. Just let this war end with Germany and Japan crushed and you'll see who we have to deal with. We suckered the Japs into attacking us at Pearl Harbor so the big boys on Wall Street could climb out of the Depression their greed had caused. And we were paying the price now.

The price might be even higher than he thought, Kleinpell mused as he watched the visiting Japanese general stroll through the camp. The general looked very fine, especially next to the always disreputable Konishi and the cowering commandant, Iwanaka. His leather boots shone brilliantly, and his cold black eyes gleamed above his thick mustache as he looked around the camp approvingly. He looks like a Turk, Kleinpell thought, and turned back to the blackboard where he had sketched the outlines of the Jurassic period for the two or three students who were still showing up for his class.

That was one of the things he and Downs had agreed upon totally, he thought: the classes had to be kept going. The Englishmen in the jungle having tea—it wasn't unreasonable. But it was probably all for naught. The Japanese general was not interested in their welfare. They were in his way, and like Genghis Kahn or Attila or Tamurlane, other great Asian butchers, he would obliterate them all without a twinge of conscience if it suited his interests.

Unlike many of the internees, Kleinpell was neither surprised nor puzzled later that afternoon when the Japanese brought in a crew of Filipino laborers and set them to digging a large trench outside the camp. Several people speculated that the ditch was simply an extension of the network of tunnels, ditches, and foxholes the Japanese had been digging for themselves ever since their return in mid-January. Kleinpell thought otherwise. The ditch was for them, not for the Japs. The only question he had now was when the guards would gun them down. Would it be during roll call when they were all in one place under the eyes and guns of the corner guard posts?

He confronted George Grey with his fears as the lanky diplomat walked past his classroom. George said nothing, but he pulled his underwear up above his trousers and held the seam near the top button away from his skinny waist so that Kleinpell could see it. A shiny American dime gleamed in the midafternoon sunlight. Grey put a finger to his lips and walked away, leaving the iconoclastic geologist to his musings. It was hardly fair, he thought: he had almost gotten himself reconciled, like Seneca, to his fate, and now he was being told to hope again.

V

Los Baños Internment Camp: Thursday, February 22, 6:20 P.M.

From the Diary of George Mora:

"A colonel from the regional staff visited the camp today and the committee asked him for food. He said, 'So sorry.' This was a war zone and food was short everywhere. He said conditions were no different now than when we had been 'free' in January, when the Japs left the camp. Would we like to be set free now? The committee had said this was up to the Japanese. Of course, the minute we walk through those gates we'll be enemy aliens in a war zone. Our only protection is right here, but we need food. You will not get more, you may get less, is what I understand the Jap's message to be.

Another man died last night, from beriberi, which is from starvation. We may have to eat the palay. They are set on starving us to death.

But there was a little bit of a silver lining around our black cloud a while ago, though I'm trying to keep from getting too optimistic. From about 4:40 until 5:00 P.M. a flight of P-38s attacked a point in the hills behind the camp. They bombed and strafed and started a fire. They were so close we could see the bombs leaving the planes! There are a lot of rumors going around. One says that the Japs are retreating southward and are expected to pass through Los Baños on Saturday. We've also heard that our forces took Muntinglupa and are pressing a three-pronged drive this way. Everyone is jubilant right now instead of downcast and they figure that it is a forerunner of the end. Some think it is significant that the Japs did not have the evening roll call tonight, for the first time since they started having them last fall.

I'm curious to see what will happen tomorrow, and fighting to hold off the optimism."

VI

Los Baños: Thursday, February 22, 11:00 P.M.

Please listen, Helen Espino was saying wearily to the elderly man who had answered her quiet knock. You must leave the village right now and go to the hills. My husband is there with many guerrillas, and you will be safe. The old man stared at her sleepily. Why should they flee now, after three years of living under the Japanese? he protested. The Americans were surely coming, and they would all be safe. Had she not given him the proof herself, in the form of a newly minted American coin? It was foolish to leave now, of all times.

Exasperated, Helen pleaded with the old man. He didn't understand anything, she said angrily. Something was about to happen soon at the camp at the college, where the American civilians were. Caution curtained the old man's eyes: he had lived for a long time knowing as little as he could about the camp. He didn't want to know anything about it now. Helen understood: it was safer to know nothing when the Japanese asked questions. But this was different, she insisted. If the Americans sent in a force to rescue the prisoners, as they had at Santo Tomás, then the village could become a battlefield. Even if it didn't, the Japanese would be furious at the attack. They were convinced, or they pretended to be convinced, that every Filipino was a guerrilla and would have been helping the Americans do whatever they were going to do to rescue the internees. Was the old man so stupid that he did not know about reprisals?

He yawned in her face and gently closed the door. Helen walked away downhearted. They had all taken the dimes, all of the fifty or sixty people she had told to get themselves and their families, and anyone else they could take with them, to the hills. Only a few had understood what she was trying to tell them. They had all taken the symbol of the coins the wrong way, not as harbingers of destruction by the Japanese but of salvation by the Americans. But the Americans were still far away, in any numbers, and the Japanese were all around them. Poor fools, she thought, poor fools. Then she set out to find her husband in the hills near Los Baños: "Colonel Price."

VII

Los Baños Internment Camp: Thursday, February 22, 11:45 P.M.

It looked like a scene from a romantic novel: a young man and a woman standing close to each other in the starlight, saying good night after a quiet game of bridge. But the young man was telling the young woman that the chances were fairly good that they might be murdered in the morning.

George Grey was apologetic as he explained to his former secretary, Marge Pierce, what he had learned. And what he had withheld from her until now about another, more appealing, possibility for the next day. Marge listened quietly as he told her that he had been working with local guerrillas for the past week, sneaking out of camp to meet them in the village. Very few people knew what he was going to tell her, and she had to swear to keep it secret: there was to be a surprise attack by the Eleventh Airborne and the guerrillas early the next morning. But she should also know that the Japanese were believed to be planning a mass murder, firing the barracks and machine-gunning them all as they rushed outside. It was an open question which would come first, their death or their rescue. He shouldn't have said anything, George whispered, but they went back together a long way.

Marge Pierce had come a long way, too, from suburban Los Angeles and Banning High School in Wilmington. Lively and outgoing, she had majored in drama at City College of Los Angeles and starred in *Kiss Me, Kate* and other productions. But the applause didn't translate into invitations to audition for Broadway, and she sensibly enrolled in the Sawyer School of Business in Los Angeles. After graduation she accompanied a friend of her mother's on a visit to Cebu, the island in the Philippines where Ferdinand Magellan lost his life. As the only American girl on an island full of lonely American sailors, she had a much better time of it on Cebu than Magellan had. Three months later, when the invitation came to join the staff of Francis Sayre, the U.S. high commissioner in Manila, she took it gladly. The next two years, as the lights of peace faded in Europe and in Asia, were undimmed for the effervescent secretary. George Grey, her frequent escort to the various governmental functions, was the assistant legal officer in Sayre's office; he had an easy Western attitude, totally different from the stuffy Sayre, Marge thought, but the old man must have seen something special in George to bring him all the way out to the Philippines with him. It was just George's bad luck that when Sayre took his staff to the Rock—Corregidor—when the war started, George was in the hospital with dengue fever. By the time he was on his feet the Japanese had moved into Manila, and George was stuck with the rest of them.

On the morning of January 2, 1942, Virginia Hewlett and Marge were at their desks when Virginia looked out of the window at the American flag hanging limply from the pole in the acrid air. When the flag came down that day, it would be for the last time, they both knew, for a long time. Together they went in to see George Grey: the flag should be burned, they said, rather than allowed to fall into Japanese hands. Grey agreed. Marge, Virginia, and Elise Flahavan, another secretary, and Grey went down to the front yard, where he lowered the flag. They then went into the garden behind the house, where Grey paced off thirteen steps south from a towering flame tree there—one for each stripe of the flag—and another thirteen steps east, toward home. He spread the flag on the ground and placed three smaller flags on top of it. He gave each one of the three women a match, and the four Americans stood, each at a corner of the flag, and recited the Pledge of Allegiance. The four corners of the flag were lighted simultaneously; the smoke drifted into the heavy morning air as George stirred the burning flags until they were no more than a small pile of ashes.

The ashes cooled quickly. George placed them in a Hershey's cocoa tin from Commissioner Sayre's pantry. There was still room for a tightly folded sheet of paper, wrapped in oilskin. On the paper Marge Pierce had typed the following:

> "We, the undersigned, being American citizens, do on this second day of January, 1942, solemnly and with reverence take it into our hands to burn the flag of the United States of America to prevent it from falling into the hands of the Japanese army, and to bury the ashes together with this record on the grounds of the high commissioner's office."

That was more than three years ago. In the meantime Marge had shared many things with George Grey. She had comforted him on the night he learned that his Filipino fiancée was murdered by the Japanese, along with her entire family of eight people, for having a radio in their possession. She had cheered him during that silly softball game after the Red Cross comfort kits had arrived—apparently the kits were intended for a colder climate than the

Philippines, for they contained long woolen underwear for the men and flannel nightgowns for the ladies. The men suited themselves up in the long undies for an old-time softball game, while the women adapted the nighties for special cheerleader costumes, and everybody had a howling good time, thanks in no small part to the total bewilderment on the faces of the Japanese guards. And they had sat quietly together knitting. An elderly Chinese amah had given them both lessons and, using the cotton string wrapped around parcels in the comfort kits, she had made a skirt, a slipover, and a jacket, while he had labored long and at last successfully on a sweater.

They were like brother and sister, George said once—Marge grimaced but kept silent—and now that things looked at once bleak and hopeful, he felt she had a right to know as much as he did.

VIII

Mamatid: Thursday, February 22, 11:45 P.M.

Hank Burgess wandered through the campsite of the First Battalion with Lieutenant Colonel Gibbs. The men and the drivers were sacked out for the most part. They had spent the day being briefed on the mission—after two days of apparently aimless travel at a diagonal to Los Baños before they suddenly cut across country to the staging point. The alligators had rumbled in at dusk with their surprised commander, a courtly, polished man in his early forties. A sergeant interrupted their conversation with a disturbing message: A Filipino had just wandered into the camp and wanted to know if he could join the raid; he had heard that they were going to rescue the prisoners at Los Baños.

Hell, he didn't need this, Burgess thought as he walked over to the guard post. He wondered where Swing was; the general told him he intended to come by this evening, but he hadn't shown up yet. The Filipino was a fisherman in his forties who lived in a nearby village. He was missing half of his teeth and looked twice his years as he spat tobacco juice between grinning responses to

Burgess' questions. Why did the man think they were going to Los Baños? Where else? the man had replied, did they think he was stupid? No, Burgess said, they thought he might be a spy. If so, the man replied, why would he walk into their camp and reveal himself? Burgess puzzled over that one; perhaps the fisherman's friends, if they were Japs, had pushed him out as a pawn. If he failed to return, then they would know something was up. But that seemed farfetched. The hell with it, Burgess decided. They would either have to shoot him or take him with them. He chose the latter course and bundled the fisherman into the nearest amtrac for the ride to Los Baños.

IX

Eleventh Airborne Headquarters, Parañaque: Thursday, February 22, Midnight

Henry Muller, Doug Quandt, and General Swing stood around the sand tables for the Los Baños operation and considered what they should do now. A P-61 reconnaissance plane had just reported large numbers of enemy troops on the move in the Los Baños area, including what looked like trucks leaving from the internment camp.

It was either an alarming coincidence or something much worse: the American security had been breached, as Muller had feared all along, and the Japs were doing one of several things. They were moving the prisoners at Los Baños to another location; they were fleeing the camp again, leaving the prisoners behind as they had done before; or they were moving reinforcements in and around Los Baños to try to ambush the First Battalion and B Company when they arrived. Should they call off the raid at this late moment? It was Swing's decision to make. Characteristically, it did not take him long. The mission would go on as planned, he told Muller. There was no need to explain why. It was obvious that while they could easily pull back Ringler and Burgess, they had no sure way of warning Skau and his men, who were spread over several square miles of rice paddies by this time. The Division Recon Platoon and the guerrillas had reached the point of no return. They would hit the camp no matter what Swing did now, and when they did they would have to have someplace to take the internees—assuming, as he did, that the camp defenses itself were not the real problem, so much as the Japanese forces nearby. Swing had no other choice to make.

But it would not be a comfortable night. He told Muller to hunt up that young lieutenant, the West Pointer, whom Burgess had sent over to take him to Mamatid, and to have his Piper Cub ready for takeoff at 6:30 A.M. He wanted to watch everything from the air. In the meantime, he wanted an advanced division command post set up at Calamba and the Second Battalion of the 511th put on alert to support Soule and LaFlamme on the ground, if necessary.

By the time the suspected spy showed up at Mamatid and General Swing heard about the troop movements around Los Baños, scores of men were moving toward the camp. Ben Edwards was with a squad of six guerrillas and a corporal named Hotchkiss. Skau had told him to take his party to the southeast corner of the camp, the area he knew best from his firewood forays; they had left San Roque by banca shortly after dark and arrived without incident at the approach to the National Road about midnight. At that point one of the guerrillas frantically signaled the rest to halt —200 yards away the glowing ember of a cigarette pierced the darkness, and they heard voices speaking Japanese.

It was only a work party, they realized as they crept slowly around the soldiers, who were trying to repair a bridge. There were no further contacts, and by 6:45 they were securely hidden in the dense underbrush near the southeast gate, waiting for the first parachute to snap open in the morning sky. That was their signal to attack.

Throughout the night the guerrillas and the Recon Platoon had been moving into place, according to plans that had been set at the last briefings the morning before. Captain Tan's D Company set off overland from Nanghaya, cross-country through coconut plantations and rice paddies, arriving at the top of Faculty Hill at 4:00 A.M. The Huks and the Chinese Forty-eighth Squadron left shortly after Tan and were likewise in position by dawn; the Huks secured the cornfields east of the college, and the Forty-eighth stationed themselves from the line between the college railroad junction and the first bridge leading to the rock quarry. The Markings went by boat to San Roque, then proceeded to the point at Mayondong; there they set up roadblocks to prevent the Japanese from reinforcing the twenty troops at Mayondong and waited for the arrival of the amtracs. The PQOGs established themselves between the college junction and the camp.

The main guerrilla force, perhaps 100 members of the Hunters ROTC, left Nanghaya by boat shortly after midnight. The silent fleet of dozens of native craft of all sizes and descriptions eased their way along the shoreline, being careful to avoid the fish traps and floating islands of water hyacinths, until they reached the mouth of the Bay River. There they slipped quietly into the knee-deep water and reassembled near the village of San Antonio. A half dozen PQOG guides met them there to take them through the rice paddies to Los Baños, a distance of some eight miles. Heavily armed with extra incendiary and phosphorus grenades, in addition to their ten-pound M1 rifles and extra ammunition, the paratroopers struggled to follow the lightly clad guerrillas through the rice paddies. With each labored breath echoing hollowly underneath their helmets, they inhaled the gnats and mosquitoes that swarmed through the damp tropical night. By 6:00 A.M., an hour before the strike, the Hunters and the Eleventh troopers were well behind schedule, the results of slips off the earthen bridges into waist-deep water and erratic guidance by the PQOG guerrillas.

Elsewhere things were proceeding as planned. Burgess and Gibbs saw the First Battalion board the amtracs at 4:00 A.M. With the infantry troops were the nearly 100 men that made up Captain Lou Burris' D Battery of the 457th Field Artillery: four gun crews of six men each plus machine gunners and communications personnel. Burris, a lean, deceptively easygoing southern Californian, had received his orders earlier that afternoon from Doug Quandt with quiet pride. His battery was known to be the assignment of last resort for a lot of hard cases in the Eleventh, but he had shaped a bunch of malcontents and misfits, as they were widely perceived, into a tough and efficient fighting force. He assumed that he and his battery had been chosen for this mission because his four guns were the only assault guns available—and because they had performed so well during the recent landing at Nasugbu. He called his officers and NCOs together quickly. Get provisions for your men for three days, he told them. And that was all he could tell them. It wasn't until later that evening that he had a chance to read his orders, which were astonishingly precise in their details, right down to which prisoners were staying in which barracks.

Those details were a tribute in part to the memory of a man whose name Lou Burris would not hear until forty years later, but who was very much with the Eleventh Airborne as the amtracs ground their way into the water in the predawn blackness. Pete Miles, desperately tired from his long journey and from the tension that accompanied his mission, had nevertheless talked the planners of the rescue into letting him return to his friends at Los Baños. He could be of no further use in Parañaque, he argued. They owed him this favor. He had to go back. Now, as the soldiers around him wondered nervously whether the bonfires that the Filipino villagers around Los Baños had unaccountably lit would tip their hand to the enemy, Pete Miles sat with the nervous fisherman who had wandered into Burgess' camp. No, he assured the fisherman, he would certainly not be shot. Not, at least, by the Americans.

16

THE ANGELS LAND AT DAWN

I

Nichols Field: Friday, February 23, 6:30 A.M.

Major Don Anderson looked from his window at the quiet, bulky shapes of the paratroopers climbing the ladder into his lead plane. Behind him, almost invisible in the predawn darkness, the eight other planes sat in line. He checked his watch: 6:26. Fourteen minutes to takeoff, four 'til engine start-up. The jump master stuck his head in the door of the cockpit. Ready when he was, the sergeant said. Anderson nodded and leaned back. It was the quiet time, he thought, just before action. Time to get nervous and think about everything that could go wrong, like an actor waiting in the wings before the stage lights go on and the curtain comes up.

He had some pre-performance butterflies in the gut, Anderson had to admit. But they weren't from fear of screwing up. It wouldn't be a milk run, that was for sure: to get nine planes over the drop zone, the first, his, at precisely 7:00 on the dot, no give or take a minute or two, would be a challenge. And they'd be low enough for the Japs to throw rocks at them if there were any around. But Doug Quandt had assured him that the guerrillas were covering the slopes of Mount Makiling like a rug—nobody would be shooting at them. And there would be plenty of fighter protection from P-38s, at least a dozen of them scheduled to strafe the roads north and south of Los Baños to keep the Japs in line.

And he certainly wasn't worried about his own competence, or that of the other eight pilots. They had all been doing this for two years, all the way from the jump schools at Bragg and Benning, then training with gliders in Nebraska. They were a pickup group, to be sure, but among them they'd flown missions everywhere in the Pacific from Guadalcanal to New Guinea to the Philippines, and they had been pulled together for this mission because they knew how to fly these lumbering buggies low and slow—not like those clowns who'd dropped the 511th at Tagaytay Ridge at 140 miles an hour and spread them over five miles of rock.

No, they would all be just fine once they were in the air. But first they had to get into the air. Peering down the remains of what had once been a major airfield, Anderson wondered again whether or not they would all get off the ground. Three weeks of battle had left it looking, only a few days before, more like Verdun than a runway, and he had not been overwhelmed by the hurried patch job done by the engineers. He had walked the length of the runway the day before, noticing the soft spots where the crater holes had been filled with gravel, half of which exploded outward every time the wheel of a big plane hit it. The next big wheel to hit one of those half-empty holes might burst or twist, buckling the strut and sending the plane into a cartwheel.

The bad spots were clear enough to a pilot's keen eyes in the bright light of day and could be avoided. But at 6:40 the sun would be not quite over the horizon, and the runway patches and ruts would all run together with the asphalt surface in a deceptive black sameness—unless it was gray with the low-clinging, early-morning ground fog, which would be even worse.

Anderson had talked the situation over with the other pilots. They were worried, too. "How about setting the drop time back to seven-fifteen from seven o'clock?" he had asked Doug Quandt. He'd have brought the matter up sooner, but he'd only been informed of the raid that morning. Quandt was doubtful: there were more than 100 men prepared to start shooting at the guard posts at 7:00, spread all over the damn jungle right now and not set to be in position until just before the attack. There was no way for them to be notified of a change in time. If they started firing and there was no support from the air, the Japs could put up a pretty stiff defense. They'd certainly have time to kill a bunch of people inside the camp, as they had at Palawan. But he'd ask the old man.

General Swing sat up on his cot looking tired and grumpy; he'd been up all night and was catching a nap when Anderson arrived at the HQ with his request at about 1:00 P.M. on the twenty-second. He swung his legs around so that his feet were on the floor and took off the jungle sweater he had been wearing, tossing it into the corner. Quandt introduced Major Anderson and explained the pilot's request clearly and neutrally. Swing thought for about five seconds. Then he looked the young pilot in the eye. "Young man," he said, "the time is seven sharp, and you'd goddam better be there."

At 6:40 Don Anderson's plane, followed by eight others, taxied into place, roared down the pocked and pitted runway, and immediately climbed 3,000 feet into the morning sun.

II

Los Baños Internment Camp: Friday, February 23, 7:00 A.M.

George Skau was still three hundred yards from the camp and his assigned position when he heard the heavy throbbing sounds of the C-47s. Damn! he thought—his Filipino guides had picked the worst possible time to get him and his men lost in the rice paddies approaching Los Baños. They were all bathed in sweat despite the early morning coolness from their frantic last-minute dash. Halting his men and the guerrillas, Skau watched as the first V formation of planes approached—so low! he thought. And so slow—they lumbered along at less than 100 miles per hour. Skau signaled to his men and they charged at a dead run toward the compound. From the corner of his eye the lieutenant saw the plume of white smoke from Haggerty's phosphorous grenade, marking the drop zone. Two miles away, he knew, similar grenades were telling Gibbs where to land his amtracs. He glanced up quickly as the lead C-47 passed overhead, in time to see the first man out— Captain John Ringler. "Move it!" he shouted. They had to hit the guards before B Company hit the ground.

* * *

Everything had happened so quickly that by the time Skau's men hit the camp the guards were still at their exercises, as promised. Skau led his men on a dead run past the enemy soldiers, ignoring them for the moment as they raced for the stacked and locked weapons fifty yards away. They won the race, and the frantic guards scattered for the fences. Most of them headed for the ravine behind the hospital, the same route so often taken by departing internees. Some of them made it; most did not. Skau had dropped his bazooka and grabbed a carbine after the guards' weapons had been seized. The commandant's headquarters was the next building. As he ran up the steps a Japanese officer ran from behind his desk and dived through the window at the rear of the office. Skau shot him in midair and he was dead before he hit the ground.

The attack was so overwhelming and so violent that by the time Ben Edwards and his squad entered the fence by the southeast corner he could only see one Japanese soldier. It was a guard from the post where Ben had accidentally tossed a smoke grenade instead of a fragmentation grenade. The guard dived into a culvert and a paratrooper casually tossed a grenade behind him. The muffled thud was not loud enough to drown out the soldier's death cries. Another guard closer to the barracks Ben had been assigned to clear of internees also tried to escape by hiding in a pipe. A guerrilla stood at one end firing into the pipe, forcing the guard to crawl out the other end, where a second guerrilla with a bolo beheaded him.

In the midst of this carnage, Ben found himself thinking that the tracer bullets whizzing through the camp looked like floating red tennis balls. He felt a light stinging sensation on his bare shins and saw that they were bleeding from shell or rock fragments. He moved on, past the piggery and Harold Bayley's shack. Bayley, he could see, was just poking his head out from under a huge kettle. Ben waved him back and ran on. It wasn't all over yet, by any means.

When John Ringler and the first stick of jumpers left the lead plane, Bob Fletcher had not seen them. He had been deep in the bowels of the first plane in the third V, on the middle stick, and he wasn't anxious to look to see what was happening. When his turn came he vowed to jump with his eyes shut—he wasn't sure he'd have the guts to go if he looked down. But at the last moment he couldn't resist looking. When he did, he froze—not from fright but from indecision. Below him, swinging back and forth like a giant pendulum, was a trooper whose static line had caught on the underpart of the plane's fuselage. If Fletcher landed on the trooper, he would kill him for certain, and probably himself as well. But if he didn't go, the timing of the jump would be thrown off so much that they would land far from the drop zone. He watched the unlucky soldier swing beneath him, tugging frantically at his emergency release, waited until he was out of sight underneath the plane, and leaped as far out from the open door as he could. His chute opened properly; he twisted his head in the direction the plane was heading, toward Makiling. The dangling trooper had finally freed himself and was floating down beside him 100 yards away. But when he turned back toward the drop zone, Bob saw Tom Zaharias plummeting through the air, in free fall. His chute, the special camouflaged chute Fletcher was supposed to have, was not opening, the Filipino realized with horror. Finally, hardly 100 feet from the ground, the chute opened and the big sergeant landed—landed hard, but safely.

Fletcher was happy to realize that he had remembered to flex his knees and roll when he hit the ground. He was still beaming with pride at his successful first jump when a pal, Mike Desko, ran up to help him out of his harness and to point out to him that he was likely to blow himself up if he didn't clean the dirt out of his carbine muzzle, which he had neglected to keep out of the mud. Desko, Fletcher, and Zaharias ran toward the camp. The company had all landed in the drop zone but didn't stop to regroup. Each had his assignment at the camp, and they were all to get there without delay.

On the south side of the camp Freddy Zervoulakas waited anxiously for the first chutes to pop. He was not afraid—not in the presence of the big American beside him, the radio operator from New Jersey who had taken him under his wing. There had been some time in Ortiz's camp for John Fulton to show the boy something about hand-to-hand combat, especially against a soldier with a bayonet. Two days of drill with the six-foot-two-inch,

190-pound American had given the slightly built eighteen-year-old confidence that he could hold his own against any Jap soldier, though he knew that the American could have broken his back in a minute in a serious fight. No, his bad moments had all come the night before. The first had been about midnight, when Fulton asked him how close he thought they could get to the camp. Freddy had said about twenty-five yards, in the high grass. Fulton had stretched out comfortably for a nap; Freddy didn't understand how he could be so cool, especially after operating a radio behind Jap lines for three weeks, waiting for them to home in on him with their direction finders. Freddy wondered if he would see his family again. Tears rolled down his cheeks and he said to himself, "Mama, Papa, I love you all." Then he felt Fulton's big hand on his shoulder. He would be Freddy's family, he said. He'd never had a kid brother before. They'd both be fine.

Freddy fell contentedly asleep. The next bad moment, a few hours later, was of a different kind. It was 4:00 A.M. and Eddie, the advance scout, stopped them with the word that a four-man Japanese patrol was about to pass them. Fulton and Freddy hid beside the road as the patrol passed, then watched as they stopped a young Filipino woman who was walking down the road, carrying a baby. The Japanese sergeant questioned the young woman abruptly as the guerrilla patrol watched. She shook her head angrily, and the sergeant pushed her to the ground. She lay there with the baby as a soldier thrust his bayonet at her. Freddy pulled out the enormous revolver that he had somehow acquired but felt Fulton's huge hand cover his. "We can't do anything, Freddy. You shoot them and we've destroyed the mission."

They could do it quickly and quietly, Freddy insisted. No, Fulton said. Remember the cable. The cable . . . Two days earlier, on February 21, Espino ("Colonel Price") had given Fulton a radio message that added a sense of desperate need to his mission. The message was coded "Urgent," from Espino to Vanderpool: "Have received reliable information that Japs have Los Baños scheduled for massacre Suggest that enemy positions in Los Baños proper as explained Muller be bombed as soon as possible." Freddy understood. If the Japs planned to massacre the internees so they couldn't be rescued, then any clue that rescue was on the way—such as a vanished patrol—might mean the execution time would be moved up: they would arrive in time to bury the people they had intended to save.

They watched in silence as the sergeant dragged the woman to her feet and the patrol disappeared down the road. Freddy and Fulton had hit the main gate with fifteen other guerrillas at seven sharp and were on their way to the gymnasium when Freddy knelt to take aim at some fleeing soldiers. Suddenly he felt a rough hand enclose his shoulder and found himself facedown in the dust. He heard a bullet hiss past his ear and the chatter of a carbine above him. Fulton had seen a guard sighting on Freddy and saved his life by knocking him down. He grinned broadly at the boy as he pulled him from the dirt. "You're okay, kid. Told you I'd look out for you, didn't I?"

George Mora gave up the attempt to record the events of the day in his diary when an American paratrooper burst into his barracks followed by three Filipino guerrillas wearing bright feathers behind their ears and shouting Mabuhay! Get ready to move out, the soldier yelled, "Toot sweet!" He disappeared. Bullets continued to rattle through the nipa walls as George strapped on the bayonet he had found in the jungle while on wood-gathering patrol. He assumed that the main advance of the American Army had arrived and that they were clearing the area of all Japanese soldiers. It didn't occur to him that this was a special mission just for them.

George had to get from barracks No. 25 to his parents in barracks No. 7. There were hundreds of men racing through the camp—Japanese guards fleeing with guerrillas in hot pursuit, charging in and out of the barracks, and bullets flying everywhere, so George cut through the lines of barracks. The married couples and their children, he noticed, had taken cover in the ditches outside the barracks, covering the children with their bodies. He saw flames beginning to spread through barracks No. 3, one of the pair the guards occupied. Not more than 100 feet away, in barracks No. 7, he found his mother in a panic but his father casually stirring a pot of boiling rice mush for their breakfast. George told them to forget about breakfast and get packed; he said he didn't know if they would be coming back, so they had better take whatever was valuable with them. He'd be back in a couple of minutes, George said.

The flames were beginning to spread to the second Japanese barracks, No. 4, as George left for his own. P-38s were cavorting through the air. A girl he did not recognize was being carried by two Filipinos on a stretcher; she was holding her side and crying with pain. He hurried into his cubicle and threw everything he could think of into a box: a poplin jacket, the notebook he had been writing in and a pen, the records for the class of '47, his good Keds.

The mush was still boiling on his parents' stove when George rushed in and dropped his box on the floor so hard that it fell apart. He put on the new Keds—new in 1941, but still not worn —and tossed the old shoes into a corner. A soldier ran through and ordered them all outside. They left the mush on the stove and moved cautiously into the street, carrying two suitcases, a handbag, a ragged bundle of clothes that his mother had thrown together, and a small bag of canned goods, their only remaining food.

The street outside the barracks was crowded with people now, all moving toward the athletic field. What looked like tanks to George were rumbling along the edges of the camp, plowing into and through the ditches dug by the guards. One of the tanks was dragging a length of clothesline that nearly tripped George as it roared by. Another, painted blue, roared toward the piggery. Two paratroopers stood talking, one an officer and the other a corporal, who was holding his bleeding arm. George and his parents stopped as they walked by the soldiers. Did they know about Konishi? they asked the soldiers. The officer wrote the name down in a notebook.

The prisoners had been reacting to their sudden deliverance as might be expected—in 100 different ways. A woman shouted at Ben Edwards as he entered a barracks full of older men and carefully placed a smoke bomb in one corner to get them to leave. He couldn't understand what she was saying until he saw she was pointing at Sniffen, the black marketeer. "Kill him!" she shouted. Sniffen was hurrying toward the amtracs with two large suitcases, carrying his fat Siamese cat and followed by his obese wife, Genevieve. A group of prisoners swarmed over a Filipino guerrilla who was drawing a bead on an escaping Japanese guard, smothering him with hugs and spoiling his aim. Another guerrilla was mistaken for a guard and threatened with death at the hands of prisoners until a paratrooper intervened.

John Wightman had accepted a cigarette from a tall trooper named Grant Gentry and smoked it so quickly, in three gasping puffs, that the cinder burned his fingers.

Charles and Henrietta Glunz, the elderly missionary couple, had learned of what was happening from the woman in the cubicle, who was scraping the grease from her frying pan (sounds traveled through the walls as though they were curtains). "John," Henrietta heard the woman say to her husband, "what are those swooshing sounds?" "Madam," the husband had replied, "those are bullets." "Oh, is that so?" the woman had replied, resuming her scraping. Charles himself had been stirring their morning pittance of rice when an explosive bullet landed a few feet away. Going to the door, he observed a frantic Japanese soldier rushing past him, his eyes glazed with fright and his bayonet fixed. Charles merely stepped back and returned to his rice as the soldier fled from the barracks.

They had heard American voices shouting a minute or two later, and Charles wanted to stop the soldier who dashed past him to ask where his hometown was, but he felt shy about bothering someone who was so busy. They ignored a Filipino guerrilla who ordered them to get out of the barracks because they still had not finished packing. But when a towering American sergeant gently said, "Sir, you must leave now," the couple had picked up their diary and the rasp that cost Charles ten dollars and gone out to the loading area. There Charles had gathered up several of the .50-mm shells that littered the ground as souvenirs for their three grandchildren. Charles had lived for many years in dangerous parts of the world, and he knew something about weapons. He was surprised to see that the .50-caliber shells were so much larger than the .45-caliber shells with which he was familiar.

Carol Terry, whose faith had been so severely tested by her illness and feeling of humiliation, crouched behind her stacked suitcases and stared blankly at the paratrooper before her. Why did he look like a German soldier? she wondered. The last American soldier she had seen wore the shallow saucerlike helmets that the doughboys in World War I had used. This man was wearing a huge helmet that covered his ears and shadowed his eyes, and she was momentarily frightened. "You got five minutes, miss," he said, "to get all your stuff and yourself outside." It took her three minutes of total immobility to realize that her prayers had finally been answered—and only sixty seconds after that to get moving as she had been told.

When her husband, Coit, rushed in to tell her what was happening, Louise Craven reacted quickly. She put the baby she had just finished nursing, or attempting to nurse, into his basket and stuffed his clothes into a pillowcase. A few more clothes at hand were tossed into another suitcase. Then she and Coit both looked over their heads to the rafters where most of their possessions were stored. They agreed to leave the heavy and inaccessible suitcases behind and started to leave with the baby. Then Louise turned to reenter the barracks. Coit watched, amazed. "Where in the world are you going?" he shouted. Louise told him: she had eaten every meal for the past year and a half off that one terrible china plate with the big chip out of it. The plate was on top of the small clay stove behind the barracks, and she had sworn to smash it into pieces the day they were freed. That's what she was going to do now, she told her husband. Smash that damned china plate! Coit took her firmly by the elbow and led her away from the barracks. He was very careful not to laugh.

When they reached the staging area some of the internees were reminded of the scene at Santo Tomás three years earlier, when they had been deposited with all their worldly goods in the courtyard of the old university. Then they had been alarmed and angry but unhurried, and some, like George Mora's family, had been able to provide for themselves very well. Now they were on the one hand exhilarated at their sudden release from captivity and death and on the other bitter at being forced to leave behind their few miserable possessions. Many, like Ernest Mora and Frank Bennett, had been wealthy men and were now paupers.

The internees had shown up with all sorts of possessions: carefully packed and utterly worthless broken toys, cans of Spam, bags of clothes so ragged they were beyond mending, boxes of *Reader's Digest*s and *Time* magazines from before the war—all the residue and detritus that, otherwise meaningless, had been their only links to the world they had known. Gently but firmly, the soldiers told them they could only take a bag or two each. They had to choose.

Watching them as they milled about in the staging area, waiting for the amtracs to drop their gates and give them refuge, the soldiers could sense the violent waves of emotion that surged through the crowd.

It was only a little more than an hour since the raid had started, and they had gone through the fullest range of human emotions during that time—from apprehension on the part of many that they would be executed at the morning roll call to stunned incomprehension at their good fortune, and finally, to a state of dizzy and rapturous happiness. After three years, unbelievably their troubles were over. For the many internees who were missionaries and nuns and priests, the moment was God-given, and the tired, dirty young men of the Eleventh Airborne were the heaven-sent angels who had landed at dawn. They clustered around the soldiers, pressing them with questions and receiving—against Ringler's orders—food and cigarettes in return. The chatter was wonderfully inane. A young girl asked a soldier if they were Marines. No, he said, they were GIs, paratroopers. What were GIs? she asked. It was a term, like pinup girl, amtracs, and a thousand others that she had never heard before. Soldiers, he replied, grinning. "Oh," she sighed. "I've been waiting for three years for the Marines," she said and turned sadly away. Another paratrooper thought he was having better luck. None of them had seen a pretty American girl for more than a year, and despite their hunger, all the girls looked blooming from the excitement. He was given a hug by a scantily clad young woman. "Hold on, sister," he said. He was busy but he'd see her later. Unfortunately, she really was a "sister"; the next time he saw her she had found her nun's habit and was boarding an amtrac, the name of which, implausibly, was "the Impatient Virgin."

Harold Bayley, for his part, had been burning with curiosity for some time about the meaning of those letters on the pack of cigarettes he had been given. "What *does* LSMFT mean?" he demanded of a young private. The private, a blond, innocent-looking lad of about nineteen, said, "Let's screw; my finger's tired."

Hank Burgess was having his own communication problems at that moment. The most worrisome was that he had not been able to make radio contact with the 188th, and he had no idea how far down Highway 1 LaFlamme and Soule had come with the support he would need if the Japs came up from the south in force. He had sent Amos Giddings off to scout a bridge right after they had crashed through the camp gates, and Giddings had nearly got himself killed. Trapped behind a tree by a Jap machine gun, he had reached into his baggy trouser-leg pocket to get a grenade only to find that all the powder had fallen out because the caps weren't screwed on tightly. Fortunately, Giddings had been as cool under pressure as he had been careless beforehand; he'd leaned up against the tree while the bullets whistled past him, scraped enough powder from his pocket to reload the grenades, and taken out the machine gun. But he suggested, upon returning to report to Burgess, that there might be more resistance than they had anticipated.

Lieutenant Colonel Gibbs had been particularly alarmed by the activity in and around the camp. It was obvious that Burgess was not going to get all these people loaded before noon, he said—by which time the Japs would surely have light artillery and mortars to threaten their retreat across the lake. The amtracs would be sitting ducks. He thought it would be best if he took the stretcher cases who were now being loaded and left the Eleventh and the internees to be evacuated by truck.

Burgess considered his response. He didn't even know if the 188th was going to arrive at all, much less with the trucks. What, he was about to ask, did the colonel expect the major to do with the more than 2,000 people in his charge, if not load them onto his scows and get the hell out of here? At that moment Ringler and Skau reported, their shirts black with sweat. The camp was secure, they said, but they were having a hard time getting the older people, especially, out of the barracks. The four officers stood and looked at the blazing Japanese guards barracks. Half the camp was about to go up in smoke. They might as well do the whole thing. "Fire the rest of the barracks," Burgess ordered. That would get them all out if nothing else would.

Within twenty minutes black, billowing clouds of smoke had risen from the upwind side of the camp and hundreds of internees were streaming toward the evacuation area by Baker Hall. By 9:15 Gibbs and his fifty-two functioning amtracs were on their way to the beach with some 1,400 internees. They would have to come back across the lake to pick up the remaining internees and the soldiers in the afternoon.

The loading had gone more quickly than anticipated because one of the few significant errors in intelligence concerning Los Baños was the estimate of the number of stretcher cases that would have to be given special attention. Even Pete Miles had failed to correct the standing impression that as many as 500 persons, or nearly a quarter of the camp's population, were seriously incapacitated. As it turned out, there were only about 150 people who were too weak or too sick to make their own way to the amtrac loading area.

Among those who were unable to walk to the amtracs was a very recent patient in the camp hospital, a Catholic missionary named Sister Mary Trinita. Sister Mary had been allowed to live in a French convent until April 1944, when she was taken to Santiago Prison for interrogation about her suspected activities in aid of the Filipino guerrillas. Her punishment would be slight if she signed a confession immediately, she was told. When she refused, she was returned to her cell. At 2:00 A.M. she was awakened and questioned for three hours, a pattern that would be repeated at various times of the day or night for the next four weeks. Sister Mary was subjected to the water treatment three times, but she steadfastly refused to sign a confession, and the questioning eventually ceased in mid-July. But she languished in her cell, losing seventy-five pounds, until she was eventually transferred to Los Baños on January 1, 1945.

Ironically, one of those who had to be carried aboard was Pete Miles himself. Ben Edwards had not seen Miles since the engineer left for Parañaque several days earlier and was shocked to see him being carried by on a stretcher, his face drawn and pale under his light blond beard. He held a Garand rifle across his chest. What was wrong, Ben asked. Had he been hit? No, he was just plain tired, Miles admitted. Somehow, when it was clear that the operation was going to be a success, or at least that they had managed to surprise the Japs and everyone seemed to be safe, all the energy had simply drained from his body. He'd collapsed in a heap. He glanced down at the Garand and told Ben to keep it safe for him. It wasn't a damn bit of good as a weapon, but he'd sure like to have it as a souvenir.

Fully loaded at last, the amtracs rolled through the front gates that they had smashed two hours before. Hundreds of villagers stood by their houses, waving and cheering, and ignoring, like the internees, the occasional rattle of bullets bouncing off the steel skins of the alligators. At the beach most of the machines rolled without hesitation into the lake, astonishing many of the passengers. There had been no time to explain to some that these were not real tanks but amphibious tractors. Not armadillos but turtles, as one GI put it. Charles Glunz was not surprised, however. Fascinated as always by mechanical contrivances, he had admired the way the tailgate on his vehicle operated by means of a wire rope and a windlass, and he knew that the rubber gasket at the base of the tailgate must be intended to keep out water. However, his wife was worried that their small bag of possessions, sitting on the floor of the amtrac, would get wet because she could see water seeping in under the floorboards. Charles stood up and looked out to see how the other vehicles were getting rid of the water. Aha, he said with satisfaction as he sat down beside his wife. There were streams of water pouring from pipes across the front of the vehicles. They must have double bottoms and pumps that would keep them perfectly dry. There was only one problem, Charles realized. For the first time since he had been imprisoned, and since aspirin had become all but unavailable, he had a headache.

There were other headaches, some potentially deadly, for the approximately 500 internees and the paratroopers who had to hike the nearly three-mile distance to the beach. Japanese machine guns chattered fiercely from the depths of the jungle, and from caves beneath the headlands that rose from the beach. Burris had solved the problem of the cave guns in a very ingenious manner —it was impossible to train his assault guns directly upon the enemy, so he aimed them at the palm trees on top of the cliff above the cave. The resulting showers of splinters, leaves, and shattered coconuts probably didn't hurt the enemy gunners, Burris knew, but it sure made them quiet down.

The scattered fire from the jungle was no more effective, fortunately, but the straggling line of hikers had no way of knowing that. One big soldier named Jake Muntz shielded a baby in his arms, glowering fiercely at his buddies' taunts and offering to settle any questions about his virility when they got to the beach. A woman who was leaving the camp with the fruits of a different kind of labor—the music she had written over the past three years —grimaced from the pain of the twine on her thin fingers, and smiled gratefully when Lou Burris offered to carry some of her compositions. Shots rattled the leaves above their heads, closer than most had been up until now. The captain watched with wondering admiration as the woman dived for cover in a ditch, executing a perfect three-point roll. When the firing ceased she dusted herself off with all the aplomb of a seasoned combat veteran, retrieved her tattered parcels, and continued on her way to the beach.

Another determined woman, Isla Corfield, struggled along the dusty road carrying the heavy suitcases that contained her diaries of the past three long years carefully hidden from the Japanese under the floor of her barracks. Her daughter Gill carried a small red suitcase. Three nurses who had commandeered a garbage wagon came by and offered to help with Isla's bags, but a wheel soon came off. The Englishwoman hoisted the heavy bags from the cart and struggled on down the road, but her strength gave out. She sank to her knees beside the road. She would have to leave the diaries, leave three years of her life in a ditch. "Oh God," she sighed, "poor old diary." She fell back, drained of energy and full of intense frustration. "Hi, Missy! Can we help?" She looked up through her tears and saw two guerrillas, no bigger than their rifles, she thought. The Filipinos shouldered her bags and they moved on, following in the dust of the amtracs.

By eleven o'clock the camp was cleared and almost everyone was gathered at the beach. Hank Burgess had solved his earlier communications problems with Lieutenant Colonel Gibbs when he had told the colonel point blank that this was his mission, not the colonel's, and that he would, by damn, get these people loaded onto his alligators. The problem of communicating with the internees had been solved by burning the barracks in which they were cowering. But the failure to find out what the 188th was doing still remained: even the distant shelling they had heard earlier ceased. If Gibbs didn't get back with his amtracs soon to take the rest of them back to safety, there would be 1,000 people sitting on an indefensible beach for the Japanese to destroy at will.

LaFlamme's 188th had been stalled, Burgess later learned, by a blown bridge across an arroyo. The troops that the reconnaissance plane had spotted the night before and that Swing had decided to ignore had been moved north in response to Japanese intelligence reports on the movement of the amtracs out of Manila. Fortunately, the amtracs had been mistakenly identified as tanks; the Japanese had assumed the tanks would be proceeding along Highway 1, not floating across the lake, and had moved to intercept them when they were not.

For the moment, though, all Burgess knew was that General Swing was on the radio. Flying several hundred feet overhead in his spotter plane, Swing congratulated Burgess on the success of the mission. How long would it take Burgess to get the rest of the internees loaded onto the amtracs when they returned? Burgess replied that it should take about two hours if they were lucky. Swing then said that after the rest of the internees were safely on the amtracs it might be a good move for Burgess to take the Eleventh back through Los Baños and link up with the 188th.

Burgess broke off the radio contact and stood silent for a moment. A twenty-six-year-old major from the Wyoming National Guard had just heard a general considering an order to commit the lives of some 500 men to a military objective. To the north, between him and the 188th, lay at least three and perhaps ten miles of territory infested with Japanese troops, including those at the impregnable rock quarry; to the south lay the major Japanese defensive force for central Luzon, some 10,000 veterans of every campaign from Manchuria through Leyte.

Around him on the beach perhaps 1,000 people sat wearily on the sand. The initial exuberance of both the prisoners and the soldiers had worn off and they chatted quietly in small groups. The firing from Mayodong Point had dropped off. Except for the ragged clothes of the internees, the stained olive-drab uniforms of the soldiers, and the scattered piles of suitcases and boxes, the scene might have looked like the tag end of a beach party, it was so quiet.

But to Burgess it was the eye of the hurricane. His tanned, trim soldiers might look invincibly fit to the hungry internees, each one worth his weight in puny Japs, but Burgess knew better. They had been going on sheer adrenaline, all of them, for a month now, and for the past two days they'd had next to no sleep. They had given all their rations to the prisoners. Now they were being faced with the prospect of a six- or eight-hour forced march through enemy territory. The young major watched General Swing's plane disappear and told his signalmen to stow the radio. They wouldn't be needing it anymore. Then he waited for the amtracs to return.

Irene Wightman was one of those who waited anxiously on the beach for the returning amtracs. She knew nothing of the decisions that were being made—knew only that she felt a deep and abiding happiness when she saw the last of the soldiers who had come to rescue her board the amtracs and leave the beach at Mayondong Point safely behind. The desperate attempts of the enemy to hit the departing amtracs with mortars lobbed from the headland above the beach were alarming—geysers spouted uncomfortably close to the slow-moving alligators, but the drivers were able to prevent the enemy from bracketing them by weaving unpredictably as they pulled out of range.

As the sound of the mortars receded, Irene sat snugly with her baby beneath the feet of a paratrooper who was busily firing his machine gun in the direction of the cave that Lou Burris had showered with coconuts, and that was now active again. She gazed with admiration at the soldier. Her husband, John, like most of the men in the camp, had lost so much weight that she hardly knew him as the man she had married. The blond young paratrooper, bareheaded and shirtless in the muggy heat, was tanned, tautly muscled, intense. . . . He was beautiful, Irene mused, just plain beautiful. Like a Greek god. Or like a Hollywood star who had just walked off of a movie poster into her life . . . to save her. Imagine that!

Suddenly Irene felt a sharp burning sensation on her lower neck, a searing, soaring pain. Oh my God! she thought, biting her lip. To go through all of this and then get shot. Across from her, through her tears, she saw blurred, happy faces. She hugged her baby, nearly forgotten in her adoration of the young paratrooper, to her breast. It's not fair, she thought through her pain. It's just not fair. . . .

Thirty minutes later, when the amtracs landed, Irene Wightman was loaded into an ambulance along with a wounded soldier, who sat stiffly in the front seat holding a large blood-soaked bandage over his upper arm and shoulder. The driver asked Irene how she was feeling, and she was embarrassed to have to admit that the pain was almost gone. Let's have a look, he said, lifting up the back of her blouse. When he did so, a 30 caliber shell fell onto the ground—a spent shell from the gun her Greek god had been operating with such flair had blown into the air and down her back! Her only wound was a slight burn from the hot shell.

Irene blushed, the wounded GI smiled faintly, and the ambulance took off for New Bilibid Prison. On the way, Irene's two older children and an elderly man in the back seat kept exclaiming over the abundance of fresh fruit for sale at stalls along the road and begged the driver to stop. Irene was embarrassed by their lack of consideration for the wounded soldier, and she told the children to be quiet. The soldier motioned the driver to stop at the next stall. Then he got out and, holding his shoulder, bought a bunch of bananas for the hungry children and the old man, whose hands quivered so that he could hardly raise the fruit to his mouth.

AFTERMATH

The Death of Lieutenant Konishi

We have no record of the feelings of Diana, the All-American Girl, about her return to New Bilibid Prison at Muntinglupa from the beach at Mamatid (it was the same place where she had spent some time a few years before the war). For the rest of the ex-internees, we can assume that the irony of being rescued from one jail only to move into another was not lost on most of them but that it meant less to them than the aroma of fresh bread, chow lines where they could eat themselves sick, and did, and hot showers.

For the internees the war was over: by March 8 the last of them had left the carefully prepared facilities at New Bilibid—either, like Frank Bennett and the Mora family, to return to their ruined homes and businesses in Manila, now securely in American hands; or, like Harold Bayley, Isla Corfield, and William Donald, to their homes halfway across the world.

For the men of the Eleventh, February 23 was merely another long day's work, a little shorter than some because they were through by late afternoon, a little longer on civilized amenities than many because they had a hot meal—a most welcome meal because they had given their rations to the internees. And it was much more gratifying than most; it was not simply that none of them had been killed or even seriously injured, miraculous though that was. It was rather that all their military prowess, training, and luck had combined to save lives rather than to take them.

But the resolution of the plight at Los Baños was not entirely a happy one. On the evening of February 23, Federico Ramos, a professor at the college at Los Baños, left the village to stay with friends on Faculty Hill. A few nights later they watched flames rising from the Roman Catholic church, where some of the townspeople had taken refuge. Helen Espino, who had warned the townspeople to leave, also watched from a safe vantage point in the hills. Two weeks later American forces advanced to Los Baños. The next time Hank Burgess and his men saw the village it was in ashes. The Japanese had tied hundreds of people—men, women, and children—to the stilts that held their houses above the ground. Then they had set fire to the houses. The stench of the carnage was beyond description. Burgess estimated that about 1,400 people had died.

In July 1945, Hank Carpenter, a Colgate-Palmolive executive who had been interned at Los Baños, was playing golf at the Wack Wack Golf Club in Manila when a work crew passed him; it was filling in some of the holes left by the fighting. One of the laborers had a familiar limp. It was Lieutenant Konishi, who had been captured and assigned to help clean up some of the rubble left in the wake of the fighting.

On May 27, 1946, Colonel Ed Lahti and Lieutenant Colonel Henry Muller were sent by General Eichelberger from Japan to Luzon Prisoner of War Camp 1 to interview Major General Masatoshi Fujishige, former commander of the Japanese Eighth Infantry Division, which was responsible for defending Japanese positions around Los Baños. Fujishige, wrote "Fly" Flanagan later, "was a small, middle-aged man, very soldierly in appearance. He was cooperative and volunteered information freely; he had a keen memory and appeared to enjoy the discussion of his campaign. He was proud, self-confident, and even boastful, but not arrogant.

"His ruthlessness and cruelty were revealed by a captured order in which he directed: 'Kill all American soldiers brutally; do not kill with one stroke. Kill all Filipinos who oppose our emperor.' During his trial as a war criminal he fully admitted to the massacre of thousands of civilians and added that 'he had been conducting a war and left such mere details to his staff.' For his war crimes Fujishige received the death penalty."

On June 24, 1946, Lieutenant Konishi was accused in an affidavit filed by the chief of the Legal Section, General Headquarters, Supreme Commander for the Allied Forces, of four counts of murder. The specifications were as follows:

SPECIFICATIONS

1. In that Sadaaki Konishi, on or about 28 February 1945 and during a time of war between the United States of America, its allies and Japan, did, at or near Los Baños, Laguna Province, Philippine Islands, willfully and unlawfully order or permit members of the Imperial Japanese Army then under his command to kill David Gardner, an American citizen, his wife, Florence Gardner, their infant son, James Gardner, Silverio Seguerra, an unarmed noncombatant Filipino citizen and shoot fifty other unarmed, noncombatant Filipino civilians, in violation of the laws of war.

2. In that Sadaaki Konishi, on or about 6 March 1945 and during a time of war between the United States of America, its allies and Japan, did, at or near Los Baños, Laguna Province, Philippine Islands, willfully and unlawfully order or permit members of the Imperial Japanese Army then under his command to kill Ang Kai and about sixty other unarmed, noncombatant Chinese and Filipino civilians, in violation of the laws of war.

3. In that Sadaaki Konishi, on or about 6 March 1945, and during a time of war between the United States of America, its allies and Japan, did, at or near Los Baños, Laguna Province, Philippine Islands, willfully or unlawfully order or permit members of the Imperial Japanese Army then under his control to attempt to kill Ang Kim Ling and Ang Elisa, unarmed, noncombatant Chinese infants, in violation of the law of war.

4. In that Sadaaki Konishi, on or about 28 February 1945 and 6 March 1945, and during a time of war between the United States of America, its allies and Japan, did, at or near Los Baños, Laguna Province, Philippine Islands, willfully and unlawfully order or

permit members of the Imperial Japanese Army then under his control to burn and destroy private dwellings and other personal property of Chinese and Filipino civilians, in violation of the laws of war.

Dated: 24 June 1946   Signed,
                             ALVA C. CARPENTER
                             Chief, Legal Section.

                             General Headquarters
                             Supreme Commander
                             for the Allied Powers

AFFIDAVIT

Before me personally appeared the above-named accuser this 24 day of June 1946, and made oath that he is a person subject to military law and that he personally signed the foregoing charge, and further that he has investigated the matters set forth in the charge and that it is true in fact, to the best of his knowledge and belief.

                             Signed,
                             MANNING D. WEBSTER
                             Captain, JAGD

In his initial summing up, the prosecutor said that Lieutenant Konishi "made several raiding expeditions after the rescue into Los Baños as a member of the Saito Battalion. The Saito Battalion was connected with the Seventeenth Regiment, which was headed by Colonel Fujishige, and Colonel Fujishige, for his conduct and his responsibility for the operations there in Los Baños, has been executed. The evidence will show that between the dates of February 23, 1945 and March 6, 1945, Colonel Fujishige gave an order to Captain Saito to ruthlessly wipe out the population of Los Baños.

"Now just to tie in with the connection of the accused with the Saito Battalion, we have seen that he was a member of the internment camp. When it was abandoned, of course, his little outfit had nothing further to do. Major Iwanaka was away on another mountain, but before leaving he assigned Konishi and ten or twelve Formosan guards to the Saito Battalion, which then had the duty of defending Los Baños and other places from the Americans."

The prosecution then called Japanese officers who testified that Captain Sinsaku Saito had received written orders from Colonel Fujishige "to kill all guerrillas, men, women, and children in Los Baños." The date of the orders was February 26 or 27. There follows detailed testimony about the burning of the church that had been intended to offer safety to the people of Los Baños.

Many years after the war was over, Tavo Ingles, the guerrilla leader, would argue that the abrupt departure of the American soldiers after the rescue at Los Baños had left the Filipinos there exposed to the fury of the Japanese. That the civilians were murdered in retaliation for the successful rescue seems self-evident from the date of the Fujishige order. But it is also self-evident that a lightly armed force of several hundred American soldiers could have accomplished nothing but their own deaths at the hands of an immensely larger enemy force if they had stayed—and that nothing in the rules of military warfare suggested that they should have stayed. The terrible truth is that the Japanese military policy, as it was later determined, ignored such rules.

What the 1,000-page trial transcript of Lieutenant Konishi reveals, aside from the atrocities perpetrated after the rescue, is the extent of the peril for the civilians who were in his charge. His enmity for the civilians in his charge had long been evident. Given his later actions, their fears, and those of their rescuers, that plans for their summary execution on February 23, though hard evidence is lacking, seem plausible enough. It seems fair to say now that the arrival of the Angels at dawn did indeed mean their deliverance from death, as well as from captivity.

Lieutenant Konishi was found guilty of the charges against him and hanged. A Maryknoll nun, Sister Theresa, later reported that shortly before his death Sadaaki Konishi became a convert to Christianity.

DRAMATIS PERSONAE

TERRY ADEVOZO served as Secretary of Labor in the Philippine government before his death in 1972.

DON ANDERSON is the manager of a lumber company in Davis, California.

HAROLD BAYLEY attended the fiftieth reunion of his class at Trinity College in June 1984. He died after an operation for cancer later that summer.

FRANK BENNETT rebuilt his business after the war. He now lives in Rancho Bernardo, near San Diego.

TOM BOUSMAN is a Presbyterian minister in Santa Paula, California.

HENRY BURGESS is a lawyer in Sheridan, Wyoming.

LOU BURRIS lives in Thousand Oaks, California, and works for the city of Los Angeles as a real estate appraiser.

ALEX CALHOUN retired to San Francisco. He is now deceased.

LELAND CHASE lives in Walnut Creek, California.

JOHN CIERECK lives in Coral Springs, Florida.

CATHERINE COTTERMAN HOSKINS lives in Los Altos, California, and ELIZABETH COTTERMAN MORGAN lives in San Mateo, California.

COIT CRAVEN died in 1972. LOUISE CRAVEN lives in Rockville, Maryland.

HAROLD CURRAN's researches continued after the war in the jungles of South America. He died in 1953 at the age of eighty-two.

WILLIAM DONALD died in Shanghai, November 9, 1946, at the age of seventy-one.

BEN EDWARDS lives on Bainbridge Island, Washington, and makes frequent trips to the Philippines.

ROMEO ESPINO retired in 1981 as President Marcos' chief of staff. He and his wife, Helen, now operate a small hotel in Manila.

EDWARD M. "FLY" FLANAGAN's last post was as commanding general, Sixth Army. He now heads a legal firm in Beaufort, South Carolina.

BOB FLETCHER joined the U.S. Navy after the war and is now retired and living in Lakeside, near San Diego.

HARRY FONGER returned to the United States in 1967. He lives in a church retirement home in Rosemead, a suburb of Los Angeles.

JOHN FULTON survived a bout with cancer in 1954; he taught literature at a college in Paterson, New Jersey, until his retirement in 1983.

GRANT GENTRY lives in Parkridge, Illinois. He is president of Foodfair.

GEORGE GREY retired after a career with the Foreign Service and died in Las Vegas in 1981.

JIM HOLZEM lives in Edinberg, Texas.

GUSTAVO "TAVO" INGLES lives in Manila, where he runs an import-export business.

HENRY SIOUX JOHNSON is a professor of psychology and Asian studies at California State University, Long Beach.

ROBERT KLEINPELL retired from the University of California at Berkeley and lives in Isla Vista, near Santa Barbara.

COLONEL EDWARD LAHTI is retired and lives in Herndon, Virginia.

HANK MANGELS lives in Los Angeles and frequently travels to the Philippines on business.

BURT and GEORGE MARSHALL retired after careers as firemen and now live in El Cajon and San Diego.

FATHER WILLIAM MCCARTHY lives at the Maryknoll Fathers and Brothers seminary in New York City.

COLONEL GLENN MCGOWAN is retired. He lives in San Diego, California.

TOM MESEREAU left the Army in 1948 for a career as a business executive. He lives in Laguna Beach, California.

PETE MILES died in Manila in 1962 of a heart attack.

GEORGE MORA attended the University of Missouri after the war and studied journalism. He now works for First Interstate Bank and lives in a suburb of San Francisco.

HENRY MULLER retired from the Army as a brigadier general to his home in Santa Barbara, where he owns and operates a garden-supply company.

DANA NANCE worked in Oak Ridge, Tennessee, for the Atomic Energy Commission, and now lives in Guadalajara, Mexico.

RALPH and GRACE NASH live in Scottsdale, Arizona, where Grace teaches music.

MARGE PIERCE retired after a career with the Foreign Service and lives in Seal Beach, California.

COLONEL DOUG QUANDT is deceased.

COLONEL JOHN RINGLER retired after thirty years as an airborne officer. He now lives in Fayetteville, North Carolina.

CARMEN RIVERA lives in Los Angeles and works as a nurse.

BOB SAMSELL lives in North Hollywood, California.

GEORGE SKAU died in a plane crash in 1945, on Okinawa.

ROBERT "SHORTY" SOULE is deceased.

GENERAL JOSEPH SWING died in December 1984, in San Francisco. A dinner given there August 30, 1984, commemorated the surrender thirty-nine years earlier of Japanese ground forces to General Swing, who had been chosen for that honor by General MacArthur.

CAROL TERRY TALBOT went to India as a missionary after the war. She lives in Seal Beach, California, and is writing her autobiography.

JAY VANDERPOOL served in Korea and in Vietnam before retiring to Sarasota, Florida, where he now lives.

JOHN and IRENE WIGHTMAN live in Chula Vista, California. John is still actively involved in his public-relations business.

BILL and POLLY YANKEY live in Marathon, Florida. Bill retired as a captain in the U.S. Navy.

LES YARD lives in Seal Beach, south of Los Angeles. He is writing a book about the war in the Philippines.

TOM ZAHARIAS was killed in an automobile accident in Idaho in the mid–1950s.

FRED ZERVOULAKAS lives near San Francisco.

NOTES

Chapter 1. Conditions at LBIC before rescue: various interviews and responses: Bayley, Brockway, Craven, Johnson, Kleinpell, Yankey; Lucas-Corfield, *Prisoners of Santo Tomás,* p. 186; McCarthy, "The Angels Landed at Seven," p. 2.

Chapter 2. Prewar Manila, beginning of hostilities, Response, Bayley; American Rule, Friend, *Between Two Empires,* pp. 82–86. Hartendorp, *Japanese Occupation of the Philippines,* pp. 1–7; Prising, *Goodbye, Manila,* pp. 12–13, 47–59; Schultz, *Wainwright,* pp. 44–45; Homma and Japanese attack; Kennedy, *Pacific Onslaught,* pp. 60–69; Schultz, *Wainwright,* p. 61, pp. 81–82; MacArthur and WPO: Manchester, *American Caesar,* pp. 186–187; Patillo, *General MacArthur: The Philippine Years,* pp. 178–181; Schultz, *Wainwright,* pp. 106–110; attitude toward Japanese soldiers: Manila *Press,* Dec. 18, 1941, p. 1; departure of government official and MacArthur for Corregidor, Quezon inauguration, looting, newspaper reports, Hartendorp, *Japanese Occupation of the Philippines,* I, 4–7.

Chapter 3. William Donald, Lucas-Corfield. *Prisoners of Santo Tomás,* pp. 21–23; Izzawa visit, Hartendorp, *Japanese Occupation of the Philippines,* I, p. 280; Executive Committee, Hartendorp, *Japanese Occupation of the Philippines,* pp. 9–14; living conditions, Hartendorp, *Japanese Occupation of the Philippines,* I, pp. 15–41; loudspeaker, Prising, *Goodbye, Manila* pp. 126–127; Quezon and MacArthur, Manchester, *American Caesar,* p. 279.

Chapter 4. Los Baños transfer and internee reactions: Lucas-Corfield, *Prisoners of Santo Tomás,* pp. 83–95; Hartendorp, *Japanese Occupation of the Philippines,* I, pp. 227–238.

Chapter 5. Calhoun, Leach, Grinnell on conditions at Los Baños: Hartendorp, *Japanese Occupation of the Philippines,* I, 532–542; Japanese Commandant Tanaka: Fonger interview; housing, sanitary conditions: Mora interview; food and kitchens: Bennett interview, Mora interview; Los Baños Executive Committee attitudes, responsibilities, organization: Lucas-Corfield, *Prisoners of Santo Tomás,* pp. 133–136, Bayley response, Yard interview, Minutes; Morrison infraction: Lucas-Corfield, *Prisoners of Santo Tomás,* p. 126; pilfering and theft: Wightman interview; Glunz story: untitled memoir; black marketeers and prostitutes: Lucas-Corfield, *Prisoners of Santo Tomás,* pp. 145–152, McCarthy, "The Angels Came at Seven," p. 5, EPC Testimony, pp. 162–163.

Chapter 6. Founding, staffing, and operation of college, social functions: Mora diary, student records; Kleinpell classes and background: Brockway response, Mora interviews, Kleinpell interview; Nash transfer to Los Baños, camp concert, Japanese soldier: Nash, *That We Might Live,* pp. 100–106; Burt Fonger, Nash, *That We Might Live,* pp. 111–115, Johnson interview.

Chapter 7. Medical conditions: Wightman interview; Talbot interview; Nance, Minutes; food and rations: Bennett interview; Posner death: Minutes; Stephens, *Santo Tomás,* "Fort Santiago: An Oriental Inquisition," pp. 324–345, is the fullest and most graphic account of conditions at Fort Santiago; Green theft and Nance comments, Minutes; dog incident, Yankey response.

Chapter 8. Bayley-Nash incident: Bayley response, Nash, *That We Might Live,* pp. 121–122; Japanese departure: Lucas-Corfield, *Prisoners of Santo Tomás,* pp. 174–178, Nash, *That We Might Live,* pp. 132–133; Minutes; Pinky–Judge Crater story: Yard interview; Japanese return: Bennett interview.

Chapter 9. Hell incident: Lucas-Corfield, *Prisoners of Santo Tomás,* pp. 180–181, Mora interview; Japanese return: Nash, *That We Might Live,* pp. 135–138; Mangels incident: Mangels interview; Bayley and Major Urabi: Bayley response; Curran brothers incident: Yankey response: Lewis death: H. Espino interview; Edwards interview; *Minutes:* cf. Dr. Nance's report: "I have examined the body of George J. Louis, who was shot this morning by the Japanese. The body was picked up by our stretcher bearers about 100 yards south of the fence along barracks No. 14. The body had been pierced by two bullets. One bullet had a wound of entrance above the outer border of the right clavicle and an exit wound along the upper border of the corresponding scapula. This missile grazed the scapula but struck no vital organs—did not even enter the chest cavity—and was in no sense a mortal wound. The other bullet entered the skull in the right frontal region and blew his brains out in the left occipital region. It would appear that this man was executed or given the coup de grace after having sustained a minor injury."

Chapter 10. Fletcher narrative: Fletcher interview; MacArthur plans: MacArthur, *Reminiscences,* pp. 210–211; U.S. naval attacks: Steinberg, *Return to the Philippines,* pp. 78–80.

Chapter 11. Eleventh Airborne background and formation: Flanagan, *The Angels,* pp. 2–8; Eisenhower opposition: Devlin, *Paratrooper,* p. 246; Swing Board and maneuvers: Flanagan, *The Angels,* pp. 11–12; Devlin, *Paratrooper,* p. 248; Eleventh Airborne mission on Leyte: Smith, *Return to the Philippines,* p. 223; 511th mission under Haugen, Flanagan, *The Angels,* p. 39; New Guinea training, Flanagan, *The Angels,* pp. 24–25; Stadtherr drop: Flanagan, *The Angels,* pp. 41–42; Burauen attack: Flanagan, *The Angels,* pp. 49–50, Devlin, *Paratrooper,* p. 560; Mesereau interview; Eleventh Airborne decorations: Flanagan, *The Angels,* p. 65; MacArthur visit: Flanagan, *The Angels,* pp. 62–63.

Chapter 12. Summary of losses: Manchester, *American Caesar,* p. 472; Yamashita defense plans: Smith, *Return to the Philippines,* p. 97; objections to MacArthur plan: Manchester, *American Caesar,* p. 472; 511th mission: Flanagan: *The Angels,* p. 67; Palawan massacre: Russell, *Knights of Bushido,* pp. 112–116; Cabanatuan rescue: Hartendorp, *Japanese Occupation of the Philippines,* p. 558; rescue at Santo Tomás: Steinberg, *Return to the Philippines,* p. 114.

The liberation of Santo Tomás was a dramatic and dangerous affair. The Japanese used the internees as hostages to secure their own release, and it was not until February 5, some thirty-six hours after the Americans first entered the gates of the university on the morning of February 3, that the internees were free. Even then they were forced to remain within the confines of the wall because of the battle continuing in the city around them. On the night of February 7 the Japanese shelled the university, killing twenty-two and wounding thirty-nine people; on February 10 six more people died and sixteen were wounded. On February 23—the day that was to prove so lucky for the internees at Los Baños—Carroll, Grinnell, the head of the Santo Tomás Executive Committee, and three other members of the committee were buried: they had been taken out by the Japanese and beheaded on January 15. Hartendorp, *Japanese Occupation of the Philippines,* II, pp. 542–547, 561–562.

Chapter 13. Guerrilla activities: *Terry's Hunters,* pp. 218–21; Vanderpool letter, *Voice of the Angels;* Grey meeting with Ingles: *Terry's Hunters,* p. 230, *Minutes;* Executive Committee meeting: *Minutes;* internees' departure: Edwards response, interview.

Chapter 14. Planning for rescue and background: Muller interview; Burgess, "Reminiscences," p. 6; McGowan, Clearwater reunion; Skau mission: Burgess, "Reminiscences," p. 6, Bailey, "Raid at Los Baños," p. 66, n. 29: "Each landing vehicle, tracked, of the 672nd Amphibian Tractor Battalion could transport twenty-four combat-equipped soldiers. The amphibious assault force of approximately 460 men, therefore, required only about twenty amtracs with the remainder for the freed prisoners. For passengers loaded with less than full combat equipment, the passenger-carrying capacity increased substantially. For example, in ferry operations, each amtrac could carry forty-five people"; Ringler role: Burgess, "Reminiscences," p. 15; Ringler, Clearwater reunion; Soule role: Burgess, "Reminiscences," pp. 16–17; Flanagan, "The Raid on Los Baños," p. 71; Corregidor, Manila fighting: Steinberg, *Return to the Philippines,* p. 121; Fujishige defense plans: Smith, *Triumph in the Philippines,* p. 427; Miles contribution: Burgess, "Reminiscences," pp. 7–8, Edwards response, Muller interview.

Chapter 15. (i) Executive Committee meeting: *Minutes;* radio incident: Nance letter; (ii) Edwards: Edwards response; (iii) Company B: Marshall memoir: Fletcher interview; Ringler, Clearwater reunion; Holsman, Clearwater interview; (iv) Kleinpell: Kleinpell interview; (v) Mora: Mora diary; (vi) Espino: Espino interview; (vii) Grey: Pierce interview; (viii) Burgess: Burgess, "Reminiscences," pp. 17–19; (ix) Planning decision: Flanagan, *The Angels,* p. 95; Skau movements: Edwards response; guerilla movements: *Terry's Hunters,* pp. 228–31; Burris mission: Burris interview; Swing: Burgess "Reminiscences," p. 18.

Chapter 16. Flight plans: Anderson, 1982 Reunion; attack: Burgess, "Reminiscences," pp. 19–24; McCarthy: "The Angels Came at Seven"; Edwards response; Fletcher interview; Mora diary; Wightman interview; Glunz memoir; Terry interview; Craven response; Bayley response; Burris, Clearwater Reunion; Corfield: Lucas-Corfield, *Prisoners of Santo Tomás,* p. 198.

Aftermath. The story of Konishi's deathbed conversion was reported in a letter to the Eleventh Airborne Division Newsletter, "The Voice of the Angels," November 1983, by David Blackledge, an ex-internee and retired Army colonel. Everything about Sadaaki Konishi is mysterious. His activities before World War II, his rank or grade in the Japanese army, his motivation for his mistreatment of the internees at Santo Tomás and Los Baños, the extent of his personal involvement in the murderous aftermath of the rescue, how he was finally brought to trial, the conduct of the trial itself, and his ultimate fate. My investigation of the record of Konishi's trial as a war criminal persuaded me that Konishi's story would probably make a satisfactory book in itself, but one that others would have to pursue. Tantalizing questions arise in reading the 1,000-plus page transcript and the supporting documentation. Was Konishi in fact a member of the Black Dragon society, a terrorist organization in Japan before the war? Had he systematically accumulated enough money during the war to pay for the services of an Australian attorney to defend him? Was he in fact doomed to die of tuberculosis—a fact disclosed to the reader of the transcripts only after the judge complains that he is having a hard time understanding counsel for the defense because of the mask he is wearing?

In the November 1984 "Voice of the Angels," Blackledge wrote that he had received correspondence from John P. Kozeletz, a veteran of the 187th Airborne Division, indicating that Konishi was not hanged on June 17, 1947, as Blackledge had said. General MacArthur had deferred the execution until April 12, 1949, in order to allow time for a review by the Supreme Court of the trial. Noting that he had "an extract from the personal records of the U.S. Army chaplain who baptised a Sadaaki Konishi and gave him the last rites just before the sentence was executed" in 1947, Blackledge suggests that perhaps "bureaucratic legalities continued the appeal process after the sentence had been carried out even before the stay of execution was received." Readers interested in pursuing the question may contact Blackledge or Kozeletz through the Eleventh Airborne "Voice of the Angels," Box 373, Johnson, AR 72471.

SOURCES

I. Publications about Los Baños Internment Camp

Many people have written about Los Baños over the past forty years, but only one at any length, and none with the intention of providing an overview of the kind that this book attempts. Celia Lucas' *The Prisoners of Santo Tomás,* based on the diaries of Isla Corfield, is the longest single account published for a general audience about life at Los Baños and about the rescue. As the title suggests, the greater part of the Lucas/Corfield book is about experiences at Santo Tomás; and it is, of course, the perspective of only one person. But it is an accurate and readable account, one that I both enjoyed and benefited from having.

Grace C. Nash has kindly given me permission to adapt several passages from her privately printed account "That We Might Live," 1982.

Publications about the rescue at Los Baños:

Edward M. Flanagan was a young lieutenant with the Eleventh Airborne in the Philippines at the time of the rescue. He wrote the first extended account of the event as a chapter in his history of the Eleventh Airborne Division, *The Angels,* in 1946. He revised and expanded this account for an article, "The Raid on Los Baños," published in 1983. I am indebted to Lieutenant General (Retired) Flanagan for his researches and grateful for his encouraging responses to my questions in my correspondence with him.

Major Maxwell C. Bailey, U.S. Air Force, published an excellent account in *Military Review,* 1983, which adds valuable information on the contribution of the Air Force to the rescue.

II. Books about the Philippines

272 Of the many works that I found useful and that are represented in the

following bibliography, one stands out as essential: A. V. H. Hartendorp's monumental *Japanese Occupation of the Philippines.* Hartendorp, a prominent journalist and longtime resident of Manila, was
interned at Santo Tomás for the duration of the war. He gathered
materials from every available source during the war, when it was
dangerous to do so, and wrote the connecting narrative for the two
large volumes that resulted from his efforts.

III. Unpublished Sources

a. These include

(a) Transcripts of remarks made at the following reunions of ex-
internees and ex-soldiers: 1965, San Jose; 1981, Anaheim; 1982,
Anaheim; 1983, Anaheim; and at the 1983, Clearwater, Florida,
Eleventh Airborne reunion.
(b) Individual accounts, memoirs, reminiscences, and diaries
(c) Minutes of the Los Baños Executive Committee
(d) Testimony at the War Crimes trial of Sadaaki Konishi
(e) Responses to author's queries
(f) Interviews with the author

b. The individuals whose contributions to this account in one or more
of these ways were particularly valuable include:

Harold Bayley, e, f.	Gustavo Ingles, b, f.
Frank Bennett, f.	Robert Kleinpell, f.
Lou Burris, f.	Hank Mangells, f.
Thomas Bousman, f.	John Manning, e.
Alex Brockway, e.	Tom Mesereau, a, b, f.
Henry Burgess, a, e, f.	George Mora, b, e, f.
Mrs. Coit Craven, e.	Henry Muller, f.
Ben Edwards, e, f.	Dana Nance, e.
Helen Espino, f.	Grace Nash, a, b, f.
Romeo Espino, f.	Carol Talbot, a, b, f.
John Fulton, b, f.	John and Irene Wightman, f.
Harry Fonger, f.	W.B. ("Bud") and Polly Yankey, e.
Charles Glunz, b.	Les Yard, f.

IV. Documents

1. After Action Report Mike 1 (Operation U.S. Army, Headquarters, XIV Corps, 29 July 1945.

2. Combat Notes Number 5, Assistant Chief of Staff, G-3, Head-quarters, Sixth Army, 21 March 1945.
3. Combat Notes Number 7, Assistant Chief of Staff, G-3, Head-quarters, Sixth Army, May 1945.
4. Enemy Property Commission Hearings Before the Committee on Interstate and Foreign Commerce, House of Representatives, 80th Congress. First Session on HR 873, HR 1823, HR 100, HR 2823. U.S. Government Printing Office, 1947.
5. "Luzon, Philippine Islands Campaigns, 31 January to 30 June 1945," Eleventh Airborne Division Report.
6. Order of Battle of the United States Army Ground Forces in World War II, Pacific Theater of Operations. Office of the Chief of Military History, Department of the Army, Washington, D.C., 1959.
7. Records of the Office of the Judge Advocate General (Army) (The Trial of Sadaaki Konishi). Record Group 153, Vol. II, 40-1936 and 41-6. 1946.

V. Newspapers and Periodicals

1. Bailey, Maxwell C. "Raid at Los Baños." *Military Review,* May 1983, pp. 51–65.
2. Flanagan, Edward M., Jr. "The Raid on Los Baños." *Army,* June 1983, pp. 64–72.
3. Jacobs, Bruce. "The Angels of the 11th Airborne." *Saga,* February, 1958.
4. McCarthy, Fr. William R. "The Angels Came at Seven." *Columbia,* April 1950, pp. 3–15.
5. Tulay, Filemon V. "Liberation of Los Baños." *Philippines Free Press,* Manila, February 18, 1950.
6. Walsh, Louis A. "The Raid on Los Baños." *The Static Line* (11th AB), December, 1980.

The Voice of the Angels, the newsletter of the Eleventh Airborne Division Association, Box 373, Johnson, AK 72741, has published many items about Los Baños, written by ex-soldiers, ex-internees, and ex-guerrillas, and by others such as the present author. Among the more valuable contributions, both for the range of interests they represent and for this book, were the following:

Blackledge, David. Letters concerning the fate of the Japanese officer, Lt. Konishi, November, 1983, p. 23, November 1984, p. 4.

Burgess, Henry. "Reminiscences of the 11th Airborne Division," December 1981.

Fulton, John. "Radio Operator Behind the Lines," September 1983, p. 4.

Mann, Judy. "Heroines," from *The Washington Post,* April 6, 1983, about Mary Harrington Nelson, Navy nurse, June 1983, p. 21.

McCarthy, Fr. William. "Claim for Reparation by Father McCarthy." August 1982, p. 2.

Quandt, Col. Douglas P. "Fifth Wheel," September 1983, pp. 5, 7, 10–11.

Vanderpool, Jay D. Excerpts from letter to David Blackledge, March 17, 1982, reproduced March 1983, p. 13.

VI. Books

Agoncillo, Teodoro A. *The Fateful Years: Japan's Adventure in the Philippines, 1941–1945.* Manila: R. P. Garcia Publishing Company, 1963.

Benedict, Ruth. *The Chrysanthemum and the Sword.* London: Rutledge, 1967.

Byas, Hugh. *Government by Assassination.* New York: Knopf, 1942.

Carr-Gregg, Charlotte. *Japanese Prisoners of War in Revolt.* New York: St. Martin's Press, 1978.

Clavell, James. *King Rat.* Boston-Toronto: Little, Brown and Co., 1962.

Coleman, John S., Jr. *Bataan and Beyond: Memories of an American POW.* College Station, TX: Texas A&M Press, 1978.

Cornell, M. W. *I Fed the 5000.* London: The Mitre Press, 1975.

Craig, Albert M., and Shively, Donald H. *Personality in Japanese History.* Berkeley, CA: University of California Press, 1970.

Crouter, Natalie. *Forbidden Diary: A Record of Wartime Internment, 1941–45.* New York: Burt Franklin and Co., 1980; American Women's Diary Series.

Daniel, Roger. *The Politics of Prejudice: The Anti-Japanese Movement in California and the Struggle for Japanese Exclusion.* New York: Atheneum. (University of California Publication in History, Vol. LXXI).

Day, Beth. *The Manila Hotel.* Manila, Philippines: National Media Production Center, 1977.

Devlin, Gerard M. *Paratrooper!* New York: St. Martin's Press, 1979.

Flanagan, Edward M., Jr. *The Angels: A History of the 11th Airborne Division, 1943–1946.* Washington, D.C.: Infantry Journal Press, 1948.

Friend, Theodore. *Between Two Empires: The Ordeal of the Philippines, 1929–1946.* New Haven, CT, and London: Yale University Press, 1968.

Gilkey, Langdon. *Shantung Compound: The Story of Men and Women Under Pressure.* New York: Harper and Row, 1966.

Gleeck, Lewis E., Jr. *The Manila Americans 1901–1964.* Manila, Philippines: Carmelo & Bauerman, Inc., 1977.

Glines, Carroll V. *Four Came Home.* Princeton, NJ: D. Van Nostrand Co., 1966.

Glunz, Charles and Henrietta. *From Pearl Harbor to the Golden Gate.* Unpublished memoir; no date.

Goffman, Erving. *Asylums.* London: Harmondsworth, 1970.

Gordon, Ernest. *Through the Valley of the Kwai.* New York: Harper & Row, 1962.

Gunnison, Royal Arch. *So Sorry No Peace.* New York: Viking Press, 1944.

Hartendorp, A. V. H. *The Japanese Occupation of the Philippines.* Manila, Philippines: Bookmark, 2 volumes, 1967.

Hartendorp, A. V. H. *The Santo Tomás Story.* New York: McGraw Hill, 1965.

Ienaga, Saburo. *The Pacific War: World War II and the Japanese, 1931–1945.* New York: Pantheon Books, 1978; first published in Japan, 1968.

James, Dorris Clayton. *The Years of MacArthur.* Boston: Houghton Mifflin, 1970 (vol. 1), 1975 (vol. 2).

Johnson, Forrest. *Horn of Redemption.* New York: Manor Books (paper), 1978.

Kawasaki, Ichiro. *Japan Unmasked.* Rutland, Vermont, and Tokyo: Charles E. Tuttle Co., 1969.

Keats, John. *They Fought Alone.* Boston: Lippincott, 1963.

Keith, Agnes Newton. *Three Came Home.* Boston: Little, Brown & Co., 1947.

Kennedy, Paul. *Pacific Onslaught, 7th December 1941-7th February 1943.* New York: Ballantine Books, 1972.

Kirkup, James. *Filipinescas.* London: Phoenix House, 1968.

Kreuger, Walter. *From Down Under to Nippon: The Story of the Sixth Army in World War II.* Combat Forces Press, 1952.

Lucas, Celia. *Prisoners of Santo Tomás.* Based on the diaries of Mrs. Isla Corfield. London: Leo Cooper, Ltd., 1975.

MacArthur, Douglas. *Reminiscences.* New York: McGraw Hill Book Co., 1964.

Maki, John M. *Japanese Militarism.* New York: Alfred A. Knopf, Inc., 1945.

Mallonee, Richard C. II. *The Naked Flagpole: Battle for Bataan. The Diary of Richard C.* Mallonee, R. C. Mallonee II, ed. San Rafael, CA: Presidio Press, 1980.

Manchester, William. *American Caesar: Douglas MacArthur 1880–1964.* New York: 1978.

Manchester, William. *Goodbye, Darkness: A Memoir of the Pacific War.* Boston-Toronto: Little, Brown & Co., 1979, 1980.

MacArthur, Douglas, General. "Reports of General MacArthur." *Japanese Operations in the Southeast Pacific Area, Vol. II, Part II.* Compiled from Japanese Demobilization Bureau and Records. U.S. Government Printing Office, 1966.

Mellnik, Steve (Brigadier General). *Philippine Diary 1939–1945.* New York: Van Nostrand Reinhold Co., 1969.

Mitchell, Richard H. *Thought Control in Prewar Japan.* Ithaca, New York, and London: Cornell University Press, 1976.

Morison, Samuel Eliot. *Strategy and Compromise.* Boston: Little, Brown & Co., 1956.

Morison, Samuel Eliot. *History of the United States Naval Operations in World War II, Vol. 13, The Liberation of the Philippines: Luzon, Mindanao, the Visayans, 1944–1945.* Boston: Little, Brown & Co., 1959.

Nash, Grace C. *That We Might Live.* Privately published, 1981: Grace Nash, 7001 E. Balfour, P.O. Box 1753, Scottsdale, AZ 85252.

Nitabe, Inazo. *Bushido.* Rutland, Vermont, and Tokyo: Charles E. Tuttle Co., 1969.

Ooka, Shohei, translated by Ivan Morris. *Fires on the Plain.* Knopf, 1957; Penguin Edition, 1969.

Patillo, Carol Morris. *General MacArthur: The Philippine Years.* Bloomington, Indiana: Indiana University Press, 1981.

Parkin, Ray. *The Sword and the Blossom.* London: The Hogarth Press, 1968.

Prising, Robin. *Manila, Goodbye.* Boston: Houghton Mifflin Co., 1975.

Redmond, Juanita. *I Served on Bataan.* Philadelphia: Lippincott, 1943.

Reel, A. Frank. *The Case of General Yamashita.* Chicago: University of Chicago Press, 1949.

Reyes, Jose G. *Terrorism and Redemption: Japanese Atrocities in the Philippines.* Manila, 1947.

Romulo, Carlos P. *I Saw the Fall of the Philippines.* Garden City, NY: Doubleday, Doran & Co., 1943.

Royama, Masamichi and Tekeuchi, Tetsuji. *The Philippine Policy: A Japanese View.* New Haven: Monograph Series No. 12, Southeast Asia Studies, Yale University, 1967.

Russell of Liverpool, Lord. *The Knights of Bushido.* London: Cassell, 1958.

Schultz, Duane. *Hero of Bataan: The Story of General L. M. Wainwright.* New York: St. Martin's Press, 1981.

Simons, Jessie Elizabeth. *While History Passed: The Story of the Australian Nurses Who Were Prisoners of the Japanese for Three and a Half Years.* Melbourne, London: Wm. Heinemann, 1954.

Smith, Donald. *And All the Trumpets.* London: Godrey Bles, 1954.

Smith, Robert Ross. *The War in the Pacific, Vol. 10, Triumph in the Philippines.* Washington, D.C.: U.S. Government Printing Office, 1963.

Spence, Hartzell. *Marcos of the Philippines.* New York and Cleveland: World Publishing Co., 1969.

Steinberg, Rafael. *Return to the Philippines,* Vol. 15, Time-Life series on World War II. New York: Time-Life Books, 1979.

Storry, Richard. *A History of Modern Japan.* London: Penguin Books, 1960.

Tanin, O. and Yohan, E. *Militarism and Fascism in Japan.* London: Martin Laurence, 1934; Westport, CN: Greenwood Press, 1973.

Toland, John. *The Rising Sun: The Decline and Fall of the Japanese Empire 1936–1945.* New York: Random House, 2 volumes, 1970.

Van der Post, Laurens. *The Prisoners and the Bomb.* New York: Wm. Morrow and Co., 1971.

White, W. L. *They Were Expendable.* New York: Harcourt Brace and Co., 1942.

Wolfert, Ira. *American Guerilla in the Philippines.* New York: Simon and Schuster, 1945.

INDEX